Traveling on the Edge

Traveling on the Edge

Journeys in the Footsteps of Graham Greene

JULIA LLEWELLYN SMITH

St. Martin's Press   New York

www.stmartins.com

ISBN 0-312-28292-3

First published in Great Britain under the title *Travels Without
My Aunt: In the Footsteps of Graham Greene* by Michael
Joseph/Penguin Group, Penguin Books, Ltd.

First U.S. Edition: November 2001

10 9 8 7 6 5 4 3 2 1

To my granny, Joyce Forrest

CONTENTS

ACKNOWLEDGEMENTS

I met hundreds of people in the course of writing this book, many of whom appear in these pages. Most are mentioned by name, some – who would not welcome the attention – appear under pseudonyms. I would like to thank everyone who travelled with me as well as the many people who took the time to speak to me and in many cases offering me and my travelling companions food, accommodation and tours of their home towns.

In addition I would like to thank: Ian Thomson, Andy Wood, Leah Gordon, David Mathieson, the Oxfam press office and Sebastian Doggart.

At home: Louise Haines and Susan Watt, Richard Max, Alex Smith and Maryam Shahmanesh. Con Coughlin, Liz Derow, Tanya Seghatchian, Sarah Smith and Kate Townsend were all sources of strength. At work, I am very grateful to Graham Paterson, Dominic Lawson, Rosie Boycott, Lindsay Cook and Tiffanie Darke. Ed Victor and Lizzie Kremer were brilliant agents and Rowland White, my editor, never flagged in his enthusiasm and support. Most of all, thanks to my parents and to David Osmon.

Obviously, I owe an enormous debt to Graham Greene and his estate. Other books which were extremely helpful included the first two volumes of Norman Sherry's biography, *The Life of Graham Greene*; *Graham Greene: The Enemy Within* by Michael Shelden, and *Graham Greene; On The Frontier* by Maria Cauto. Paul Hogarth's *Graham Greene Country* was invaluable.

INTRODUCTION: Brighton

*It was weak of me but I did not then realize the depth of my
aunt's passion for travel. If I had I would have hesitated before
I made the first fatal proposal: 'I have nothing particular to do
today. If you would like to go to Brighton . . .'*

TRAVELS WITH MY AUNT

On a cold December night, in 1926, Graham Greene, a
22-year-old Englishman, was in Brighton convalescing from
appendicitis. He was depressed by his illness and by the fact
that his first two novels had been rejected by every publisher
he had approached. Greene walked down to the seafront, sat
down in a shelter and watched 'the thin phosphorescent line
of the surf smoothed back by a frosty wind'. In the dark, he
failed to notice another man sitting there and was startled by
his voice. 'Do you know who I am?' the man asked. 'I'm Old
Moore.' Greene had no idea what he was talking about. 'I live
alone in a basement. I bake my own bread.' Greene still did
not make the connection to the annual volume of anonymous
astrological predictions until the man added humbly: 'The
Almanac, you know, I write the Almanac.'

The encounter enchanted Greene and touched his imagination. More than a decade later, in one of his most popular
novels, *Brighton Rock*, he was to use his memory of this man
as the basis for Prewitt, the sleazy lawyer. Prewitt is an old
man with a hag of a wife, a passion for tinned salmon and a

lust for typists. He fights the urge to expose himself in a public park. As he considers his wretched life he is reminded of Marlowe's Doctor Faustus. 'You know what Mephistopheles said to Faustus when he asked where hell was: "Why, this is Hell, nor am I out of it."'

The Brighton that Greene depicted in *Brighton Rock* is hell, or something close to it. It is the story of Pinkie, a teenage gangster of staggering evil. At the start of the novel, Pinkie kills Hale, a journalist, by pushing a stick of Brighton rock down his throat. Hale is in Brighton on a Whitsun Bank Holiday, leaving cards from his newspaper – with a cash reward for anyone who finds them. After the murder, Pinkie's gang continue to scatter the cards across town to create an alibi. But one card is found by Rose, a waitress, who knows that the man who left it was definitely not Hale. To silence her, Pinkie is forced to quell his sexual revulsion and marry her; a wife is not compelled to give evidence against her husband. Yet Pinkie is also being pursued by Ida, a blowzy former showgirl, who met Hale minutes before the murder. A string of killings ensues as Pinkie tries to conceal the crime. Eventually he persuades Rose to join him in a suicide pact – which he intends to break. But just as Rose is about to shoot herself Ida arrives with the police. Pinkie throws himself over a cliff and is dashed on the rocks below.

Pinkie epitomizes wickedness. 'I wanted people to believe that he was a sufficiently evil person almost to justify the notion of Hell,' Greene later explained. Yet Greene also did everything he could to shift our sympathies in Pinkie's direction. However much we pity them, it is hard to identify with vulgar Ida or feeble-minded Rose. Pinkie is a far more attractive proposition precisely because he is so single-minded in his depravity. Even in death, he emerges as a winner of sorts because he chooses his own damnation. By jumping into the abyss, he proves that he can forego the divine love and mercy that other – weaker – people crave.

In Pinkie's Brighton we are in Greeneland – the fraught, amoral universe where nearly all Greene's subsequent characters lived. From Vietnam to Paraguay, Haiti or Sierra Leone, Greene chose settings for his novels in which accepted standards of morality were absent. The wicked thrived, the good were somehow ridiculous. It was a world that Greene had begun to explore already in Liberia, West Africa: 'this supernatural world which is neither good nor evil but simply Power.' When you read *Brighton Rock*, you feel as if you are playing hide and seek in the dark – with your adversary, the author, constantly moving the furniture.

On a blustery Whitsun morning, more than sixty years after the publication of *Brighton Rock*, I boarded the London to Brighton train just as Hale did on his final, fatal journey. The main differences were in the details. He would have been on a steam train, surrounded by boisterous families. I shared the compartment of the bright blue and yellow Connex South Central train with a floppy haired man who talked continuously on his mobile phone and a couple of silent, shaven-headed and multi-pierced lesbians. Yet, across the decades, we shared the view of shabby south London tenements dissolving into the green of the Sussex Downs.

As the train pulled in to Brighton, I felt the same sense of release that Greene's Bank Holiday crowds felt as they 'rocked down Queen's Road standing on the tops of the little local trams: stepped off in bewildered multitudes into fresh and glittering air'. Brighton's station stands on the crown of a hill. On the horizon, I could just make out the pale glint of the sea. I walked down the long Queen's Road which becomes West Street at the Clock Tower, past casinos, Chinese takeaways and newsagents, their façades faded by the sun. The seagulls wheeled and cried, the light was dazzling, dynamic. One moment my nostrils were filled with a heady whiff of ozone, the next with the tang of stale chip batter. I was filled with a sudden bubble of happiness, as if I had swallowed a pint of champagne. Brighton has that effect on people.

I had always loved Brighton since my first visits there as a teenager. I came from Oxford, famous among other things for being the town in Britain furthest from the sea. In school holidays, my friends and I would spend three long hours on a hot train so we could spend an afternoon screaming on the helter-skelter, eating salty fish and chips, paddling in the cold sea, and hobbling painfully over the stony beach in a dance that locals laughingly described as the 'Brighton two step'. Brighton represented reprieve from our everyday lives of netball, chemistry, homework and television.

Greene's bleak portrayal of the town upset the authorities, who 'proved a little sensitive to the picture I had drawn of their city', but in truth he loved Brighton, too. He first visited it as a convalescent child at the age of six and saw his first film there, *Sophie of Kravonia*, a story of a kitchenmaid who became a queen. As an up-and-coming author, he went there frequently, to escape from his small children. After a few weeks spent writing in a rented room, he would return to London, inspired and invigorated.

On the surface, Greene's Brighton has changed considerably since his jaunts there in the 1930s and 1940s. The 'street parallel to the railway behind the terminus' where poor Prewitt lived with his slattern of a wife had been demolished to make way for the station car park. The surviving two-up two-downs, such as the one he would have inhabited, were tidy beiges, pale pinks and yellows. In our post-industrial age the soot that once had 'settled continuously on the glass and brass plate' was no longer a problem. There were flyers on the window panes: 'Genetic Engineering. Is there something fishy going on?' Some had been converted into shops selling Japanese furniture or vegetarian shoes.

I was on the fringes of the North Laines, one of the most fashionable shopping areas in Europe. The tourists who in Greene's day would have entertained themselves with 'this sun, this music, the rattle of the miniature cars', were all consumers now and found their happiness browsing in the patchouli-scented clothes markets and organic bread shops. A man cycled past with a live rabbit in his bicycle basket and a dreadlocked busker sat on the pavement playing the didgeridoo.

Much of Greene's Brighton had been destroyed. Nelson Place, the slum tenement from which Rose 'had emerged like a mole into the daylight' was cleared after the war. The Cosmopolitan Hotel, where the gangster Colleoni lived – 'where did you bring a swell blonde to if not to the Cosmopolitan' – was modelled on the Bedford Hotel on the seafront, where Charles Dickens wrote *Dombey and Son*. It had burned down in 1964. The Royal Albion, Greene's favourite hotel bang opposite the Palace Pier, where Pinkie saw 'a well-known popular author' displaying his 'plump too famous face in the window' had also been destroyed in 1998, by a fire caused by a pan of frying eggs. Now it was surrounded by scaffolding. A faded sign over the burnt-out entrance bore the royal crest and the words underneath: 'Licensed for public dancing'.

On the Palace Pier Spanish language students puzzled over pictures of cats captioned 'Happiness is a warm pussy'. Under the dome of the amusement arcade young men in baseball caps fought aliens and fed one-armed bandits. Outside there was no wind to dispel the cloying smell of candy floss and the jangle of the carousel. On the beach below, couples fully clothed in coordinating sportswear watched a salsa band. To Pinkie, the sea was 'poison-bottle green', today it was milky blue like the eyes of a blind man. Snow's, where poor Rose worked, was gone, replaced by seaside cafés such as Buddie's, open twenty-four hours and offering *tagliatelle carbonara* along-side cod and chips. Lace tablecloths had been replaced with laminated tartan. The staff was no longer poor young girls waiting for husbands but cheerful Australians in white shirts and black trousers.

A few hundred yards away on the seafront sat the Star and Garter pub, now known by the nickname the townsfolk had always given it – Dr Brighton's. Inside, the 'private saloon' where Hale took refuge from Pinkie's gang had been demol-ished – along with 'the two bars and a glass partition' through which he watched Ida singing drunkenly. Now there was just one airy L-shaped room. The 'inscriptions of a philosophical nature' that once covered the walls had been replaced with framed advertisements for Bacardi and Chesterfield cigarettes. A small stereo behind the bar played George Michael. Hale and Pinkie were alone in the saloon bar 'apart from the company of an old commissionaire, who slept over a pint glass of old and mild'. I shared the room with a shaven-headed barman and three gay men who sat talking quietly at the bar. A poster informed me that on Friday nights the pub would be hosting a 'Kinky Boots Event'.

But for every Dr Brighton's, there was a Cricketers' in Black Lion Street, which remained a monument to Edwardian kitsch – red and white flock wallpaper, red lampshades with tassels, a low ceiling with a collection of chamberpots hanging from it. At the back of the room, a fire burned in a grate. Next to it hung a tarnished oval mirror. There was a bowl of fruit on the bar, while above it a sign with peeling gold letters on a white background proclaimed the place to be a 'Bonder of spirits, brandies, choice brands'. Surrounded by so much junk you barely noticed the fruit machine or the jukebox.

Both the Star and Garter and the Cricketers' feature in another, much later novel of Greene's – *Travels With My Aunt* – published in 1969, which tells the story of Aunt Augusta, an elderly lady with a colourful past and her nephew, the retired bank manager Henry Pulling. This unlikely duo embark on a series of trips. 'Brighton was the first real journey I undertook in my aunt's company and proved a bizarre foretaste of much that was to follow,' says Henry. They check in to the Royal Albion, because Aunt Augusta likes to be at the 'centre of all the devilry'. Henry wants a 'bath and a glass of sherry, a quiet dinner in the grill, and an early bedtime.' Augusta, as ever, has other ideas and the pair find themselves drinking sherry (Henry) and port and brandy (his aunt) in the Star and Garter, before continuing to the Cricketers' for a 'substantial snack' of warm sausages laid out in a basket on the bar and washed down with draught Guinness.

Today, lunch at the Cricketers' consisted of a baked potato and tuna. I sat on a round, red upholstered stool by the window with its view of Food for Friends, offering global vegetarian and vegan foods. Henry Pulling had seen a second-hand bookseller 'with a complete set of Thackeray for sale at a very reasonable price'. Then it came to me. Brighton was different now – but only in the inessentials. 'Look at me, I've never changed. It's like those sticks of rock, bite it all the way down, it'll still read Brighton,' Ida tells Rose, and the same simile applied to the town itself.

Brighton was – and always had been – a place of escape, for family outings and dirty weekends. In T. S. Eliot's 'The Waste Land', Mr Eugenides, the Smyrna merchant, asks a young man to a 'weekend at the Metropole Hotel' and indeed in the 1930s, many of Greene's contemporaries, such as the poet

Stephen Spender, would take off for a few sleazy days in Brighton with a working-class boy of their fancy. In the 1950s and 60s, the town became a magnet for leather-jacketed Rockers and furry-parka'd Mods who flocked there on their scooters every Bank Holiday weekend in search of temporary liberation from their dreary day-to-day existences. Today the town was a mecca for New Age gurus, anarchists, street performers, drug addicts, homosexuals and organic vegetable growers, all drawn to Brighton because of its situation on the very edge of Britain, because of its devotion to pleasure, because of its sense of endless possibilities.

No wonder Greene felt so happy there. The headmaster's son from the quiet Hertfordshire town of Berkhamsted had suffered since childhood from an overwhelming desire to get away. As a child he devoured books such as *King Solomon's Mines* by H. Rider Haggard which recounted the adventures of Allan Quatermain in darkest Africa. In *Ways of Escape*, his aptly named autobiography, Greene wrote: 'The mood for escape which comes to most men in middle life . . . with me arrived early, escape from boredom, escape from depression. If I had been a bank clerk, I would have dreamed of betraying my trust and absconding to South America.'

If the action did not come to Greene, then Greene would go to the action. He loved to visit brothels, to take drugs, to hurt and manipulate not just his readers but the people around him. Like Pinkie, he enjoyed the frisson of flirting with his own damnation. His attitude infuriated many. George Orwell complained, with some justification, 'he appears to share the idea, which has been floating around ever since Baudelaire, that there is something rather *distingué* in being damned. Hell is a sort of high class nightclub, entry to which is reserved for Catholics only.'

Above all, Greene had a horror of the mundanity of domestic life. He shared the disgust Pinkie feels at the contents of a suburban garage whose owner 'was nameless, faceless, but the boy hated him. The doll, the pram, the broken rocking horse. The small pricked-out plants irritated him like ignorance.' When it came to the modern world in general, Greene was profoundly influenced by his idol Eliot. Yet, like Eliot, he also realized that his duty as an artist lay in shoring its fragments – making a new order out of the confusion he saw around him. The world of *Brighton Rock*, with its soundtrack of cheap songs and cast of small-time fall guys and spotty secretaries sunning themselves on deckchairs, was straight from the mould of 'The Waste Land'. Today, Greene implied, the most primeval powers of evil rested in Pinkie's scrawny frame.

The western world needed to reconstruct and recover. Europe was on the brink of war. To understand the new society emerging, to 'recall the point at which we went astray', Greene needed to investigate 'seediness' – which he defined as the primal matter out of which society had been constructed. 'It's the same draw that a child has towards making a mud pie,' he said in an interview with *The Listener* in 1968. 'Perhaps it's a certain remaining infantility in one's character. The seedy is nearer the beginning, isn't it – or nearer the end . . . No, it's not that I enjoy puddling in the mess, but if there is a mess, I feel it's our duty to look at it.' The seediness could be found just as much in 'civilized' societies as in the jungle – 'the sky-signs in Leicester Square, the "tarts" in Bond Street, the smell of cooking greens off Tottenham Court Road, the motor salesmen in Great Portland Street' all held 'great appeal' for Greene. Naturally, he was drawn to Brighton which had always teetered on a tightrope between the squalid and the elegant. 'The shabby secret behind the bright corsage, the deformed breast,' thought Pinkie, who is in the course of a day moved between the ornate vulgarity of the Cosmopolitan to Rose's slum dwelling with 'only one door and a staircase matted with old newspapers'. The caramel and cream Regency houses that 'ran away into the west like a pale Victorian watercolour', built as winter retreats for the eighteenth-century aristocracy, now housed bed and breakfasts with worn swirly carpets, floppy beds with stained mattresses and shower cubicles where the trickle of water alternately scalded or froze.

Yet Greene admitted that there were 'times of impatience, when one is less content to rest at the urban stage, when one is willing to suffer some discomfort for the chance of finding King Solomon's Mines, the "heart of darkness".' 'It's a restlessness that I've always had to move around and perhaps to see English characters in a setting which is not protective to them, where perhaps they speak a little differently, a little more openly,' he said.

Without these travels, Greene's oeuvre would have been much slimmer. Imagination, by novelists' standards – was not his strongest point. Virtually everything he wrote was based in reality. His characters were tormented with guilt, failure, treachery and sin – and his settings reflected these tortured inner lives. Out of his twenty-five novels seventeen are set outside England. 'I wasn't seeking sources,' he wrote in *Ways of Escape*. 'I stumbled on them, though perhaps a writer's instinct may have been at work when I bought my return ticket to Saigon or Port-au-Prince.'

I left the Cricketers' and wandered the narrow mesh of streets that made up the Lanes, past shops selling dubious antiques and expensive clothes, porcelain dolls, gold chains, oriental prints and semi-precious stones. I understand that compulsion to probe the depths of human experience, I thought. Yet in many other respects I didn't like Greene much, not least because I saw qualities in him that I recognized, to a lesser degree, in myself. Greene was misanthropic and selfish and he had a habit of treating life as a stage-play in which other people were merely characters to be manipulated and these qualities contributed to my feeling that although he was a great writer, he was not the greatest.

My fascination with Greene came from somewhere quite different. It had been sparked two years previously and 5,000 miles away on the run-down island of Haiti. I was there in order to research another book, but my bedtime reading was Greene's 1966 novel *The Comedians*, which happened to be set in the Gothic folly of a hotel where I was staying. At night, to the background strains of cocks crowing and stray dogs howling, I lay in bed reading Greene's description of this 'shabby land of terror', impressed at the evocation of his surroundings and struck by the sense that nothing fundamental had changed about the place.

I began to catalogue mentally Greene's destinations. So many of them were in lost, lonely, neglected parts of the world that had always interested me. I didn't want to write another biography of Greene – that has been comprehensively done – instead, I wanted to know more about such bizarre surroundings, to know how very different other lives could be.

Not all of Greeneland appealed to me. I had little desire, for example, to see the Sweden that made up the background for *England Made Me*, as Greene himself admitted to barely knowing the country. The same applied to the then Belgian Congo, where he visited a leper colony in order to provide the setting for *A Burnt Out Case*. The novels with European settings – *Dr Fischer of Geneva*, or *Loser Takes All* – set in Monaco – were often the slimmest of Greene's works. I was looking at the places where Greene – for whatever reason – had found himself at particularly dark – or momentous – moments: Argentina during its 'dirty war', Mexico during the religious persecutions, Vietnam on the eve of war, or Cuba just before the revolution. I wondered how these countries had been affected by the change or whether the atmosphere Greene evoked still remained.

In many ways, I was unprepared for my task. I had Inter-railed across Europe as a teenager, lain on beaches in Jamaica, spent two hellish weeks in a Mercedes truck on an escorted tour across southern Africa, but apart from my trip to Haiti, I had little experience of places on the verge of collapse or war zones. I comforted myself with the fact that Greene himself had set off on an expedition to walk across the unexplored hinterland of Liberia at the age of 31, in the company of his 23-year-old cousin Barbara, a journey which he later admitted 'was, to say the least, rash'. Greene was not gung-ho. He appreciated his creature comforts, as did I, but he pushed on, compelled by a desire to test his limits and face up to his inner self. By facing the devils of the Liberian bush, he hoped to put to rest the child within, still terrified by the spectre of a witch in the nursery linen closet. In that he was partly successful. I hoped that the same would apply to me.

Greene's visits to most of the countries were brief – usually no more than two or three weeks, even if he returned for subsequent visits. I intended to follow the same pattern. He was only too aware of the novelist's shaky role when writing about a place outside his intimate experience. '[The Americans] are just as ignorant of Africa as they were of Asia – except, of course, through novelists like Hemingway. He would go off on a month's safari arranged by a travel agency and write about white hunters and shooting lions – the poor, half-starved brutes reserved for tourists.' But impressions of a resident are necessarily different from those of a visitor, and when it comes to the truest insight neither has the monopoly.

I left The Lanes and re-emerged into sunlight by the Clock Tower, turning left to return to the seafront past the ugly concrete Paradox discotheque featuring Club Barcelona's 'Brighton's Best Over 25 Night'. Until the early 1980s this was Sherry's Dance Hall, with its 'little tables, the dancing partners with bright metallic hair and little black bags' where Pinkie took Rose. Back on the seafront the Palace Pier lay just as Ida had seen it, 'long, luminous and transparent, like a shrimp in the sunlight'. The sea stretched flat and grey all the way to France. Now I was thinking not of Greene – but of his alter ego – the travelling Aunt Augusta.

Aunt Augusta was greatly influenced by Henry's Uncle Jo. 'He wanted to slow life up and he quite rightly felt that by travelling he would make time move with less rapidity,' she explains. To this end, he set off on a round-the-world tour, but had to be carried off the train when he suffered a stroke at the start of his journey in Venice. Undaunted, Jo decided to find a house with 365 rooms, so he could continue to spend every night in a different place. When this proved impossible he settled on 52 rooms – one for every week of the year. After he suffered a second stroke in room 51, the doctor forbade him to be moved. But Jo disobeyed, crawling from his bed down the hallway towards room 52 – the lavatory. He collapsed and died in the passage.

'He died on his travels . . . As he would have wished,' says Aunt Augusta admiringly. Later on, she tells her nephew that she too wishes to prolong life as much as possible.

'. . . how many rooms have you occupied so far?' asks her nephew.

'A great many,' my aunt said cheerfully. 'But I do not think I have yet reached the lavatory floor.'

At the start of my travels, these were the words that stayed with me.

1. Mexico

This hating and hateful country

THE LAWLESS ROADS

I

To reach the centre of Mexico's troubles you need only take a short drive from the backpacker mecca of Palenque. The winding road carries you up out of the steamy tropical plains where the great Mayan ruins lie, into the *tierra templada*, the temperate region of vast coffee plantations, cattle ranches and marijuana farms. In the broccoli-green hills around you, there are gangs of paramilitaries, employed by the local landowners, whose role it is to kill any Indian who stands up for his rights. The traffic frequently slows behind convoys of tanks. At the side of the road, six-year-old children trudge barefoot, bent under the sacks of firewood on their backs. Indian women with worn faces wash bare-breasted in a stream. Men with machetes at their sides sift methodically through rubbish dumps.

My friend Guy and I were driving through this landscape in a white Volkswagen Beetle and I was very scared. Hold-ups were common on this road. This was the heartland of the Zapatistas – the rebel army who were fighting for the rights of the Indian people. It was a place where violent shoot-outs were common, where foreigners were not supposed to go.

We were heading for a church in the village of Bachajón, where we had an appointment with a priest. This was not the destination we gave the young soldier who stopped us at a checkpoint. The Beetle in front of us was being searched methodically, while its elderly driver sat smoking on the verge. On either side of the road, more soldiers were hiding in the undergrowth, holding the end of a spiked metal chain. If you ran the checkpoint, they pulled the chain taut, puncturing your tyres.

'We're going to Yajalon.'

'Yajalon?' The soldier turned to the tank parked behind him, with a 'what will these crazy gringos think of next?' look.

'Yes, Yajalon. A *muy famoso escritor Ingles* stayed there once. His name was Gray-ham Green-ee.'

The name rang no bells, but the excuse was so bizarre he waved us through. As soon as we left the main road, the tarmac deteriorated into a potholed mess. On either side of the road stalks of maize swayed forlornly in the breeze. Occasionally, a stetsoned cowboy galloped past us. The sky was black with an impending thunderstorm. In the surrounding mountains green-uniformed soldiers hidden under shiny green canopies of banana trees scanned the valley with binoculars.

Our first stop, Bachajón, was a fly-blown cluster of low whitewashed houses. It was siesta time and the town was ominously silent. We stopped at the simple white church with a maroon front door. A middle-aged man with a greying beard and glasses, wearing a faded denim jacket and jeans, walked warily down the nave to greet us. He was called Raffael and looked nothing like a priest. In Mexico, it is unwise to wear clerical dress. This church, he said, was one of the few still open in this state, Chiapas, today. In the past few years paramilitaries had closed forty in the area. A year previously, they had attacked and wounded two bishops on the outskirts of the town. Seven foreign priests, most of whom had lived in Mexico for decades, had recently been expelled. Two Jesuit priests had been sent to prison for five days, accused of being part of a street blockade which, in fact, they had been nowhere near.

'The name of the paramilitaries is *Paz y Justizia* – peace and justice,' Raffael said with a snort. 'They're a ghost army. The government and the landowners pay them to carry out their dirty work, so the real army keeps its hands clean. Last year, they massacred forty-five people – mainly women and children – as they were leaving a mass in the village of Acteal. They murder anyone they suspect of being a Zapatista and they rape their wives. They shoot at priests who try to help. The other day they killed an Indian couple. They cut off the husband's head then they slit open the wife's belly and put it there, so it looked as if she was pregnant. Another time, they opened the woman's belly and took her baby out.'

It was cold in the church. Raffael spoke in a murmur and looked around nervously. 'My position here is very weak,' he said. 'It's only because I'm Mexican that they haven't kicked me out yet. You shouldn't stay too long, it will look very bad. You could find yourself on a plane back to London by tonight.'

II

When Graham Greene went to Mexico, in 1938, the church was just coming to the end of a decade-long period of persecution by the state. Churches were burned, effigies of saints destroyed and priests executed. The socialist President Calles accused the priests of promoting superstition amongst the poor and encouraging their backwardness. Today, the government-funded paramilitaries are still killing clergy. The difference is that now they think the priests are teaching the peasants too much.

Greene was thirty-three and depressed when he set off for Mexico to investigate these atrocities for the Catholic newspaper *The Tablet*. He was not sorry to leave. In London, Shirley Temple was suing him for a review of her film *Wee Willie Winkie*, in which he concluded that the star's 'well-shaped and desirable little body' was displayed in too provocative a manner for a nine-year-old. The recent publication of *Brighton Rock* had done nothing to dispel Greene's disgust with the impermanence of modern life and its lack of moral direction. Europe was on the brink of war, polarized between the ideologies of Fascism and Communism. There was great pressure on young British writers to side with the latter, not least when it came to the Spanish Civil War. Some, most notably George Orwell, risked their lives to fight Franco's army. But Greene, although he claimed to dislike Franco, said he was unhappy about the left's persecution of the church. In some areas, priests were being murdered by the Republicans, churches gutted and nuns raped. Still a recent convert to Catholicism, he refused to take sides.

Sometime before he had left for Mexico, Greene returned to his home town of Berkhamsted and was appalled by the social chaos he found. A boy of twenty and a girl of fifteen had committed suicide by laying their heads on the railway line – a story also recalled by Pinkie in *Brighton Rock*. She was pregnant with her second child, the first had been born when she was twelve and her parents 'could not fix the responsibility . . . between 14 youths'. The local shops were selling a new game – Monopoly – which, for Greene, summed up the sterility of contemporary life: 'a few acres of land, a desirable residence for as long as the marriage lasts, the soil exacting no service and no love – no responsibility for the child on the line'.

In the midst of such depravity Greene wondered if faith offered the only means of coping. 'Even if it were all untrue and there were no God, surely life was happier with the enormous supernatural promises than with the petty social fulfilment, the tiny pension and the machine-made furniture,' he wrote in *The Lawless Roads*, his Mexican travelogue.

In Mexico, the disillusioned writer hoped to find some answers. The church had rarely had an easy time there. Ever since the revolution of 1910, it had been attacked continually by the state. Greene was inspired by tales of enduring faith and he became even more enthusiastic when he learned the story of Father Pro, a Jesuit who, at the height of the intolerance, remained at loose for two years in the southern Mexican states of Chiapas and Tabasco, dressed in 'a dark lounge suit, soft collar and tie, a bright cardigan'. Constantly evading the police, he held mass in private, heard confessions in the dark and gave the Sacrament to hundreds of people. Eventually, he was captured and executed. To Greene, Father Pro's tested faith was a symbol of how belief in the Catholic Church could help the individual to transcend these troubled times, if not provide a solution to a world on the brink of anarchy.

Greene was hoping for a replay of his adventures in Liberia two years earlier, a journey in search of his spiritual origins, for what might have existed before the corruptions of materialism set in. As ever, he was also excited at the prospect of adverse conditions. Shortly before his departure, he wrote excitedly to his brother, Hugh: 'The reading is as morbid as Liberia's. There seem to be even more diseases and an average of one shooting a week.' Yet almost as soon as he crossed the Texan border, disillusionment set in. His long-cherished dream quickly turned into a nightmare. At San Luis Potosí, halfway between the border and the capital, he witnessed a cockfight and was disgusted by the rituals performed around it. 'That, I think, was the day I began to hate the Mexicans,' he wrote.

By the time he reached Mexico City, Greene was declaring the country and everything connected with it 'hideous'. The same adjective is applied to everything from the trinkets sold in the market, to a politician's house, to a priest, to an old woman. He sneered at the other tourists, whose minds were 'sprightly with the legend of a happy and picturesque Mexico'. He found the food: 'repellent . . . if it isn't hot with sauces, it's nothing at all'. In some 'random thoughts' about the Mexicans, jotted down in the space of a train journey from Oaxaca to Puebla, Greene wrote: 'How one begins to hate these people . . . If this is what Spain is like I can understand the temptation to massacre.'

He vented his hatred in *The Lawless Roads*, one of the most bilious travel books ever written. Reading the book, a month before my departure, I was shocked by Greene's venom. Nothing in Mexico seemed to please him. The ugliest of motives were attributed to everything. When he sees men embracing in the street, he speak of: 'this immaturity, which gets most on the nerves in Mexico'. He is ill at the ruins of Palenque and wakes to find his guide leaning over him in concern. 'He had a feeling of responsibility, and no Mexican cares for that. It's like a disused limb they have learned to do without.'

I wondered if modern political correctness was what rendered my reading so uneasy, but contemporary reviewers also disliked Greene's tone. 'Wherever he went, ugliness stalked him and leered at him from things and beasts and humans,' wrote the *New York Times*. '. . . One suspects that even at the North Pole, Mr Greene would be harassed by mental mosquitoes'.

Yet, good was to come out of the experience. The peevish rantings of *The Lawless Roads* were recycled and transformed into what many regard as Greene's greatest novel, *The Power and the Glory*, the story of the 'whisky priest', ageing and alcoholic, on the run from the authorities. He is the last priest in Tabasco to have avoided capture and he is dogged by a Judas figure in the form of a wily *mestizo* – half-caste – who eventually betrays him. The priest dies without absolution but immediately after his execution another priest arrives in town looking for shelter.

But the novel could not appease the people of Tabasco and Chiapas, the southern states that Greene described so venomously. In San Cristóbal de las Casas, the mountain city that was the climax of Greene's journey, I visited Don Andrès Aubry, a French priest and the archivist of the diocese. He lived in a low pink house, typical of the town, with a red-tiled roof. I walked there up a steep, cobbled street that reminded me of a Yorkshire pit village. Dogs were lying everywhere, sleeping in the thin mountain sunshine. Don Andrès was a sort of Friar Tuck in mufti. He wore a baggy grey cardigan and a blue shirt with a button missing at the belly. He had a grey beard, a pointed face and chain-smoked local cigarettes. His dark sitting room smelt of the ashes from the previous night's fire. A decanter sat on a round table and the room was full of left-wing tracts and periodicals. He was very friendly until I asked him if he knew of Graham Greene.

'*Malheureusement!*' he cried. 'Oh! That book he wrote about Mexico. What a disaster! You know, I adored him when I was a teenager but after I read that I couldn't bear him any more. What he did here was incomprehensible. You know they couldn't even call that book *The Lawless Roads* here. They had to find another title for it. It ended up being *Un Otro Mexico* – Another Mexico. The whole thing was a caricature, he looked at Mexico through *des lunettes selectives*. It was all very distressing.'

An American woman who ran one of the city's English-language bookshops stocked the paperback but was no less outraged. 'Oh, the first time I read that book I was so angry, I threw it across the room,' she cried. She had a white, powdered face and wore big glasses that obscured her heavily made-up eyes. 'He's so bigoted. All those references to those little brown people who don't speak English and how the beer's too warm and nah, nah, nah. Well, like, hello! He's in Villahermosa for God's sake. What did he expect? At least he liked San Cristóbal, even though he got dysentery here. Hah! When I read that bit I laughed and laughed. But I have to say, he got the place right. If you walk up Real de Guadalupe where he celebrated the secret mass, you'll see. It hasn't changed a bit.'

The Mexico of my imagination had always been a dry and dusty place, of mules and cacti, of desolate canteens where you were served by dusky girls in full pink skirts and men in sombreros played mariachi music. But Greene had set his novel in 'the swampy puritanical state' of Tabasco, where crocodiles floated in the marshes and monkeys screamed from their jungle creepers. It sounded at best unpleasant, at worst dangerous. I had no desire to go there at all.

Greene went to Mexico to report on religious persecution, but by the time he had organized his journey, the rug had been pulled from under his feet. 'The pressure from the Catholic population was beginning to make itself felt' and across the country, the churches were re-opening. To find examples of martyrdom, Greene had to head south to Tabasco, where the purges had been carried out most enthusiastically by the state governor Tomás Garrido Cannabal, the model for *The Power and the Glory*'s idealistic lieutenant determined to create a just society.

Cannabal was a passionate, scrupulous man with two hatreds: alcohol and organized religion – both of which he saw as holding his people back. Under his regime both were banned. There were public burnings of statues of saints and mass singing of atheistical songs. Crosses were torn from their wearers' throats. Churches were used for the exhibition of livestock, with a donkey being named Christ, a bull God, a pig the Pope and a cow the Virgin of Guadalupe. The word *Adios* – goodbye – was banned because it literally meant: 'To God'. Gravestones were abolished. 'We die like dogs,' a local woman told Greene.

Yet he was too late, even for Tabasco. By the time he arrived, Cannabal had gone into exile in Costa Rica. He died in Los Angeles, California, in 1943. The atrocities Greene hoped to report on never materialized, although persecution of the clergy continued and the churches remained closed, thanks largely to the state's extreme isolation. In 1938, the only way to reach Villahermosa was to take a forty-two hour boat journey from Veracruz to the port of Frontera, followed by eleven hours in a paddle steamer down river. Today, I was relieved to learn, Villahermosa was just an hour's flight from Mexico City, in a tidy Boeing with telephones in the back of the seats. Its passengers were Mexican businessmen and women, executives of the oil companies that now flourished there.

Yet from the air, Tabasco looked as inhospitable as ever. The state consists of more water than land. My friend Guy and I could see nothing but silver-grey lagoons choked with water hyacinths and floating logs – or possibly crocodiles. Egrets perched in the trees like question marks. 'It was,' as the whisky priest observed 'as if this part of the world had never been dried in the flame when the world spun off into space.'

'This is my home,' said the man next to me, sadly. 'It rains all the time here. It is the second-wettest place in the world.'

'Where is the wettest place in the world?' I asked.

'Oh, I don't know. Somewhere in Africa.'

His name was Mr Prats and he was Mexico's answer to Oliver Reed. There was little hair on his head, but plenty fizzed out of the neck of his shirt, pink and white with a green ink stain on the pocket. He had been born in Mexico City, but for the past ten years he had lived in Villahermosa, where he managed a group of canning factories. Every time the drinks trolley went past he demanded another tequila.

'The place has improved you know,' he said. 'When I first came here it really was the swamps. The heat and the mosquitoes were terrible; now you have many more modern conveniences. I'll never forget the first time I returned home – the relief as the bus climbed up the mountains and I felt cool air again. It really was an escape. I read *The Power and the Glory* and I had so much pity for that priest. He wasn't just running from his persecutors you know, but from that environment. Having to sleep outdoors in this climate – it must have been hell on earth.'

He gave me an odd look. 'Why on earth are you here? Why don't you go to Cancún like all the other tourists?'

It was an unpropitious start. I read the guide book. 'Villahermosa used to be a dirty town but is now improving, though it is very hot and rainy . . . it can be difficult for lone women; local men's aggressive behaviour is said to be due to the effect of eating iguanas.'

Of course Greene loathed Villahermosa, where the lights were switched off at 9.30 p.m. prompt and the only alcohol available in the sweaty heat was flat warm beer. In 1938, the city had only 'one possible hotel', with a shower that didn't work and the food was 'unspeakable, worse than anything I had had or was to have in Mexico'. Despite Greene's loathing of cultural imperialism, he would surely have preferred today's city, which boasted a super-express highway, dozens of shopping malls, a five-star hotel, a Blockbuster, a Domino's Pizza and a KFC.

The lobby of the Hotel Miraflores, on one of the city's main pedestrianized streets, was full of men in suits and ties and women in silk shirts and high heels. It was early December and over our heads hung a vast Norman Rockwell poster of a jolly postman being chased by three apple-cheeked American schoolchildren. 'When a Child is Born' was piped through the dining room. Outside it was 90 degrees, but the air-conditioning kept the bloated mosquitoes at bay.

The bellboy showed us a double room on the seventh floor. 'No,' I said. 'I want a room with two beds.'

He looked at me in suppressed amusement. 'But this room is much nicer. The twin rooms are very small.'

'I don't care. I want two beds.'

He giggled. 'OK, if that's what you want.' He picked up the phone and called reception, smirking over his shoulder at Guy.

'Bad luck, *amigo*,' he whispered, as he showed us to our much pokier twin.

Guy was mortified. 'They must think I'm a total loser.'

'Why don't you tell them that I'm your sister?'

But Guy was too embarrassed to do this either. As we left the hotel for our evening stroll, the doorman had to stifle a chuckle. Two maids nudged and pointed at us. I smiled demurely, in what I hoped was a good impression of a determined virgin.

We strolled a few hundred yards to the Plaza de Armas on the banks of the wide river. It was a Sunday evening, just as it had been sixty years previously when Greene observed the evening parade there. 'Women in one direction, men in the other. Young men in red shirts milled boisterously around the gaseosa stands.' Now the gaseosa stands sold Squirt, a popular Mexican fizzy drink, from green and white crates and couples were embracing on the white iron benches. Music drifted from a cassette stand. Families were everywhere. A mother yelled at her small daughters not to touch the bird shit, a grandmother strolled arm in arm with her son. Their presence gave the city a safe, old-fashioned feel, much like the one sensed by Greene in Monterrey: '. . . it was as if these couples hadn't the need for lechery, their nerves were quieter'.

The dentist, the prison, the treasury that Greene described had all gone, replaced by shoe shops and restaurants. The ruined church had been fully restored. The 'continual sour smell' of the Grijalva River still permeated the air – but the only boat on it now was the Captain Beulo floating restaurant with its speciality of roast armadillo.

In the pedestrianized city centre, everyone was eating: hotdogs from paper napkins, ice cream from sticky cones, sweet corn and mayonnaise from paper cups. Oil had made Tabascans rich and, like their American neighbours, it had also made many of them fat. At nine o'clock the shops were still packed. In a beauty salon a man was having his hair blow-dried. Pop music boomed from every doorway. Only the scores of vultures screaming angrily on television aerials took you back to Greene's city, with its long Sunday nights with nothing to do but 'sit in Victorian rocking chairs swinging back and forth waiting for sunset and the mosquitoes'. Today, 'Behind the wire-netted window of a private house', families sat in darkness around flickering television screens.

Greene had arrived in Mexico on the heels of a social revolution. President Cárdenas had embarked on a programme of land redistribution, so that nearly all of the country's arable land was shared out among the peasants in the form of agricultural cooperatives. More than one in three Mexicans had received land. At the same time, he boosted the power of the unions. Just as Greene arrived in Mexico City, Cárdenas performed his most radical reform, the expropriation of oil from foreign companies. 'The country was stupefied and scared for its savings, and the exchange rate began to rocket down.'

President Cárdenas was one of the earliest members of the Institutional Revolutionary Party, or the PRI as everyone called it. Today, the PRI still exists – in fact it has ruled Mexico without a break for more than eighty years. But somewhere in the 1980s, along with most of the world, it discarded its socialist roots and became a party that Reagan and Thatcher could be proud of. The President of Mexico, Carlos Salinas, was determined to make his country the antithesis of Cárdenas's He attacked the unions and repealed Article 27 of the constitution, which guaranteed communal holdings for indigenous people. On 1 January, 1994, Salinas signed the North American Free Trade Agreement – NAFTA – making his country a bastion of free trade and private enterprise.

But hours before the signing, as Salinas's guests were welcoming in the New Year at a party in Mexico City, the host was summoned from the room. An aide had bad news. In the southern state of Chiapas, a group of masked, armed guerrillas had invaded the town of San Cristóbal de las Casas. They called themselves the Zapatistas, after the hero of the Mexican revolution, Emiliano Zapata. Their leader was a former college lecturer known as Subcomandante Marcos. Their demand was the reinstatement of Article 27 and withdrawal from NAFTA.

After this, things began to go very wrong for Mexico. As Manuel Camacho, who was appointed Commissioner for

Peace in the region, told me: 'The government had known
for years that the Zapatistas were gathering, but they had their
own reasons for pretending to know nothing about it. Salinas
was going to sign NAFTA, so they wanted Mexico to look
good and they thought that if there was trouble they could
get rid of the Zapatistas without much noise. The army did
deal with the Zapatistas quickly. But not quickly enough. By
the time they had got moving in Chiapas, so had every
journalist and every aid organization in the world. They
couldn't wipe them out. There would have been an outcry.'

As the Zapatistas advanced, international investors fled. A
car bomb exploded in Mexico City, in Puebla an electricity
tower was blown up. The Zapatistas were known to have
stolen a ton and a half of dynamite from the army, enough to
destroy any major oil installation in the country. A few months
later, the stock market crashed. By the end of that year, a
presidential candidate had been assassinated and the Mexican
peso had collapsed. Prices rose. Standards of living went dramatically down. The dream the PRI had promised the people
was over before it had even begun, but in the next election
the party still won by a landslide.

In Villahermosa everything still seemed civilized enough.
Guy and I sat outside a café on the main pedestrianized street.
The waitress came to take our order.

'Two beers, please.'

She returned with two coffees.

'We asked for beer.'

'We don't have any. This is a coffee bar, you know.'

A man at the next table was listening to us. 'You are from
where?' he asked.

He didn't like our answer. 'England? So you are harbouring
that criminal who used to be our president.'

Guy, unlike me, knew what he was talking about: 'No,

you're thinking of Ireland. That's where Salinas is living now. Ireland has no extradition treaty with Mexico. He's safe there.'

The man liked Guy's answer. His name, he said, was René. In Mexico this was a very bad name. 'You know the Muppet Show? You know Kermit the Frog? Well, in my country his name is René la Rana. You wouldn't believe what a bad time I had at school.'

René was a travelling salesman from Puebla, near Mexico City, whose mission was to flog tights with the curious brand name of Dorian Grey. He had small, smiling eyes buried in fleshy Indian cheeks and a shiny, floppy fringe. He had just come from evening mass in the twin-spired cathedral that Cannabal had razed and turned into a children's playground. 'So busy, I couldn't even find a seat,' he said. 'We Mexicans are *muy creyente*. You English are not, I think. We can do nothing without our Virgins. We have Virgins for the taxi drivers, the bus drivers, the workers in the Volkswagen factory. We even have a Virgin of the pantyhose. Below her, in a glass case we display all the different brands and styles available. There is a Virgin for socks, too.'

René had never heard of Graham Greene, but he knew all about Tomás Garrido Cannabal. 'In Tabasco, he is a hero,' he said. 'The largest park is named after him, so are several streets. What he did to the priests was terrible, but most people think he was a good governor. He did many things to promote the material well-being of the people. He promoted rights for women. He introduced sex education into schools. He encouraged the people to take control of their own destinies. In many people's eyes, the church was a complacent, greedy organization and Cannabal was a great revolutionary.'

Today, however, the Mexican government is about as radical as Mrs Beeton's *Book of Household Management*. René recalled: 'Our chief of police had a collection of 2,000 cars.

His house was so large it was later turned into a university. The ex-president's brother stole $80 million from us and put it in a Swiss bank account. *Es in-cre-ible.* Unbelievable. So, in the circumstances, who can blame us for putting our faith in a man who was born from a virgin and rose from the dead?'

One of the eternal mysteries of Mexico was how no one had a good word to say about the government, yet every taxi bumper and shop window was plastered with stickers pledging undying love to the PRI.

'Bribes,' said René. 'If they display them they're given a crate of beer. Or hopelessness. Five, ten years ago, we got angry with our government. We tried to change things. But they didn't work. Now we just despair. We figure since there will never be any change, why not accept five hundred pesos from the PRI and put their posters everywhere.'

On the street, the Mexicans you saw looked like René. They had heavy eyelids that gave them an air of ineffable patience, hook noses and thick lips. They were the living embodiment of the Mayan carvings that decorated the great pyramids of the Yucatan. In contrast, the PRI candidates, so prominently displayed on every lamp-post, had long noses and thin lips, indicating their direct descent from the conquistador elite. Their names too spoke of long-distinguished lineages – Madrazo, Bartlett – all figures from Greene's travels, sixty years previously.

'They're their sons,' confirmed René. 'In Mexico, there are never any changes.'

III

It was not until the following morning, when we left Villa-hermosa in a rented Volkswagen Beetle that we realized precisely how little Greene's Mexico had changed. The landscape was as lazily primitive as ever. We drove through a string of hot quiet towns. Turkeys gobbled in the dust. Men were hacking at palm nuts with machete blades. A child pulled at an obstinate cow and a black hairy pig strained at its chain. A man lay comatose in a hammock strung across his porch, while a toucan swung above him in a cage. Once, we swerved to avoid a dead armadillo.

Hiring the car had been an ordeal. The droopy-moustached man from the rental agency had insisted on laboriously checking every feature of the vehicle against a list. 'Windscreen wiper? Ashtray? Radio?' There was no radio, but he spent a good five minutes suspiciously tapping the fittings just to make sure.

Guy was feeling ill. His face had a strange grey sheen to it. 'Could you hurry up?' he barked eventually. The man gazed at him reproachfully.

'I have to make the check.'

'Don't speak to him like that,' I hissed. 'It's not his fault he's slow. It's the Mexican way.'

'Which is exactly why their country is going down the drain. Now I know why they call it a Mexican stand-off.'

At least now there were roads in Tabasco. The only way Greene could reach Villahermosa was by boat from the port of Veracruz. When Greene's guide heard of this plan, he was horrified. 'Nothing – nothing will ever make me go on that boat again. You don't know – it's terrible.' Sure enough, Greene endured forty-two hours of seasickness, claustrophobia and terror on a rotting barge that he 'wouldn't have

gone down the Thames in'. When it arrived in Frontera, he
had to join a paddle steamer for a hellish, ten-hour journey
down the River Grijalva. Today, the same trip took just
forty-five minutes. It would have taken considerably less had
it not been for *Topes*.

I saw the first sign for Topes about a mile out of town. 'Can
you see it on the map?' Guy asked. We were driving along a
wide, flat road flanked by swamp land choked with giant water
hyacinth. 'Ooff'.

We had hit a speed bump.

I scanned the map. 'No, I can't. Ooff. Next time you see
one of those things, slow down.'

Thirty or so speed bumps later, we deduced that *Topes* was
the Mexican word for speed bump. In fact, they were a
Mexican obsession. They punctuated every highway in the
land and were responsible for the extraordinary number of
Beetles in circulation lacking a front bumper.

'Fucking *topes*,' René ranted, when we returned to Villahermosa. 'They are Mexico's only contribution to the world. Do
you know how much tax we pay? Thirty-five per cent? It's
bloody going up another five per cent next year. At least for
your taxes you get hospitals and universities. What do we get?
Topes.'

Frontera was a fly-blown port at the mouth of the wide
Rio Grijalva. Greene had renamed it Obregon and set the
opening scenes for *The Power and the Glory* there:

Shark fins glided like periscopes at the mouth of the Grijalva River
. . . three or four aerials stuck up into the blazing sky from among
the banana groves and the palm-leaf huts; it was like Africa seeing
itself in a mirror across the Atlantic. Little islands of lily plants came
floating down from the interior, and the carcasses of old stranded
steamers held up the banks. And then round a bend in the river

Frontera . . . the Presidencia and a big warehouse and a white
blanched street running off between wooden shacks.

Despite its desolate appearance, Frontera had once been the
gateway to southern Mexico. Steamboats had ploughed up
and down the Grijalva. Today, most of the boats that left
Frontera were fishing dugouts. In the main square, 'the two
stalls that sold mineral water' still stood, surrounded by empty
metal tables. Only the hairdressers and dentists that to Greene
were the 'inevitable' components of small-town life had gone,
replaced by their modern equivalent – shoe shops and chem-
ists. The regulation branch of Alcoholics Anonymous was
tucked down a side street. Two supermarkets sat side by side.
Loudspeakers hooked above their entrances crackled with
news of the best bargains. On the other side of the square,
outside the customs house, a sailor all in white was smoking a
cigarette. It was as if an extra from *South Pacific* had wandered
on to the set of *High Noon*.

We checked in to the Maya de Grijalva hotel a few yards
from the waterfront. The dingy tiled lobby looked untouched
since Greene's day, with the exception of some Kodachrome
posters of motorboats. The proprietor had a droopy, once
handsome, face. He wore baggy jeans and a white jersey top
and was amazed, but pleased, to see us. 'Foreigners never
come here. You do realize we have no hot water. *No – hot –
water.* Will that be all right for you?'

We showed him a picture taken by Greene of his hated
steamer, the *Ruiz Cano*. 'Of course, I remember it,' the man
said, grinning as if at an old friend. 'It was one of five boats.
Some were wood, some were steel. They used to go up and
down the river, picking up people and bananas, and then they
set out to sea, north to Veracruz. They've all sunk now,
though.'

Our room had a tiled floor, a black wooden wardrobe, a dappled mirror and psychedelic orange and brown curtains. A ceiling fan dangled perilously from two frayed wires. I crushed an ant that was running up my arm. Guy swatted a mosquito. It was full of blood. By six, he was deep in a sweaty sleep. I went out on to the balcony. Twilight was settling over the town. A few boys were kicking a football, some men sitting on iron benches. The vultures that Greene had hated with their 'little idiot heads and dusty serrated wings' were circling overhead.

I glanced into the room next door. A fat hairy man was lying on his bed in his underpants. Sweat glistened on his belly. His floor was covered in empty beer cans. My shins began to itch and swell as the work of the mosquitoes made itself felt. 'The place will be dead by ten o'clock,' the proprietor had boasted. 'We have none of those *delincuentes* here, you know.'

Frontera was the first landing place in Mexico of the Spanish conquistadors, in March, 1519. No wonder they had got straight out. I remembered what René had said. 'Cannabal succeeded in destroying the church in Tabasco, but he wouldn't have stood a chance in the rest of Mexico. The point was so few priests could bear it here, that the Catholic church didn't have the roots that it had elsewhere. Tabasco is not a spiritual place.' The depressed American dentist, whom Greene met on the *Ruiz Cano*, had put it another way: 'They don't care about religion here, it's too hot.'

IV

For otherworldliness, you had to travel on from Frontera, back through Villahermosa and down the modern highway that led to Palenque, an ancient Mayan city whose stones were said to emanate mystic vibes. In the parlance of the New Age, Palenque was a 'vortex', a place where the earth's spiritual energies are concentrated, along with a variety of psychics, spirit channellers, healers, astrologers and ufologists all intent on finding cheap jewellery and the meaning of life.

Greene, who had not the slightest interest in Mayan architecture, was forced to visit Palenque in order to give the authorities a reason for his presence in this troubled region. It was a considerable undertaking that began with a flight in a tiny biplane from Villahermosa to the little town of Salto de Agua in the jungle. From there, the only way across the 'bare exposed plateau' to the ruins was by mule. It took Greene a day to reach Palenque: 'one of the worst days I have ever spent'. His flimsy sunhat soon turned into damp cardboard, the unrhythmic plodding of the mule jarred his spine and made his head and neck ache. He began his journey at four in the morning and arrived after nightfall at a 'collection of round mud huts'. There was no hotel. Greene slept in a hammock in the tin-roofed school to the sound of crying children and coughing cows.

In England, studying this account in *The Lawless Roads*, I dreaded Palenque. I didn't know that today you could travel there on an air-conditioned bus with on-board lavatories, reclining seats, a video showing *GI Jane*, starring Demi Moore, and a selection of German backpackers who spent the whole journey absorbed in the Lonely Planet guide. When we arrived, after two-and-a-half comfortable hours, there were fifty hotels to chose from. Ours had a swimming pool the size of Wales and was hosting a dry-cleaners' conference.

Yet the town of Palenque itself was still much as Greene had known it. There were rows of dusty streets running up the hill to the main plaza, the only difference being that today they were lined with travel agencies offering excursions to

Guatemala and healers' parlours where you could have your aura read. A wind chime dangled over every doorway. In the cafés, morose couples in matching North Face cagoules sat silently absorbed in their Booker Prize shortlisted novels, and strapping blondes in tasselled skirts drank margaritas and discussed whether they had been a Mayan or an Egyptian princess in their past lives.

Surrounded by jungle, at the foot of the Chiapas mountains, and looking out over the flat plains of the Yucatan, Palenque was one of the greatest cities in Mayan civilization. Its club-footed king, Pakal, lived for a hundred years and reigned over a culture that developed the only pre-Columbian writing in the Americas. In the ninth century it was abruptly abandoned. Nobody has ever been able to work out why. The New Agers have their theories though. 'In 900 AD, time ended,' said Anastasia, a strapping New Zealander with several rings through her lip, whom I met on the bus to the ruins. 'It's going to happen again in December 2012. That's the end of the next *baktum*. That's what the Mayans called each period of 5128 years.'

I did some frantic calculations. Guy got there quicker. 'But 5000 years ago is 3000 BC. And you said time ended in 900 AD?'

'Yeah, well there were sort of mini ends of time every now and then. That's why Palenque stopped. But 2012 is a mega end of time. A crystal city is going to descend on Palenque and carry it up into the fourth dimension. I can't wait. I'm trying to find a place to live here, so I can be around to see it. It'll be really cool.'

Greene, of course, loathed Palenque. It took him two and a half hours to travel there from the town by mule, his guide hacking through the jungle with a machete. By the time they arrived he was too exhausted and angry to do more than glance at the interiors of one or two of the 'gnarled ruins'. Petulantly, he decided: 'I had told people I was here in Chiapas to visit the ruins and I had visited them; but there was no compulsion to see them.' So he crawled in to an Indian twig hut and refused to move, despite the supplications of his anxious guide.

At that time, archaeologists were just beginning to rescue the cold stones from the jungle full of jaguars and howler monkeys, but Greene doubted they would succeed. He was wrong. Today, we walked over springy grass dwarfed by giant pyramids cut from the surrounding trees. We climbed the outside of the Temple of the Inscriptions, 25 metres high, and from the summit descended cold, slippery steps to its centre, where nearly a thousand years ago the body of King Pakal was placed in a tomb, his face covered in an obsidian death mask. We explored the palace decorated with eight-foot carvings of Mayan warriors. From its bell tower at the winter solstice, the priests and royal families had watched the sun set directly on the Temple of Inscriptions. Now, however, it was closed to the public. 'Last year, a man jumped off it,' said the guide. 'He had eaten too many magic mushrooms.'

At the entrance, a Hari Krishna centre offered vegetarian food and meditation. In the jade-green waterfall below the ruins we found two white rastas washing their crusty dreadlocks. At sunset, every pyramid was topped with a bare-chested Dutchman, with beads around his neck, having a 'moment'.

In the minibus back to town, we bumped into Anastasia again. She was talking to an Australian couple, both blonde, stocky and sunburnt.

'We don't know what to do next. We're thinking of San Cristóbal but we're not too sure,' said the man, fingering his guitar.

'Yeah,' said his girlfriend. 'It's a *siddy*.'

'It'll just be more of the usual crap,' he continued. 'Just more colonial architecture and beautiful old doorways.'

V

To Greene, San Cristóbal de las Casas was like an oasis in the desert. In Mexico City, he had visited the exiled Bishop of Chiapas, and his imagination had been touched by his descriptions of a 'very Catholic town'. In *The Lawless Roads* he wrote: 'I began to regard the city of Las Casas hidden there in the mountains, at the end of a mule track, with only one rough road running south, as the real object of my journey.'

To the whisky priest, the city was to remain a tantalizing prospect forever to be denied him. ' "It's a fine state over the border," a woman said . . . "you'd be happy there, father." ' Greene made it, but only after another arduous journey. From Palenque, he retraced his footsteps to Salto de Agua by mule. From there, he flew in a tiny scarlet plane over the mountain ridges of Chiapas to Yajalon where he waited in vain for a plane to take him to San Cristóbal 12,000 feet in the mountains. After a week, he gave up, and continued by mule.

As soon as you leave Palenque for the long climb to San Cristóbal, you are in Indian country. From the Beetle's window we saw roadside settlements unchanged since Greene's day. 'Half a dozen huts of mud and wattle stood in a clearing . . . a few pigs routed round.' Then, Greene had described the villagers as 'Stone Age creatures', 'living on the edge of subsistence' and statistics showed that nothing had changed. Nine out of ten children living in these villages were severely malnourished. There were regular deaths from cholera, TB and diarrhoea.

We stopped in one village to buy a snack. To enter a hut, we had to bend double. Three mattresses lay on a dirt floor, bedding for a family of ten. There was a porthole-sized hole cut in one wall for ventilation. Anything larger would have made the cold mountain nights intolerable. The kitchen contained a metal brazier over cold ashes, a metal rolling pin and a clay pot. There was no chimney and the walls were black with smoke. Some dried meat hung from a stick above the stove. A woman in a long blue dress and white blouse with pink flowers around the neck sold us two greasy *empanadas*. She spoke even less Spanish than I did. Her language was the Indian dialect of Tzotzil.

If there had been any changes in these people's environment, it was in the surrounding jungle, once thick and bountiful but now scrubby and sparse. The trees were all being cut down for firewood. 'The government gives them gas stoves but they just sell them in the market and use the money to buy clothes,' René had told us. And every village had a basketball court with a rusting hoop. Weeds would be growing out of the cracked tarmac. They were the legacy of one of the government's sporadic programmes to help the Indians. No one in Mexico City remembered that the average indigenous male is little more than five foot high and therefore unsuited to the game of basketball.

The Mexican revolution had promised each man ten acres of land, but in Chiapas this had never been fully implemented. The Indians, who had lived in their villages for generations, had copies of presidential decrees dating back for decades that recognized their rights to land, but their attempts to have them upheld always failed. The landowners appealed in court and used their political clout to see that those rights would never be enforced. Occasionally, Indians invaded land that they believed to be rightfully theirs and were only ejected after the army came in and massacred dozens of them.

If there was any support for the Indians, it came from the *catequistas* – lay preachers trained by the San Cristóbal diocese to go out among the Indians, speak to them in their languages and encourage them to create a better world in this life, rather than waiting for the next. Greene lamented that the priests who had been driven away had been the only ones who had 'learned the Indian dialects and acted as necessary interpreters between one village and another, who had shown interest in them as human beings'. Exactly the same was true today and the authorities did not like it.

It was on the road from Palenque to San Cristóbal that we made our detour to the church in Bachajón, and talked to its priest. From there we travelled on down an increasingly battered track to Yajalon, a 'long mean tin-roofed village beside one of the tributaries of the Grijalva river'.

In *The Power and the Glory*, Greene renamed Yajalon La Candelaria. During his week there, waiting for transportation to San Cristóbal, his mornings were passed drinking ginger beer and eating chocolate at the cantina. The afternoons he spent drinking coffee with a Norwegian widow of a coffee farmer. Her daughter, who was being educated by correspondence from America, was the model for the character of Coral Fellowes, the saintly British girl who befriends the whisky priest. A local clerk, 'a mestizo with curly sideburns and two yellow fangs at either end of his mouth', who ate every night at Greene's lodgings and whom he 'grew to loathe' was transformed into the Judas figure who betrays the whisky priest.

There were times when it was hard to comprehend quite why Greene had hated Mexico, and the friendly, courteous Mexicans so much. But in Yajalon it was easy. The only pretty thing in the town was the pebbly stream crossed by an arched stone bridge that could have been imported from Dorset. In the run-down plaza, there was 'the inevitable bandstand and a statue in florid taste of a woman in a toga waving a wreath'. Excerpts from the United Nations Declaration of Human Rights were painted on the walls of every public building. The roads were full of rubble and potholes, filled with empty Coke bottles. A woman in a chemist's shop leant yawning on a grubby display case containing Oxy 10 acne cream, Huggies, and Johnson's Baby Oil. The only sign of diversion came in the form of a few posters plastered on to doors proclaiming the visit of a band called *Ladron* – thief – in two weeks' time. For the first time in Mexico, no one seemed remotely pleased to see us. Children giggled, but their fathers, in stetsons with machetes strapped to their thighs, stared unsmiling through us.

We stopped at a restaurant with a palm-leaf roof and a placard outside promising us *cocktail de mariscos* – prawns. We were as far from the sea as it was possible to be, but there was nothing else to do but dine. Two men were sitting in a corner watching a black-and-white western. The young waiter gaped at the sight of us. He rushed to the tape deck and put on a Chuck Berry cassette.

'What are you doing here?' he shouted over the strains of 'Roll Over Beethoven'.

'We heard there was a good seafood restaurant here,' I said emolliently. 'We wanted to try it.'

Our prawn cocktails were served in ice-cream glasses. They were a dusky pink and tasted of mayonnaise and chlorine.

'I'm not eating this,' Guy said. 'It'll kill us.'

Embarrassment made me eat, although to be killed by a south Mexican prawn cocktail would have been more embarrassing.

'You'll be sick,' Guy said.

'I know,' I said chewing fast. 'But at least by then we'll be out of Yajalon.'

The waiter stood mournfully over Guy's untouched glass. 'Don't you like it?'

'Yes,' said Guy. 'But I'm not very hungry. A big breakfast you see.'

We were not sorry to leave Yajalon. '*Pronto Retorno*' exhorted a sign by the roadside. Suddenly, Guy stopped. Two barefoot boys, in their early teens, on either side of the road had barred the road, by pulling taut a piece of string. 'They're holding us up.'

Another boy ran towards us. 'Don't give him all your money,' I hissed.

'Please sir, I wonder if you can help us. We are collecting for our village. We want to build more *Topes*.'

VI

Greene was not helped in his travels by the fact that he spoke virtually no Spanish. In Salto de Agua, a town now at the heart of the Zapatista campaign, he found himself 'hopelessly at a loss'. 'Always before there had been *someone* who spoke English.' His chutzpah astonished me. Sixty years on from his visit, almost no Mexican I met could speak a word of English, and those who did were to be mistrusted as con men intent on scraping a few pesos from a dumb tourist.

Luckily, Guy's Spanish was excellent. Mine was adequate and was to improve on subsequent trips, thanks to the fact that I spoke Italian (if in doubt take the 'o' off each word and speak as if you're clearing your throat) and a language cassette I had played to myself in my tiny London kitchen, in the few weeks before we departed.

The cassette seemed to be designed to ensure that the student put herself in as many compromising situations as possible. The first exercise involved being approached by a strange man in a bar. 'Excuse me,' he said, 'are you Señora Rodriguez?' Rather than being taught: 'No, now fuck off, you sleazeball,' I had to say, 'No. I am not Señora Rodriguez. But I *am* Julia. How nice to meet you.'

Starved as he was of human interaction, it was no wonder that Greene's happiest moments in Mexico took place at a *finca* – farm – just outside Palenque that belonged to the English-speaking Herr R – who reappeared in *The Power and the Glory* as the Lutheran pastor Mr Lehr. Herr R was born in Germany, but ran away when his father demanded he joined the army. He went to America, then moved to Mexico to be an agent for various firms. He settled on his own *finca*, determined, like his neighbouring landowners, to do everything he could to deprive the peasants of their birthright. 'When the *agraristas* demanded land he gave them a barren fifty acres he had not the means to develop himself – and saved himself taxes.'

Like all the foreigners Greene met, Herr R had come to Mexico to seek his fortune and been disappointed. His hope of a better life had been thwarted by the country's instability: '. . . there had been revolutions of course – he had lost crops and cattle to the soldiers and he had been fired on as he stood on his porch'. Today, the foreigners who settled in Mexico set up organic coffee shops, vegetarian restaurants, English language bookshops and high-quality bed and breakfasts. Yet politics still had a nasty habit of interfering with their dream.

We visited one such establishment run by Glen and Ellen, a middle-aged couple from Idaho, on their ranch just a few miles outside the town of Ocosingo and midway between Yajalon and San Cristóbal. We stayed in a wooden hut ('Twin

beds? Are you sure?' Ellen asked) with a hammock on the
porch. Swinging there, you looked out at neat rows of young
macadamia trees. Behind them were fields of brown and green
maize. Behind them were banana groves and behind that was
the purplish bruised wall of the Chiapas mountains. A goat
nibbled at the grass, a peacock cried and a rabbit bounded into
the woods. There was no electricity – just oil lamps and a
chilly outhouse in place of flush toilets. In the Indian villages
such conditions had shocked me, but here they seemed
romantic.

'Welcome to another shitty day in paradise,' said Ellen.

A few hundred yards away, across some farmers' fields, were
the ruins of Toniná, another cluster of Mayan pyramids. The
tour buses rarely came here. We shared the steep pyramids
and their cold inner chambers with two guides, a horse and
three cows.

'What a beautiful spot,' someone had written in Rancho
Esmeralda's Guest Book. 'What a shame the Mayans had such
a violent history.'

Today, the same sentiments applied. Ocosingo was at the
heart of the combat zone. During the 1994 Zapatista rebellion,
no one was hurt in San Cristóbal because that was where the
tourists and media were. But in this small market town, hidden
from the world's cameras, scores were killed and hundreds
wounded. Most of the victims were innocent villagers, caught
in the crossfire between government troops and the rebel
army. From the summit of Toniná, we could see the brand-
new sprawling army base. In Chiapas, soldiers outnumber
civilians by seventeen to one.

After supper, we sat by the campfire and watched the
fireflies. The night was alive with the chorus of cicadas and
bullfrogs, drowned out by an occasional crash of an explosion
from the valley.

'Don't worry,' said Ellen, seeing my face. 'It's not the Zapatistas. It's fireworks. The festival of the Virgin of Guadalupe is only five days away now.'

She was in her forties, with a pretty face and long hair that was turning grey. Glen was older and much taller. His grey locks were tied back in a pony tail. They had met in America, joined the peace corps and lived in Santo Domingo and Argentina, before settling at Rancho Esmeralda six years previously. Ellen spoke gently about how much she would have liked children. Glen couldn't see the point of them. 'I only get kids when they're six or older. Then you can put them to work on the fencing.' They drove an old yellow American school bus and looked like a pair of ageing hippies, but when they spoke their opinions were pure American.

'You must have been pretty upset when they built the army base,' said Guy.

'Well, no, not really,' Glen said. 'They're pretty quiet boys there. They've been instructed to keep on friendly terms with the locals, and if they keep the Zapatistas at bay then they're welcome.'

I was amazed. Surely every right-on person sided with the freedom-fighting Zapatistas?

'I'm sure they have a point,' said Ellen. 'But they made the people of Ocosingo endure a terrifying ordeal. Our friends were huddled in their houses for days without food. Mexicans don't keep stores, so they had to sneak out to buy things. That was when most people were killed. It was friendly fire from the army, in fact, but no one resented that. They resented the Zapatistas for coming in the first place.'

But didn't the Zapatistas have the right idea? Ellen shook her head slowly. 'They want justice, yes, but they are too ideological. They are looking for a perfect world and will not settle for anything less. Some of the less radical *campesinos* are making more practical demands. They know that things don't become perfect overnight. They are the ones we should be supporting.'

The Zapatistas had turned down government offers of drastic increases in health and education funding. They said they had heard such promises before, that the new hospitals would soon fall into disrepair, that the teachers would return disillusioned to the cities. For now, they were hiding in the jungle longing for the rainy season precisely for the reason that the whisky priest dreaded it, because all roads through the jungle would be impassable. Just a few miles away sat the army perpetually watching but never daring to pounce, lest the wrath of the developed world should fall on its head.

Had Glen and Ellen still been living in Idaho, they would probably have supported Subcomandante Marcos and his men. Living in the middle of it, things appeared quite different. 'Our friends in Ocosingo think we are crazy to live out here, in such an isolated spot,' Ellen said. The ranch had no phone. 'For months, no one would visit us here. I guess it's the most dangerous spot in Mexico, but the beauty makes up for that. Not that the local people can appreciate that. They have never been anywhere else in the world, so they have no idea about the beauty of their surroundings.'

'They have no idea about anything much at all,' said Glen.

'It's true,' said his wife. 'I was watching a beautiful sunset with the cook one evening. She turned to me and said "Doña Elena, where do you think the sun goes at night?" Trying to explain in Spanish wasn't easy.'

'We watched *Apollo 13* on video with our staff once. They were astonished. They were all saying "But did this really happen? Are you expecting us to believe that man has been to the moon?"'

Statistically, there was no reason why this should be surprising. In Ocosingo, nearly half the population can't read. There is no running water in 57 per cent of homes, no electricity in 67 per cent, and 89 per cent still do their cooking on wood fires. In the smallholdings surrounding the ranch the peasants preserved their own justice system. Wrongdoers were not tried, they were simply taken into the hills and left tied to a tree for three days with just water and corn gruel left at arm's length. Yet something was not quite adding up. Chiapas produces most of Mexico's electricity and nearly half of its natural gas. Every day twenty buses, each one carrying a dozen tourists following the gringo trail from Palenque to San Cristóbal, make a fill-up stop in Ocosingo. The foreigners descend from the air-conditioned vehicles, have a cigarette and reboard. The two cultures brush against each other continually without ever making contact.

Ellen laughed when I asked her if the locals had been welcoming. 'Not at all. They're not exactly hostile, but they are very suspicious of us. They give our staff a pretty hard time. They tell them they are earning too much money. My cook once came to me and asked if I could pay her less. I had to explain that there was nothing wrong with wanting the best out of life for yourself. But then they're pretty conformist here. They don't like Glen much, because he doesn't get drunk with them.'

'I like to drink,' Glen said, sucking on his roll-up. 'I have a beer in my hand all day long. But these guys roll up here at eleven o'clock in the morning and they're already wasted. They don't have anything to get up for the next day, so it's all right for them.'

Ellen stood up, her back to the fire. 'The problem with Mexico is that too many promises have been made by too many people. Once there was a great *finca* next door to the ranch. It was owned by a foreigner who never came here.

After the Zapatista rebellion, some peasants occupied it. The government said to the foreigner, "Let's make things easy. Sell it to us for half price and we'll give it to them." So the smallholders moved in, but of course the land can't support them all. Each family has an average of eight children – four sons who all grow up expecting to be handed ten acres and a job. And no one will say why someone who has worked hard to create a successful farm should hand it over to the people. Even the newspapers can't make up their mind if the peasants are occupying land or stealing other people's property. Often, in the same article, they refer to it both ways. Things are very confused.'

VII

We left early the following morning. Diaphanous green-grey mist was rising off the valley. Barefoot children stood in the maize fields, shouting '*gringo, gringo!*' In the Ocosingo market, Indian women sat cross-legged, a few oranges at their feet. Two men were shooting the breeze in a shop doorway. A parrot sat on a post between them, squawking greetings at passers-by. Vultures slept on telephone poles like sentries. We overtook dozens of pick-up trucks, laden with happy, singing people. A runner carrying a burning torch ran in front of each one. They were pilgrims on their way to San Cristóbal for the Festival of the Virgin of Guadalupe.

As the sun rose the temperature dropped. We were climbing out of the African lushness of the valley into a landscape of limestone cliffs and thick pine forests. It was like a shabby Switzerland. Barefoot children squatted dully at the roadside with snot running down their faces. Their bright costumes were covered with filthy padded jackets. Poverty that could seem so picturesque in the sunshine was revealed in all its squalor in the damp mist. On the occasional rock, you could make out a message in white spray paint. '*Dios es Amor*'. God is Love.

But in San Cristóbal, finally, we were in the happy land of the tourist brochures. The town sat in a bowl surrounded by mountains that Greene described as 'crouching like large and friendly dogs'. From the Basilica of Guadalupe that sat on the hillside like a miniature Sacré-Coeur you looked over a city of red-tiled roofs. Cobbled streets sloped down the hillside lined by low houses in yellow, purple and duck-egg blue. Few had windows, occasionally an open wooden door allowed a glimpse into a sunny courtyard with a fountain splashing in the middle. In Greene's day, donkeys plodded round the town, 'laden with bright chemical gaseosas for the saloons'. Today, there was constant background noise of clanking metal, from the lorry carrying gas canisters, which dragged a metal chain behind it to proclaim its presence in the neighbourhood.

All roads led to the main square dominated by the sky-blue and white town hall, and full of newspaper stalls and shoeshine stands. Children in maroon school blazers chased each other around the bandstand, old men in broad-brimmed stetsons gossiped on the metal benches.

Even Greene had been initially taken by San Cristóbal, although he felt wretchedly conspicuous as a lone stranger 'whose presence in town was known to everybody and suspected by most', while a vicious attack of dysentery left him as miserable as ever. Today, the town has become a travellers' hang-out in the mould of King's Cross in Sydney or Kathmandu, and full of placebos for the homesick. The mile-long street to the Basilica of Guadalupe that Greene had described as being lined with 'little stores selling identically the same things – pottery, guitars, serapes, candles', was now busy with Internet cafés and sushi bars, launderettes and jewellery shops.

The Hotel Español, which in Greene's day had been the only hotel in town was now the Hotel Flamboyant Español, with a blue and yellow chocolate-box exterior and rooms available at $45 a night. The girl at reception had fat legs encased in white tights, a pale face, greasy brown hair and a terrible cold. We were put in a room on the ground floor, looking out over the obligatory internal courtyard with Andrex-pink walls and splashing fountains. The Español was a fixture on the tour bus route. We were kept awake most of the night by the sound of boisterous Italians in the courtyard. Greene enjoyed a 'beautifully cooked meal, steak and greens and sweet bread' there; we had our worst breakfast in Mexico: fried eggs turned cold lying on a bed of carrot and cabbage, blotting-paper bread, slimy fried potatoes mixed with stringy onion, tumescent chunks of tinned sausage and watered-down orange juice.

In San Cristóbal, you were always cold. The city had a Saharan latitude, but it also had an Alpine altitude. Even at midday the thick-walled haciendas, built by the homesick Spanish, retained a dank chill. Outdoors, you learned to dodge the patches of shade as if they were potholes in the road, and seek out pools of sunshine. At night, fires were lit and central heating became a prize commodity. The doorstep of the electrical shop was taken over by the town's street children who gathered every evening to watch the soaps through the glass. Strapping Germans in stonewashed denims covered their daytime T-shirts with heavy fleeces and set out in search of organic vegetarian lasagna, brushing away the little girls with bare feet in long black skirts who danced around their legs shouting '*Un peso, un peso*'.

It took the Spanish four years of hard fighting before they

took San Cristóbal from the Indians in 1528. For years after
that it was known as 'Villaviciosa' because of the brutal exploi-
tation of its Indians. The conquistadors dealt with the rebels
by hurling them into the mile-deep Canyon of the Sumidero.
It was only with the appointment of the city's second bishop,
Fray Bartolomé de las Casas, that the lot of the natives began
to improve. 'To us, Don Fray is like a god,' said Miguel, a
thirty-year-old Indian, whom we got talking to one happy
hour in the Margarita bar.

Miguel had waist-length hair, a nose like a potato, a boss-eye
concealed behind a permanent pair of Ray-Bans. His friends
called him Pocahontas, but he did not find it funny. 'Even
when I was a child, my family was frightened of the gringos,'
Miguel said. 'We thought they stole children. My grandmother said "Shut the doors and windows when they come."
But now it's the opposite, children run to the tourists to sell
them Zapatista dolls.'

In the diocese of San Cristóbal, Don Fray's philosophy still
prevailed. In 1938, Greene had visited the Bishop of Chiapas
in Mexico City, who attempted repeatedly to re-enter the
state from which he had been banned. 'People had told me
he was regarded as one of the most dangerous and astute of
the Mexican bishops,' he wrote. Today, the spirit of Don Fray
lived on in the deeds of Don Samuel Ruiz, the current bishop
of San Cristóbal. The Indians call him *Tatic*, which means
father. The rest of Mexico know him as *El Rojo* – the red one.

Don Samuel was seventy-five years old. Having grown
up under the shadow of Calles's persecutions, his natural
sympathies were with the Right. But then, in 1960, on the
brink of middle age, he was posted to San Cristóbal. He
arrived in a city where Indians were not allowed to walk on
the pavements. In 1968, following the radical second Vatican
council, he attended a conference of South American bishops

in Medellín. A theology of liberation was decided on that would position the church on the side of the poor. Shortly afterwards, on the eve of the 1968 summer Olympics in Mexico City, the government massacred student demonstrators at Tlaltelolco Plaza in the capital. From then on Don Samuel pitched himself implacably against the Right. 'I thought I had been sent to Chiapas to evangelize the Indians, but it turned out that I ended up being evangelized by them,' he said.

If Greene had met a priest like Don Samuel, the tone of *The Lawless Roads* would have been quite different. In this benighted land, he searched – almost fruitlessly – for the power of faith put into effect. When he was in San Antonio, Texas, he witnessed a strike organized by Catholic Action, a body set up by the Church to put into force the 'papal encyclicals which have condemned capitalism quite as strongly as Communism'. He attended a shambolic meeting in the park and was disappointed. 'One compared it mentally with the soap-box orator and the Red Flag, and a crowd singing the "Internationale". Catholicism, one felt, had to rediscover the technique of revolution.' Yet typically, when Greene learned of the Cristeros, a Catholic rebel movement which had kidnapped a rich Mexican and held him to ransom, he was disgusted. 'It is typical of Mexico, of the whole human race perhaps – violence in favour of an ideal and then the ideal lost and the violence going on.' Don Samuel rejects violence at any price, although many of the Zapatistas disagree.

Nor was Don Samuel the only one to be radicalized. In 1993 the Vatican, worried at this fireball in their midst, decided that San Cristóbal should have a 'co-bishop' in the form of Don Raul Vera, a conservative priest. However, within a fortnight of taking up his post Don Raul gave an interview in which he announced that he had converted to the Indians' cause.

If you stayed in San Cristóbal a few days, you stood a good chance of spotting Don Samuel coming or going from his office next door to the corn-yellow cathedral. He was small with huge square glasses and wide down-turned lips like a frog's. An audience with him was not so assured. Repeatedly, I set up meetings with him; repeatedly they were cancelled. He was going to the northern zone, to Mexico City, to a conference in Guatemala. His archivist, Don Andrés Aubry, told me there was no need to meet him.

'But isn't there a parallel between Don Samuel and Graham Greene's whisky priest – both persecuted by the authorities?'

'No. Don Samuel was never drunk. He never had a wife. He never had a child,' said Don Andrés, with a jovial smile that suggested such thoughts might not be so alien to him. 'He has never doubted his role and it was doubt that made Greene's priest such a fascinating and complex figure. If you tried to turn Don Samuel into a character in a novel you would fail. He is far too straightforward to be the stuff of literature.'

There had been several attempts on the life of Don Samuel, some organized by the state, others backed by the landowners of Chiapas, who as far back as 1987 wrote to the President asking for the removal of Ruiz. They blamed him for the recent *campesino* land invasions, calling him the 'principal craftsman of the climate of agitation, disorder and violence that rules our property'.

The state-owned press called him the devil and claimed it was he, not Marcos, who led the rebels. The *coletos* – the town's hierarchy who claimed direct descent from the first Spanish settlers and owned most of San Cristóbal's hotels and restaurants – were in the habit of throwing eggs at Don Samuel or holding vigils outside the cathedral, during which they burned coffins with his name on. 'It's a tricky one for them though, because they make so much money out of journalists and international observers coming here to write about the Zapatistas,' Miguel said. 'Last year the government was getting a bit overzealous about expelling foreigners and the *coletos* had to step in and ask them to cool it.'

The truth was that revolutionaries had done wonders for San Cristóbal's tourist trade. In the main square they were selling Che Guevara T-shirts and posters of men in ski masks. The Zapatistas, after all, were the chic-est of radicals. From the depths of the jungle they sent out press releases via the Internet. Marcos had been voted the sexiest man in Mexico. Oliver Stone and Danielle Mitterrand hung out with him.

'It drives me crazy,' said Carol, the owner of the American bookshop, who had already told me of her dislike of Graham Greene. Carol sold Marcos postcards, of course – it would have been bad business not to, but she had also hung a framed copy of the Mexican constitution that reminded clients it was illegal for any foreigner to interfere in Mexican politics.

While wrapping my postcards she told me, 'I hung it there because I get so many wide-eyed fools from Berkeley coming in and saying, "I'm going to buy a balaclava and run off to join Marcos in the jungle."'

Like Glen and Ellen, Carol had discovered that revolutionary glamour decreased in direct proportion to the amount that their activities actually impinged on your lifestyle. It was one thing to sell indigenous art but quite another to have these quaint people stand up for their rights.

Even the Catholic church – both in Mexico and in Rome – shunned Don Samuel. The days when all priests were pitted against the government had passed, like so many things, with the accession of Carlos Salinas. Desperate for support on coming to power, virtually his first act was to invite the Mexican bishops – until then enemies of the state – to his inauguration. In 1992, religion was finally recognized in Mexico's constitution and priests were given the right to vote. The same year relations with the Vatican, broken off more than fifty years before, were re-established.

'Most of the bishops were delighted that they had got a foothold in the power structure – that they had become players,' said Don Andrès. 'But the so-called liberation theologists said they would rather have the church cast its lot with the poor. But now the majority of the bishops back the PRI and shun Don Samuel. It's a little like the alignment of Pilate and the Sanhedrin, who put their efforts together against a certain preacher.'

VIII

A few days later, in Mexico City, I went to see Manuel Camacho, former Commissioner for Peace in Chiapas and now leader of an opposition party, the Partido de Centro Democratico. 'Once the church's role was to defend religion against the government,' he said. 'Now they have become part of the system. The other day I was talking to a bishop who said to me: "When I think about who I would like the next President to be my heart is with Labastida of the PRI, but my head is with you." I thought I must have misheard him. But he insisted. "No, my head tells me that this country needs reforms and you represent that. But I am so much part of the system that I cannot help plumping for Labastida." And this,' said Camacho, his eyes widening behind his round glasses, 'was a good honest man. There are plenty in the church that are not. But this is how he sees the world.'

And what of Don Samuel, with whom Camacho spent fifteen agonizing days locked in the cathedral in San Cristóbal drawing up a peace accord? 'He is too religious, that's his problem,' Camacho said. 'I used to think "Please Don Samuel – look at the consequences of what you are doing." But he would just say "God will provide." Then he would add: "You know what counts is the world that's going to come." You just couldn't reason with him.'

I was sitting at the top of a long rectangular table in Camacho's office in the southern suburbs of Mexico City. I had arrived from Chiapas the night before, and was dazed by the skyscrapers, six-lane highways and apoplectic traffic policemen.

'There was nothing to connect this European capital with the small wild farm and the Indians in the hills,' Greene said. He, of course, hated the city for 'its fake smartness and gaiety', anathema to a man in search of authenticity. Yet life in the capital could seem every bit as precarious as in the villages of northern Chiapas. Everywhere there were reminders of potential disasters. The lift in our hotel bore the warning: 'The elevator will cease to function in case of fire or earthquake.' The newspapers warned of the imminent eruption of the volcano of Popocatepetl. The waiter in the rooftop bar told us of his relief when Hurricane Mitch, which devastated Nicaragua and Honduras, had stopped within a few miles of the Yucatan coast. From our room, we looked out on to Greene's 'old Spanish rambling galleon' of a cathedral, built on the remains of an Aztec temple whose steps had been soaked in the blood of human sacrifices. The cathedral's exterior was obscured by a maze of green scaffolding trying to prevent it sinking slowly into the marshland on which Mexico City was built.

The following morning we learned that a demonstration of two million people would take place that night. It would block the entire southern ring road. 'Why are they demonstrating?' we asked the breakfast waiter. 'I'm not sure. We are always demonstrating. We demonstrated when they cut off the electricity. Then we demonstrated when they turned it on again and asked us to pay our bills. Once I couldn't get home for a week. I live in the northern suburbs and the road was completely blocked.'

Since I had already lain awake half the night dreading my journey to Camacho's office this was not what I needed to hear. In San Cristóbal, you could walk home drunk at midnight. In Mexico City, the prospect of the shortest hop across town left my stomach in knots. If you took the Metro you would be pickpocketed. If you walked, a policeman would stop you, put a gun in your back and demand a credit card and pin number. If you took a taxi, you would at best be ripped off, at worst beaten up. In the end, the hotel called me a limousine and fixed a fare at fifty pesos – about $6. I clutched a grubby note in my hand. I had heard the 'no change' story too many times.

'Friday tonight,' said the driver, tailgating green VW Beetle taxis that circled the city's potholed highways like tin toys. 'Friday night is your night with your friends. Saturday with your girlfriend. Sunday with your folks. Saturday night's the best night. Eh, eh, eh?' My eyes stung and my nose watered as he unwound the window letting in some of the city's high-octane pall. The traffic was nothing like as bad as predicted. On the radio, a disc jockey was cajoling a caller to tell us the name of the boy she fancied. 'I can't,' she exclaimed, in genuine indignation. 'He's younger than me.' 'Does he like you?' asked the DJ. 'Because I do. Why don't you make a date with me?'

We stopped at a traffic light. The driver hooted, swore then leant out of the window and spat in the path of a ten-year-old boy trying to sell an Abdominizer exercise machine. We drove straight past the address I had given him. 'Shit.' The gears clunked and we rapidly reversed back down the street, oblivious to the honking traffic. I handed over the fifty peso note. 'Oi!' he shouted after my fleeing form. 'Don't I get a tip?'

The cold morning air nipped at my ankles as I waited on a sagging Paisley sofa in the waiting room. The green carpet was full of cigarette burns. Camacho, who had once been tipped as the next Prime Minister of Mexico, had fallen out of favour with the PRI. Now, he was having to get used to life on the outside. 'To be in the system is to be in heaven,' he said. 'You have money, you have friends, you have connections, you are protected. If you are outside the system you are in hell.'

Take the case of Cuauhtémoc Cardenas, the son of the President Cardenas of Greene's travels. In 1988, Cuauhtémoc broke away from the PRI to found another party, the PRD, which would have won the subsequent election if Salinas had not engineered the convenient 'breakdown' of a computer. Yet today, the policies of the PRI and the PRD were so close it was impossible to put a toothpick between them. Cuauhtémoc, it seemed, had given up the struggle.

'Cuauhtémoc was the enemy of the government and everything was done in such a way that he just couldn't place himself,' Camacho said. 'He had no access to the media, every kind of lie appeared in the newspapers. Eventually he couldn't take it any more. The PRI spends hundreds of millions of dollars on its campaigns – more than Clinton even – and no one controls it. It is totally unethical and it works quite brilliantly.'

Camacho should know. For thirty years he was a central figure in the PRI. At various times, he was Mayor of Mexico City, Minister of Regional Development and Minister of

Foreign Affairs. On New Year's Day 1994, he was on holiday in Cancún when his father-in-law alerted him in a phone call that there had been a rebellion in Chiapas. Eleven days later he was in San Cristóbal as Commissioner for Peace and en route to political downfall.

'I'd always thought Chiapas was the most important area in the country because I had seen the guerrilla movement in Central America and I could see what might happen here. When I became minister for regional development in 1984, I started to go to Chiapas often. I could see that tensions were brewing. I realized that we had to expropriate some land and redistribute it to the indigenous people. I convinced Salinas that this was the right thing to do, but I then had to convince the landowners. I tell you that meeting was the most difficult meeting you can ever imagine.' His eyes rolled dramatically. 'Finally, I succeeded. I used the line – these people are in your garden already, so why not just push back the fence? It worked and I was so excited. I returned to the capital to find that the secretary of the president and the governor of Chiapas who both had land in the area had meanwhile convinced the president that this was a terrible idea. The budget was already approved and the government was buying land to give the peasants but once Salinas's opinion had been swayed the whole plan just collapsed.'

In 1994, Camacho returned to Chiapas determined to bring peace to the region. 'I made speeches in Tzotzil, I visited the areas where poverty was at the greatest, I called the Zapatistas by their names instead of calling them killers and terrorists, I asked the Indians to forgive us for the terrible things we had done to them but nothing worked.' He laughed. 'They had taken the decision to be in a war and I could not persuade them to come to the negotiating table.

'There were elections coming up, the economy was at risk,

there were acts of terrorism in Mexico City. My last card was "Let's go and look for the Zapatistas and talk to them directly." My hotel was completely surrounded by journalists, but I left in a scarf, a hat and a coat at one o'clock in the morning and nobody spotted me. We changed cars several times and finally at five o'clock in the morning, in a very cold area in Chiapas we were waiting to have a contact with the Zapatistas. I didn't know what was going to happen. Somebody came into the car and I didn't look at him because I thought that is more respectful. I sat with my back to him but then I smelt the smoke of maple tobacco. I thought "This is Marcos!" I turned to him and we began to talk.'

For fifteen days, Marcos, Don Samuel and Camacho sat locked in San Cristóbal's cathedral negotiating a peace deal. 'At the end we were on such good terms we were showing each other our speeches in advance of making them. Marcos said, "I never thought that this was going to be honest, I always thought that you were going to trick me but you are a man of your word." We said we would sign for peace, and I returned to Mexico City, once again elated. But once again, when I got there no one was thinking about Chiapas. They were only thinking about who was going to be the candidate for the Presidency. I wait ten days before taking the decision that I won't stand. I want peace and I decide that my role is going to be the guy who made it possible. I announce my decision and then they go kill Colosio.'

Colosio was the officially approved presidential candidate. He was assassinated in Tijuana, on the American border, on the campaign trail. The assassin, a former policeman, was allowed by Colosio's bodyguards to shoot him at almost point-blank range. Kennedyesque conspiracy theories began to circulate and one of them pointed at Camacho. 'Colosio's death was like a meteorite coming down in front of you in the street.

There was nothing I could do. They were all pointing the finger saying I had organized the killing. It was left to Marcos who was supposed to be my adversary to defend me. I had to resign and once again peace was forgotten about.'

Today the PRI do everything possible to discredit Camacho. Only a month earlier the students of the law faculty in San Cristóbal invited him to speak about democracy in Chiapas. 'The government offered them all scholarships to Spain if they retracted the invitation. I am happy to say, they did not.'

Perhaps it was my gullibility but Camacho struck me as far too sincere to ever have been part of this monstrous organization. He had a nondescript face and a sweet, shy, eager manner. His desk was littered with CDs of Celtic music and the bookshelf behind him covered with pictures of his children.

When Greene went to Chiapas he exclaimed at people existing in a 'scene from the past before the human race had bred its millions'. I asked Camacho if he thought the Indians' lives had improved in any way over the past sixty years. Slowly, he shook his head.

'It's a shame and a disgrace. The PRI are doing the same things they have always been doing. They are buying votes, they are managing Chiapas like a police state. They treat the place like a banana republic.'

IX

The day before I met Camacho, I had travelled out of San Cristóbal past endless shanty towns of shacks made of cardboard and scrap lumber crawling up the skirts of the mountains. Each has a name: 'Mount Zion', 'New Jerusalem', 'Betania'. These were the homes of the 30,000 *expulsados* –

evangelical Protestants who had been forced out of their Catholic villages after they converted.

It was the Day of the Virgin of Guadalupe, the holiest in the Mexican calendar. Greene visited the Basilica of Guadalupe in Mexico City and told the story of how in 1531, only ten years after the Spanish conquest, the Virgin had appeared to an Indian peasant three times and imprinted her image on his cloak. She called him 'My son', before asking him to carry a message to the bishop to build a shrine on that spot where she might watch and love the Indians. 'It is as well to remember how revolutionary that vision must have seemed . . .' noted Greene. 'The legend gave the Indian self respect; it gave him a hold over his conqueror, it was a liberating, not an enslaving legend.'

The Indians loved the Virgin of Guadalupe and in homage to her everyone was drunk. Two young men in moulting ponchos and cotton trousers stood swaying on the verge, cursing incoherently at the passing cars. Women huddled in primeval groups, squatting on their hams in their long skirts. Some had covered themselves in plastic sheeting to keep off the rain. Others hadn't bothered. Furtively, they passed a bottle between them. Babies' heads poked out of their blue and purple shawls.

We were on our way to San Juan Chamula, a village about six miles outside San Cristóbal, in a Volkswagen minibus driven by Miguel, our Indian friend. At his side was Janice, from Boston, thirty-three years old, in flared bell-bottoms with a rainbow stripe down the seam and an embroidered blouse like those of the local women. Her hair was long and brown. Janice was attempting to learn Spanish and was a paying guest of Miguel's family. 'Miguel's mother is a beautiful person,' she told me. 'She doesn't speak a word of English, but she's still a beautiful person.'

Janice liked Miguel. The night before they had been out dancing until three. 'But I still was up at eight, because we had a breakfast date at nine. But he never showed. Hey, Miguel – I was waiting for you, you know. It's OK, I'm not mad. But you never turned up. Don't worry, I don't mind.'

Miguel was unmoved by these reprimands. From time to time, he stopped the minibus and jumped out to light a rocket at a roadside shrine. The road was lined with billboards saying: 'Disfruta Coca Cola', 'Pepsi', 'Coke is It!'

'The people of these villages worship Coca-Cola,' Miguel said. 'They believe that the gases purify the spirit. By burping, you make your soul clean again. Just like you, when you drink Coke for stomach problems. But now, in the past couple of years, the villagers have started to drink Pepsi too. There is big competition. Big trucks distribute the drinks to all the communities round here.' This explained why every member of the village of Chamula had a flash of gold in their smiles. Dentistry, just as in Greene's day, was still the 'most thriving trade in Mexico'.

In the valley below was a market square. It was dominated by a white church with an arched wooden door with a portal in psychedelic turquoise, green and pink. A recess above the door bore a statue of the virgin. We approached it over tough grass grazed by black sheep. 'Don't touch them,' Miguel warned. 'They worship sheep here. They shave off their wool, but they would never eat one.' Barefoot girls with their hair in pigtails danced around us shouting: 'One peso, you photograph me, what's your name?' Janice had brought a bag of oatmeal cookies to share with them. They looked horrified at the sight of this nutritious offering and scattered instantly in search of more promising victims. 'No children in the village go to school,' Miguel said. 'There is too much money to be made begging from the tourists.' He gestured towards a video games parlour, where half a dozen young boys were blasting aliens. 'They're not starving yet.'

Chamula consisted of low wattle-and-daub huts with tin roofs spreading out from the main square. Set back behind the town hall smothered in PRI posters was a white hacienda with green lawns and a picket fence. 'There lives a *cacique* – a village chief,' Miguel said. 'He sells the Coca-Cola and the beer too. Negra Modelo. Superior. Corona. The *caciques* have the monopoly on the beer and that makes them very rich.'

The *caciques* also organized the villages' religious rituals, charging each family an extortionate sum for the honour of organizing a festival or looking after a saint for a year or two. 'If a family converts to Protestantism, they no longer drink alcohol or take part in the rituals,' Miguel explained. 'So the *caciques* are very angry. They expel the converts and they seize their land. And then the Protestants fight the Catholics in the hills. It is brother fighting brother. It is a hatred which will endure for generations.'

One in five people had been expelled from San Juan Chamula. Recently, one of them – now a Protestant deacon – had returned to the village. The *caciques* rented a mob to surround his house. There was a shoot-out, and the deacon and five *caciques* were killed. 'I know his widow,' Miguel said. 'She just says "All my confidence and trust is in God. He is my only hope."' In Chiapas, half the population were now evangelists compared to seven per cent in the rest of Mexico. The government had kept American missionaries out of the rest of the country, but it encouraged them to come to Chiapas. 'The evangelicals, they say, "Accept your lot. God is good." This is a better message for the people to hear than Don Samuel saying "You can change your lives",' Miguel said.

The Catholicism of the Chamulans was not that of Don

Samuel. Everywhere you looked in the town there were turquoise crosses in groups of three or more. Some, just three feet high, had been planted in back gardens. Others, twice the size of a man, stood in clearings on the hills surrounding the town. On his way to San Cristóbal, Greene had stumbled across such a grove of tall black crosses, 'like wind-blown trees against the blackened sky'.

For him it was a glorious moment, a sign of longed-for spirituality in a soulless land. 'The Catholics might be dying out "like dogs", but here, in the mountainous strange world of Father Las Casas, Christianity went on its own frightening way.' His whisky priest experienced the same epiphany. 'They were the first Christian symbols he had seen for more than five years publicly exposed if you could call this empty plateau in the mountains a public place. No priest could have been concerned in the strange rough group; it was the work of Indians and had nothing in common with the tidy vestments of the Mass and the elaborately worked out symbols of the liturgy. It was like a short cut to the dark and magical heart of the faith – to the night when the graves opened and the dead walked.'

The Chamulans' faith had far more to do with the forces of the Mayan world than with Christianity. They had adopted the Catholic trappings: the saints, the rosary, medals, incense, banners and processions – but the rituals had been adapted to their own beliefs. To them, Jesus was a minor saint but the Virgin Mary was the goddess of the sun. In the church, the statues of the saints had mirrors on their chests to ward off evil spirits. Women waved cloying sticks of incense under their noses. 'They are feeding the saints,' Miguel said. 'At least there are no longer human sacrifices here.'

Greene had seen the Chamulans as wild, romantic figures, fuelled by primordial beliefs, protectors of the faith in a godless land – 'faith in the spittle that healed the blind man and the voice that raised the dead'. But today, the *caciques* were not so much protecting their gods as their alcohol monopoly. Archbishop Ruiz had appointed a diocesan priest to Chamula but they threw him out. The *caciques* were inordinately conservative. At every election, Chamula returned a 100 per cent vote to the PRI. In return, they were left to govern the town any way they chose. When evangelicals were thrown in jail, no one from central government intervened. A new parish priest had been appointed by the bishop of Tuxtla Gutiérrez. He visited twice a year to perform baptisms, but otherwise left well alone.

In the market square, a man in a black cape was holding a firework in one bare hand and lighting it with another. It exploded in the grey sky with a terrifying bang and not a spark of light. In front of the church, three drunk men were lying out cold. Groups of French and Italian tourists picked their way over them. They did not point their video cameras though. The *caciques* had a bad reputation amongst tourists. Once they had stoned to death two Australians who had taken pictures in the church.

Inside the church, the floor was covered in slippery, sweet-smelling pine needles. Long, fleshy vines dripped down the walls. Scores of stubby candles burned on the floor, warming our ankles as we moved between them, and incense billowed from large burners. There were no pews; village women with shawls around their heads sat on the floor with chickens under their arms. Their faces were old, but as Graham Greene pointed out: 'You could never tell with Indians – she mightn't have been more than twenty.' They muttered their prayers and gulped from Coke and Sprite bottles. Musicians with ancient stringed instruments played background music for aromatherapy massages. Other worshippers were slowly undressing and then dressing one of the statues on the walls, in brilliant costumes and with a mirror hanging from its neck. 'The mirror gives you direct communication with the underworld,' whispered Miguel. Beside a startled family, Janice fell on her knees, closed her eyes and stretched out her hands as she muttered a prayer into the smoky gloom.

We emerged blinking into the grey morning. A man vomited, narrowly missing my shoes. The air was thick with the smell of woodsmoke and urine. Barefoot children surrounded us. It was like returning to the Dark Ages.

Janice gazed around in rapture. 'This is seriously *spiritual*.'

We left the church and walked up the hill. Outside every home was a tiny grave marked by a small arch covered in pine needles. It was the grave of a chicken used for healing. 'They pass an egg over the head of the sick person and the sickness is sucked away,' Miguel explained with some embarrassment. We passed a group of *caciques*. They wore black tunics, had coloured ribbons in their hats and carried silver-topped canes. They waved cheerily at Miguel and he nodded respectfully back. As soon as they were out of earshot, he grabbed my arm. 'You know, people say the Zapatistas represent the voice of the indigenous people. But nothing could be further from the truth. They are far better than your average peasant – they are very brave men. They have broken with every tradition of the community. They don't get married – and everyone here is married. They don't drink. No wonder the *caciques* hate them. They will pay anyone to wipe them out.'

His diatribe was interrupted by shrill cries of joy. We turned round to see Janice running up the road in pursuit of three old women bent double under enormous loads of corn strapped to their backs.

'Oh! You're so beautiful! You are the goddesses of the corn!'

After this, the shaman was to prove almost too much. He lived in a large house on the outskirts of the town. A blue sign hung from the front door:

Traditional Healer
Salvador Lunes Collaso
Ask for him here – T'otikl H'ilol Jesus Medico Christ Doctor

Inside the floor was covered in pine needles. A shrine had been erected in one corner. It was dominated by an image of the Virgin and covered in candles, flowers and clay incense burners in the shape of oxen. Above it was a gaudy painting of the Last Supper next to a cork pinboard covered in postcards of New York, and brochures from the Marriott Hotel, Washington. 'The View', one read. 'It's a fabulous restaurant.' There were also several photos of Salvador shaking George Bush's hand. 'He was invited to a convention in Washington and President Bush asked especially to meet him,' boasted Miguel. 'He went the following year, but Clinton didn't want to see him – and look at the President now.'

Salvador was an old man. He sat in a rocking chair on the porch dressed in a leather jacket, stetson and cowboy boots. Reverently, Janice held out her hand to him. He took it and yawned.

It took a lot of prodding to get Miguel to ask Salvador about the fleeing evangelists. 'She wants to know if it is true you don't let Protestants live here,' he eventually muttered reluctantly. Salvador gave me a supercilious look. 'Not at all, *señorita*. What happened is these people wanted to practise their religion, but here we don't have another religion. So they decided to leave voluntarily. Trouble was, they weren't happy where they went, so they claimed they were expelled from here.' He turned to Miguel and muttered something in Tzotzil.

Miguel cleared his throat. 'Salvador wants you all to know that he won't answer questions today. He doesn't work because it is a holiday, but if you take a taxi here tomorrow, he will cure everything for you,' said Miguel. 'He is very good value for money.' Janice started fumbling in her pocket for a deposit.

2. Sierra Leone

The magic of the place never failed him:
here he kept his foothold on the edge of a very strange
continent.

THE HEART OF THE MATTER

I

When you check in to the brutalist concrete monolith that is
the Cape Sierra Hotel in Freetown, Sierra Leone, the first
thing they do is ask you for a $2000 deposit. Cash only. The
beautiful receptionist smiles winningly as you count out the
notes. 'I'm sorry, but we have to do it,' she says. 'It's in case
you die before you check out.'

When I went to Sierra Leone it was the most dangerous
country on earth. Civil war had been raging there for eight
years. More than 50,000 people had died in the fighting. More
than half the population of four million had been displaced.
Tens of thousands of people had had their arms, legs, lips or
ears chopped off by the rebels' machetes. Rape was common.
Cannibalism had been documented. The fighting was growing
fiercer by the day, with the prize of Freetown, the capital, just
outside the rebels' grip.

More than anywhere in Greeneland, Sierra Leone had
changed since Graham Greene's four visits there. His first was
in 1935, en route to neighbouring Liberia to collect material

for his travel book *Journey Without Maps*. His romantic hope was to catch a glimpse of primitive Man, of humanity at its purest, as it must have been before it was contaminated by civilization. He was not disappointed. 'Africa', he wrote, was the 'shape of the human heart'.

In 1942, Greene returned to Freetown as a spy for the Special Intelligence Services. As cover, he worked at the local police station. The city was of vital strategic importance to the Allies. The Vichy French held French Guinea next door and German agents were trying to smuggle industrial diamonds out of central Africa.

Greene was not a successful secret agent. When MI6 delivered him a large safe, he locked his code books in it but then could not re-open it. Eventually it had to be destroyed to rescue the vital codes. On another occasion, he was enthused by the idea of starting a 'roaming' brothel, whose girls would debrief Vichy French officers. London gave the idea serious consideration, but in the end dismissed it as too expensive.

Life in Freetown had its ups and downs, but during his year there Greene grew to love the place. Like Scobie, the protagonist of *The Heart of the Matter*, he was given a house on the mudflats below the colonists' enclave of Hill Station. It was overrun with cockroaches and rats. Once his cook went mad and chased the houseboy with a hatchet. On another occasion, Greene slipped and fell six feet into an open drain. He emerged covered in excrement.

Yet war hardly touched Freetown. There were blackouts, but no bombs dropped there. Wounded people from torpedoed ships were ferried ashore but the actual attacks took place hundreds of miles away. 'There's an awful lot of time around in a country like this,' Scobie says, and Greene had plenty of it in which to ponder his disastrous personal life. He no longer loved his wife, Vivien, yet he was also tiring of his mistress, Dorothy Glover. Both made him feel trapped and guilty. He toyed with the idea of suicide.

Ultimately, however, Freetown was one of the few places where Greene's dark side disappeared. The sights, the smells and the shambles of the city relaxed and amused him. He returned in 1949, wretched about his affair with his beautiful, married mistress, Catherine Walston, but as soon as his aeroplane landed in Freetown, he felt a weight lift away. 'I have loved no part of the world like this & I have loved no woman as I love you,' he wrote to Catherine. 'You're my human Africa. I love your smell as I love these smells. I love your dark bush as I love the bush here, you change with the light as this place does, so one all the time is loving something different & yet the same. I want to spill myself out into you as I want to die here.'

The Heart of the Matter is the story of Henry Scobie – 'an obscure policeman in an unfashionable colony' – who has an affair and then, torn between his clinging wife Louise and his young mistress Helen Rolt, kills himself. George Orwell, who hated the novel, complained: 'Why should the novel have its setting in West Africa? Except that one of the characters is a Syrian trader, the whole thing might as well be happening in a London suburb.'

The novel may not say much about African politics, but it does show Greene's growing disillusionment with God – which in turn contributed hugely to his political development. Scobie loves God, but the Church's generalities prove an inadequate solution to his private dilemmas. At the end of the novel, Greene fudges this tension by having his Catholic priest, Father Rank, rebuke Scobie's widow by telling her: 'The Church knows all the rules. But it doesn't know what goes on in a single human heart.' Privately, however, Greene was beginning to have less and less trust in an organization that allowed humans, both individually and collectively, to suffer.

The African setting began to make sense to me when I considered that, like all Greene's heroes, Scobie is a lonely man whose loneliness is compounded by his surroundings, on the margin of world events. His struggles of conscience are all the more acute because they take place in a country where morality is a relative thing. Scobie finds the Sierra Leoneans impossible to police. They are inveterate liars who cannot comprehend why it is wrong to pervert justice with bribes and blackmail. 'It is usually safe to assume, if the accusation is theft and there is no question of insurance, that something has at least been stolen,' Greene writes. 'But here one could make no such assumption, one could draw no lines. He had known police officers whose nerves broke down in the effort to separate a single grain of incontestable truth.'

Yet today these 'injustices' and 'meanness' have developed into incomprehensible depravity. Greene's record of Sierra Leone is remembered by the locals as an irrelevant piece of cosy nostalgia. '*The Heart of the Matter* is a portrait of Freetown as it used to be, when it was a sleepy, happy-go-lucky place,' John Ganda, an academic, told me in his office in Freetown. 'In those days you could stay out to the wee hours of the morning. When your brother came knocking on your door at eight o'clock at night you used to listen. But now these murderous fellows have come and made life so difficult.'

If Scobie had lived in Freetown today, fear would have banished his existential anxieties. Every time I thought about going there it was as if a shard of ice had lodged in my chest. I rang the Foreign Office for advice. 'Our advice is don't go,' a spokesman said. I rang Alex Duval-Smith, the Africa correspondent of the *Independent*. 'God, I don't envy you at all,' she said. I rang James Murray who worked for Oxfam in

Freetown. He sounded more relaxed. 'It's just like a normal city most of the time,' his voice echoed over 3000 miles.

When I rang him back on the eve of our departure, to ask about the current security situation, there was a pause too long to be blamed on the faulty telephone lines. Then an intake of breath. 'Frankly,' he said. 'It's very bad indeed.'

Portland Place is one of the grandest thoroughfares in London, a tree-lined avenue a few yards from Regent's Park. It is lined with tall Georgian mansions now inhabited by multinationals and embassies. The Sierra Leonean High Commission had dirty sash windows and a peeling front door. The consular section is in the basement, the door obscured by black rubbish sacks and piles of mouldy cardboard boxes. The waiting room is lit by a dusty 40-watt bulb. Behind the counter are piles of tatty paperwork. A poster on the wall read: *Sierra Leone – a Holiday Paradise*. The only other person waiting for a visa was a Lebanese businessman in an expensive suit with gold cuff links. 'Why are we going to this place?' he asked me expansively. 'We must be mad.'

I did not want to go alone. I asked a photographer I knew called Christopher if he would like to come with me. To my amazement, he said yes. The more I learned about our destination, the more guilty I felt about this.

Christopher and I had sometimes had a rocky working relationship. Our big bust-up came when we were despatched to northern France to report on the murder of the English teenager Caroline Dickinson. Christopher was a gourmet and he was looking forward to *foie gras*, *crêpes* and *boeuf bourguignon*. I was worried that no one at the scene would to talk to us and I was right. I ended up interviewing old ladies too senile to realize I was a journalist who would tell me in impenetrable Breton accents about their pet poodle needing to visit the chiropodist. A day passed before we found someone who spoke to us eloquently about this horrific crime and the disgraceful way it had been handled by the French police.

At the end of the interview I turned to Christopher and asked him if he had any questions.

'Yes,' he said. 'Can they recommend anywhere for us to eat tonight?'

But now there were other things beside Christopher to worry about. I had no idea about what to take to a war zone. I ended up buying a torch, sunscreen and a money belt that you attached to your leg. I took out $4000 in cash and distracted myself from my real fears with a quest for dry shampoo. Whatever happened I wanted to have clean hair.

We left very early on a Saturday morning. We were flying via Brussels and Bamako in Mali to Conakry in Guinea, next door to Sierra Leone. There is no war at present in Guinea, yet according to a United Nations scale it is the worst place in the world to live thanks to its dreadful economy, complete lack of public health and corrupt government. Yet Guinea is where aid workers in Sierra Leone are ferried for their R&R breaks. We arrived as darkness fell. The airport building was a fetid wooden hut. The greeter promised by Oxfam, so necessary at African airports, was nowhere to be seen and I prepared myself for a round of conversations about how we lacked 'proper documentation' and would have to pay a 'fine'. Instead, we were waved through passport control. At the luggage carousel, a man in a long blue gown wandered around carrying a drum and muttering angrily to himself. Christopher's bag never came. We went to lost property to fill in a form. By now our minder, Alpha, had arrived, a short young man in a dirty white robe with an expression of perpetual fury. He dragged my wheelie bag behind him as if it were a recalcitrant dog.

'You are a fool,' he snapped at Christopher in French. 'Why

did you check your bag in? You should have taken it on the plane like Madame. You know you will never see it again.'

In Guinea, the only effective method of communication is to scream as aggressively as possible at everyone. Alpha yelled at the blue-uniformed, female customs officers who hovered round us like jackals. They let us through without a bribe. He bellowed at a taxi driver, who offered him a bargain fare. We drove down a long, flat road past endless shanty towns. Fires burned at the roadside. There was nothing to redeem our surroundings. A wire sticking out of the car seat pierced a hole in my trousers. The air was full of thick brown dust. I reached for my sunglasses to protect my eyes. They had snapped in half in my bag.

We were staying at the Hotel César, a shabby collection of buildings off a dirt road so potholed it looked as though someone had made it that way on purpose. Rows of white four-wheel drives were lined up in the muddy parking lot. An obese woman swam slowly up and down the tiny pool. A sign read: BEWARE OF MAD DOGS BETWEEN MIDNIGHT AND DAWN.

The owner was a small Italian with a handlebar moustache. A middle-aged man ate pizza alone on the terrace, wiping his face continually on his napkin. We ate tough steak and chips and drank beer. We were too tired to talk much and too nervous. My room had a clean tiled floor and a saggy single bed. A huge can of insecticide sat on the windowsill of the spartan bathroom. I sprayed it everywhere and my nose ran. Rain began to hammer on the tin roof and the savage dogs barked. After a couple of fraught hours I took a sleeping pill. I fell asleep wondering if this was my last night on earth.

II

Travelling to Freetown is not like travelling to other places. 'There are terrible fuel shortages at the moment,' said Alpha. It was seven o'clock the following morning and he was driving us to the airport in a shiny four-wheel drive. 'Sometimes no plane leaves for Freetown for days. Mind you, if that happens it's better to be in Conakry than Freetown. Then there is no way out. If the rebels come, you're in the shit.'

Some days a vast grey Russian helicopter flies you across the border, some days a tiny Antonov plane. We got the latter. The seats were leaking foam rubber and the emergency exit appeared to be sealed with a sticking plaster. The captain was a moustachioed Russian in a short-sleeved shirt and Vuarnet sunglasses. After a half-hour wait, he announced there was a problem and ordered us off. We stood in the meagre shade offered by the wing. Our fellow passengers were aid workers and none looked happy. 'We're going back to our deaths,' said Paul, a stocky Australian in khaki knee-length shorts, who announced himself, improbably, to be a midwife. He clamped some earphones over his balding head and turned up the volume on his personal stereo.

We left two hours later. The flight took twenty minutes. From the air we could see no houses, just miles of quagmire and vegetation. It was a beautiful view but the canopy of jungle enclosed burnt-out villages and rebel camps.

Lungi airport, Freetown, has a reputation for corruption. Recently, however, officials had been warned that it was impolite to demand large bribes from kind aid workers.

'Have you a present for me?' asked the man who stamped my passport.

'No.'

Glum-faced, he handed it back.

The airport is probably the most inconveniently situated in
the world. It sits at one end of a horseshoe bay with the city
at the other. In peace time, a ferry links these two points but
for now it was out of action. The rebels and the swamps make
it impossible to drive so the only link to the city centre was
by helicopter. The next one, they said, would be along in a
few hours. We handed over $80 a head and they handed back
a wooden baton. This, it transpired, was our boarding pass.

Christopher and I sat waiting for the helicopter. A young
man in a stripy cheesecloth shirt was the first to spot us. 'Who
are you looking for, madam? Oxfam? Ah, very good. I am
their right-hand man. I will take you to them. They are
working just by the airport. Theirs is a drainage project.'
He held out his hand. 'I am Sami Johnson. Here is my
complimentary card.' He handed me a dirty piece of cigarette
packet with his name scrawled on it in blunt pencil. He
sounded plausible enough to me.

Within moments, Christopher and I were sitting in a
battered Ford with empty sockets for headlights bumping
down the red dirt road that led away from the airport.
Chickens pecked in the dust. Women in printed batik robes
swayed under loads that would have crippled a pack mule.
The scene was undeniably third world, but it didn't seem
particularly scary. 'Oxfam?' Sami shouted at the passers-by.
They shrugged and giggled.

After a ten-minute tour Sami was defeated. 'My colleagues
must have gone back to Freetown,' he decided. He took us
back to the airport. The bill came to $20. 'If you find out I
am not who I say I am, I will reimburse you,' Sami assured
us. 'Here is my telephone number.' Oxfam, we later discovered, had never heard of him.

Our fellow passengers were sitting in the airport café staring out of the window at the green-jacketed Nigerian soldiers who flanked the runway. They were members of Ecomog, the West-African peacekeeping troops. Their presence at the airport troubled the aid workers. A rebel attack must be imminent. Suppose there was another fuel shortage? We would have no means of escape. It was at this point that I seriously considered turning around. Had it not been for Christopher, I think I would have done so.

The rebels had last entered Freetown two months previously on 6 January, 1999. They burned the eastern third of the city to the ground, killed more than five thousand people, and asked thousands more to choose between the 'long or the short-sleeved treatment', in other words, whether their arm should be chopped off at the elbow or the wrist. More than a thousand children had been abducted to fight for the rebel forces. After a long and bloody battle Ecomog had chased the rebels back into the hills. But they could return at any moment.

Two hours later, the helicopter arrived. It was a five-minute hop across the bay. We sat with our backs to the wall on shabby grey cushions and peered over our shoulders through the portholes. I could see people digging trenches in the laterite soil. 'Mass graves,' Paul bellowed above the noise of the engines.

There was only one place to stay in Freetown and that was the Cape Sierra Hotel, about seven miles west of the city centre in an area known as Lumley Beach. This decision had nothing to do with ambience, standards of service, or value for money, and everything to do with the fact that all the other hotels had been blasted to bits. The room rate was $130 for a single and $160 for a double. It meant that Christopher and I had no choice but to share, which he was not terribly happy about.

'Are you sure you wouldn't rather pay the extra and have your privacy?' he said.

'No, Chris. I can't afford it and nor can you.' Our room had two small beds, a television, net curtains and a view of neglected scrub that must once have been garden. I could just make out the blue of the ocean. Most importantly, there was an ensuite bathroom with a shower attachment. I tried the water. It was hot. Hair washing would be possible after all.

The Cape Sierra was not the kind of place where you felt like loitering in your room over CNN and room service. We decided to go for a drive. We already had a self-appointed driver who had pounced on us at the helipad. He had a cheeky face under a skullcap and wore floor-length black robes. His name, he told us, was Alghabi Kamra and he was forty years old. He drove a dilapidated brown Datsun with faux-leopardskin seats and a bullet hole in the windscreen. The rebels had burned down Alghabi's house. Now he, his wife and his four sons were staying with relatives. By the time we had got to the Cape Sierra, he had decided that he was going to stay with us all week for $30 a day, a rate which crept up alarmingly for any drive that Alghabi considered dangerous, which in Freetown meant everywhere.

Sierra Leone is the poorest country in the world. Even before the war, average life expectancy was forty-two years. I was braced for horrors as we drove slowly down what Greene called the 'great loops of the climbing road' that led to down-town. What I was not prepared for was beauty. No one had told me that Freetown was magnificent, with a setting to rival that of Rio's or Vancouver's – between velvety green mountains and a ballpoint-blue Atlantic.

Unlike Conakry, which had been a marshy rubbish dump stretching into an oily ocean, Freetown seemed like a place that was meant to be. Gabled gingerbread houses with red tin roofs teetered drunkenly on the verge of collapse. On the skyline the crosses that topped the city's dozens of churches jostled for space with the stars and crescents of mosques. Greene was thirty-one when he 'lost his heart to West Africa' and at that moment I, just a year younger, understood his passion completely.

We drove past endless white beaches shaded with coconut palms. Once, there had been a small tourism industry in Sierra Leone. The Bounty advert was filmed just outside the city centre. German and French visitors ordered cocktails by the pool and congratulated themselves on their unusual choice of destination. Then, in a 1997 coup the rebel army shelled the Mammy Yoko hotel, trapping two hundred holidaymakers in the basement for three days. Until about a week ago, these sands had been covered in corpses. 'We thought they belonged to white men,' said Alghabi. 'Then we realized the sand had just rubbed off the top layer of skin.' A billboard informed us that: *Golden and white sandy beaches plus hospitable people make Sierra Leone the ideal place to stay.*

If you ignored the heat and the musty smell then Freetown could almost have been some faded English seaside resort. A sign pointed to Cockle Bay and we drove along Bathurst Street. On the left a roadside shack of corrugated iron announced itself to be 'Aunty Flo's Hairdressing School'. On the right was 'Sister Dorothy's Cook'ry Shop'. We passed a cottage called 'The Honeycomb' with a red plaster lion above its front gate.

In *Journey Without Maps*, Greene had complained that 'everything ugly about Freetown was European: the stores, the churches, the Government offices, the two hotels; if there was anything beautiful in the place it was native'. But now that Greene's despised colonists had jumped ship, these echoes of empire were extremely comforting. When the British were in charge the biggest problems posed by Freetown were heat and damp, rather than rampaging bands of drugged-up rebels.

When Greene drove along this road, he would have seen women selling eggs from baskets and farmers goading herds of cattle. Today, we passed a group of Nigerian soldiers, jogging. 'This is what we do in the morning,' they sang, even though it was late afternoon. From around a bend in the road, we could hear the sound of tooting whistles and banging drums. As we drove slowly on, we passed an angry band of marching men. Some tapped on our window. Others could not. Most were missing one or both arms. Some lacked a leg. Others had no ears and lips. 'They live in the amputee camp, but they are angry because they have not been fed for days,' Alghabi explained. 'They are going into the city to demonstrate.'

We carried on into the city, past the Cotton Tree, as tall and wide as a house, 'where the earliest settlers had gathered their first day on this unfriendly shore'. Today, it was almost the only landmark that Greene would have recognized. The Police Station where Scobie worked was a smoking ruin. The Ministry of Justice was a bullet-pocked shell. The Post Office, the Parliament, the High Court, every reminder of Sierra Leone's shaky civic life, had been obliterated. Yet what was most striking about the scene was not the ruins, but the sense that life was carrying on almost as it had always done. The streets were jammed with people. An old man in a skullcap and threadbare safari shorts smoked a clay pipe on the verge. Shirtless, barefoot adolescents with bodies like paperknives weaved through the traffic. A group of Greene's 'young negresses in dark-blue gym smocks' were chasing a goat along the street.

The traffic was at a standstill. Horns wailed. Our car had no air-conditioning. First one tiny child noticed two white people stuck in a car, then another, then a hundred. They banged on the window, waving maps, socks, T-shirts, cassettes, newspapers and bundles of filthy *leone* notes. 'Hey wetman!' they shouted. 'You want? You buy?'

'Wetman?'

Alghabi giggled. 'They mean whiteman. It is Krio language.'

'You could get some new clothes,' I suggested to Christopher.

He looked pained. 'They won't be as nice as the Boden shirt I lost.'

We parked by the burnt-out marketplace. We had an appointment with John Ganda, a Sierra Leonean academic, who turned out to be a former employer of Alghabi. 'Alghabi is the craftiest man I've ever known. I can't believe that of all the drivers in Freetown you found this one,' Mr Ganda said. Alghabi shrugged smugly.

Mr Ganda had large square glasses and wore a brown polyester suit. His office had been created out of a shed attached to a breeze-block building that housed one of the many aid agencies that had swooped down on Freetown like vultures. His office was dark and full of papers. A sign on the wall read: *I'm so great I'm jealous of myself.* Mr Ganda filled us in a little on the current political situation. 'Two years ago, after three decades of coups and military governments, we had elections. They were the first our country has ever had. Ahmad Tejan Kabbah was the winner. He is a very distinguished man, a former representative to the United Nations and he came in with a laudable programme, but he made one major mistake. He said, "We are going to cut down the army and downsize their rations." He ended up paying the soldiers 7000 a month ($3). This was to our detriment.'

Given the Sierra Leonean army's penchant for coups, this was an understatement. Within weeks, a faction of rebel soldiers had overthrown Kabbah and a new junta was in place. A few months later this government was ousted by Ecomog, with the help of mercenaries employed by foreign companies with business interests in Sierra Leone. Kabbah was returned to power. By then, however, a good proportion of the army had deserted to the rebel side.

'And what exactly are the rebels fighting for?'

'Nothing,' said Mr Ganda. 'Their leaders are fighting for control of the diamond fields on the north and west, but the rest are fighting because they know no other way. They simply want to terrorize. A great many of them are children. They know nothing but violence. They drink their enemy's blood to make them stronger. They drape the entrails of their victims over their roadblocks. It is an evil situation.'

The rebels might have no ideology but for the past two years they had been carrying out operation 'No Living Thing'. 'Kabbah's election slogan was "The future's in your hands", so when they cut hands off they shout: "Ask Kabbah to give them back to you",' Mr Ganda explained.

On 6 January Mr Ganda was staying with friends on the outskirts of Freetown. 'The rebels came to our house and shot a woman. Then they told us that we should sing and dance and rejoice, because we were lucky to have been spared. I was lucky. They had canisters of petrol with them, but for some reason, they chose not to use them. All I lost was my personal organizer, my watch and my wallet. The eleven-year-old boy who took them from me said I did not deserve to live.'

Mr Ganda showed me photographs of the streets of Freetown covered with mutilated corpses. 'The stink of rotting flesh from the hospital was so bad, you could smell it all along the street ten days after the fighting stopped.' He flicked through a series of Polaroids. Shocked faces stared into the lens from makeshift hospital beds. 'This is a twenty-year-old student of mine. On 20 January the rebels cut his hand off. Then they killed his father in his presence. They said, "Aren't you going to thank us for what we have done?" and when he said no, they cut his other hand off. This is Mr Jaka. He is forty-five and a security officer. They raped his wife in his presence and when he begged for her, they said, "Since you have begged we will cut off both your lips." He still doesn't know the whereabouts of his daughter.'

Mr Ganda stood up. Curfew hour was drawing near, it was time to go home. 'Do you think the rebels will come back to Freetown?' I asked.

'They are very close at the moment,' he said. 'Many of them never left of course. They have infiltrated themselves into the normal population. Some have stolen Ecomog uniforms. There are rebel cells all over the city.'

I must have looked quite faint. He gave me a kindly look. 'Is there anything else you would like to know?' he asked.

'Yes,' Christopher said. 'Where do you recommend we have dinner tonight?'

III

Greene's snobbish colonials had spent their tropical evenings drinking pink gins at the Hill Station Club, but today the aid workers and soldiers who made up the minuscule expatriate community preferred Paddy's bar near the Cape Sierra Hotel. Paddy Warren was seventy-two and originally from Kent. He had lived in Freetown for thirty-one years and was a balding gangly man with kind eyes behind thick glasses. His joint was nothing more than a strip of concrete floor with a rectangular bar in the middle shaded by a high bamboo roof. Purple geckoes with yellow heads and tails ran up the wooden pillars.

It sat on the corner of Cockle Bay with the water slapping on the rocks below. Children were fishing there. Only the occasional roar of a helicopter overhead spoilt the idyll. 'It could be so perfect,' Paddy sighed.

Paddy had lived through the past two rebel incursions into Freetown. 'I just holed myself up in the house for a week and then the curfew lifted for two days so I went to buy some food,' he giggled. 'I don't see what the rebels could possibly want with me. People always ask me why don't I leave, but where could I possibly go? I don't want to end up running a sandwich bar in Canterbury. Most of the Brits have gone, but there are a few of us hanging on. Take old Dickie Duncan. He married a local girl. We have a stroll together every evening.'

Every evening at around five, aid workers would start arriving at Paddy's in their Land Cruisers. The first Star beer would be sipped slowly, the second downed in a few greedy gulps. As curfew approached, the drinking got faster and the volume louder. At 5.50 precisely, the bar was empty. To be caught out after curfew would mean a night in an Ecomog cell. The expat vehicles raced home along the coast road, the driver clutching a bottle of Star in one hand and balancing a foil-wrapped plate of Paddy's evening special in his lap.

Paddy introduced me to Bill Stewart. He wore blue-rimmed spectacles and a stripy shirt and had the expression of a man who had just been told that his lottery numbers had come up on the week he forgot to buy a ticket.

'Bill is a Brit,' Paddy said. 'I asked him to come to the beach with me this weekend but he refused. I mean, what's the point of being here if you won't go to the beach?'

'It's bloody dangerous, that's why,' Bill said.

Bill had been in Sierra Leone for twelve years, running a travel agency that belonged to a Lebanese family, who were now living in Beirut. 'When they first offered me the job, it seemed like a good idea. You always think it's going to get better here, but it just gets worse and worse,' he said, staring morosely into his bottle of Star beer.

I fell into conversation with a turbanned Sikh. 'I am the local dentist,' he said. 'It's quite eventful being here, let me tell you. Things have really gone downhill, you know. Once, in Freetown there was a department store as big as Harrods and even up country you could buy anything you wanted.'

I asked Paddy if he had read *The Heart of the Matter*. 'Oh yes, it's a ridiculous book,' he said. 'Graham Greene got it all wrong. He didn't understand life in the tropics. In his world it was always miserable and always the rainy season. He didn't understand the joy of these people. The Sierra Leoneans must laugh more than anyone else on earth. They understand that the tensest situation can be defused if you just crack a joke at the right time.'

IV

From six at night to seven every morning, Christopher and I were locked in the Cape Sierra. Only three types of people stayed here: soldiers and mercenaries, who lounged around the bar, and hookers. In Greene's day, they worked from places like the 'tin-roofed bungalow halfway down the hill' described in *The Heart of the Matter*, but curfew had put an end to that. Business had shifted to the hotel corridors where they lingered in platform shoes, tight jeans and tops that stopped short of their pudgy midriffs. Their eyes were surrounded by smudgy kohl and their lips coated with what looked like Robertson's raspberry jam. From a distance they looked glamorous, up close their exaggerated features were faintly menacing.

'The girls can't leave until dawn now,' said a fellow guest, Tejan, who had joined us in the bar. 'Either a soldier takes them in or they sleep on the terrace. You know how old that one over there is? Fourteen. Her family have all been killed.'

Tejan was one of the mysterious characters drawn to Freetown like maggots to a rotting corpse. He was devastatingly handsome, muscular, and in his early twenties. He had been born in Sierra Leone, his father's country, but when he was very young he and his Singaporean mother moved to the more salubrious surroundings of Coventry. He did a degree in marine biology at Plymouth University but his activities in Freetown were far more fishy. He had close friends in Ecomog and he had been living at the Cape Sierra for the past six months. 'I like it here,' he said simply. 'You can do anything you like. At home, I don't know how to talk to a traffic warden. Here, I can smooth things out.'

He went on: 'In January we all sat in the bar and prayed that the rebels wouldn't get as far as us. You could hear the shots and see the fires burning across the bay and watch the planes overhead. God, it was frightening. There was nothing to do but get drunk. My bar bill for that period came to 1.3 million leones – more than $400.'

'Do I hear a British voice?' said a man behind Christopher. He was dressed in full combat gear and his face was sunburnt red. 'I'm Lieutenant Colonel John Pullinger of the Parachute Regiment. Delighted to meet you. Are you journalists? Don't s'pose you knew my wife, she used to work for the *Daily Express*.'

John was a stereotypical squaddie, bluff, pink-faced and jolly. 'You know the Foreign Office earmarked $25 million for Sierra Leone? Well, that's us. Our job is to train the army so they're ready to fight back against the rebels. Or rather to train the first army in the history of Sierra Leone that won't commit coups. Bloody awful job. They don't listen to a thing we tell them. I tell you, I'm dying to go home.'

It was eight o'clock in the evening, but it seemed much later. I had had four beers on an empty stomach, I was tired, hungry and very frightened about what the next few days would bring. I was going to be sick. 'Excuse me,' I said.

The ladies' loo was full of hookers. Up close, they seemed pathetically young. A girl in white jeans and a white top grabbed my hand. 'Please, miss, what is your name? We like you.'

'Julia,' I said, trying to push past her into a cubicle.

She seized my right nipple through my shirt and started to twist it. 'But Miss, we like you, we want you to be our friend. Will you buy us dinner? A drink?'

'Ouch!' I made it into the cubicle and locked the door. I knelt on the floor. There was banging behind me. 'Miss, we want you to be our mother!'

Clearly, there was to be no peace for the nauseous. I unbolted the door, and tried to squeeze past. The bony hand reached out and twisted again. 'Stop that!'

I hurried down the long concrete walkway that led to our room. A Nigerian soldier was being chatted up by another girl. He leaned against the balustrade, his AK47 tucked between his legs. I made it to the room and was immediately violently sick. The phone started to ring.

'Who is it?'

'Miss, it is me. I want you to be my friend.'

I slammed the phone down. There was a knock on the door. 'Go away!'

'Room service.'

I opened the door. A waiter in white evening dress was carrying a plate topped with a silver-plated dome. The outline of his vest was visible under his white shirt. 'I didn't order any food.'

'Your friend ordered for you. He thought you might be hungry.'

It was a sweet gesture, but a useless one. I pushed the fish in a peppery sauce around my plate. Another knock.

'Yes?'

'It's Christopher.'

He wanted an early night. But before he could go to bed, there was one thing he had to do. 'I'll have to wash out my boxers in the sink. They're the only pair I've got.'

I lay weakly on the bed. Christopher was splashing in the bathroom. It was nine o'clock. Curfew made the nights very long.

Another knock on the door. 'Chris, you get it.'

'But I'm naked.'

'And I'm ill.'

Christopher opened the door, a scanty hand towel wrapped around his waist. It was Lieutenant-Colonel John.

'What are you doing in your room so early?' he said. 'Listen, the lads and I thought we'd have a barbecue. Jimmy who has a cottage in the grounds was out earlier today catching fish.'

Christopher stumbled and stuttered his excuses. 'Julia not very well . . . I have nothing to wear . . . all my clothes wet.' We were a pathetic pair.

'OK!' said John, not one to take rejection personally. 'Tomorrow night maybe. Just don't eat the muck they give you here. You'll have the shits for weeks.'

'Did you eat in the dining room?' I asked when he'd gone. Christopher nodded gloomily.

He hung his boxer shorts to dry on the air-conditioning unit and turned it up to high. Scobie had endured nights intent on avoiding body contact: '. . . wherever they touched – if it were only a finger lying against a finger – sweat started'. Thanks to technology, I lay listening to Christopher's wet knickers flapping in the breeze like sails in a storm. I looked around the moonlit room wondering quite seriously if the shelf on top of the built-in wardrobe would be a good hiding place when the rebels came to get me.

In the morning, Christopher and I both felt better. It was time for a row. I wanted breakfast. I sat in the high-ceilinged dining room on a white plastic chair surrounded by Nigerian soldiers in khaki. They stared at me. I stared at the single rose in a vase on my table and the life-size china Afghan hound that guarded the entrance. I tapped my fingers to the piped Vivaldi. Forty-five minutes after placing my order, my plate of scrambled eggs and Christopher arrived simultaneously.

'Hurry up, it's 8.27,' he urged me.

'Just let me eat my breakfast.'

'No, the driver will be waiting. Come on.'

'We're paying him to wait. I'll just finish my coffee.'

A drop of perspiration landed on the table. 'We've been here nearly twenty-four hours and I haven't shot a single frame,' Chris shouted. 'Come on!'

We both fumed silently, as Alghabi drove us down the hotel drive. A few hundred yards along the road there was a checkpoint. We waved our passports at a young soldier in camouflage fatigues.

'Stop!' he yelled, tapping his machine-gun on the bonnet. He was tall with yellow eyes, the legacy of endless bouts of malaria. 'Get out of the car.'

We stood on the muddy verge. 'Go and stand over there!' His breath smelt of alcohol. He pointed us towards a middle-aged woman sitting on a stool in the patchy shade of a tree. Alghabi opened the boot for him and he rifled through it muttering under his breath. Five minutes later, Alghabi was waved on. He drove the ten yards up the road and we got in again.

'Someone's got a hangover,' he chuckled.

We continued to what had become known locally as the Amp Camp. From the road, it looked like we were approaching a society wedding. Rows of brightly coloured marquees flapped in the breeze. The canvas was home to more than five hundred people, sharing three latrines and five tap heads. 'We are living here under protest,' said Sok Dankwah, who showed me around.

Sok introduced me to some of the camp's inhabitants. Most were illiterate villagers from the vast, thickly forested interior, who had walked for days to reach the safety of the capital. Mercifully the January attackers had not advanced as far as the camp.

'This is Ali,' said Sok. 'He was shot. Mohammed here was butchered in the head. They cut his ears off. Poff.'

Sekou Kono was a strapping teenager, dressed in denim cut-offs. The sleeves of his T-shirt hung loosely over his non-existent arms. 'It was two o'clock in the morning when the rebels came to his house,' Sok told me. 'They cut off both his arms. It was a moment of frustration and trauma. He wanted to buy and sell and trade. But now he can do nothing. His family are all dead, he cannot farm. He cannot even wipe his own arse. He cannot even commit suicide. The rebels turned him into the living dead.'

How do you comfort someone like Sekou? I couldn't squeeze his arm or shake his hand to wish him luck. I ended up placing both my hands on his shoulders. It was the first time in Sierra Leone that I really wanted to cry.

Finna Kamara was thirty-eight, came from the bush and now lived with her nine children in a stifling tent built for four. She had a turban on her head and was dressed in a patterned flowing robe, which she lifted to reveal the stump where one of her legs had been. 'They cut off my seven-year-old daughter's two arms,' Sok translated. 'Two more of my children were crippled. The rebels kneecapped them with their guns. We hid in the bush and when the rebels had gone we came to Freetown. But we do not like life in the city, we want to go back.'

'Do you think the rebels will come back?'

'No, we do not think they will return because we pray to God for this.'

'If they did return, would you want revenge?'

'No. No revenge. God will punish them. We just want to return to the bush.'

Sok was exasperated by the words he was translating. 'That's the trouble with the Sierra Leoneans,' he said. 'They put too much trust in God.'

Lizards were running around in the dust. A child stood over a potty that swarmed with flies. Women in long skirts and bras were washing at a standpipe. It was a scene from the *Nine O'Clock News* come to life, yet what struck me most was the air of normality. A fast game of football was being played in the mud and in one corner of the camp women were tending plots of cassava and spinach. 'If the rains come, this will be turned into a garden,' Sok said. The Sierra Leoneans were masters of rickety improvisation.

A child in a Mickey and Donald T-shirt and no pants clung to Sok's legs. 'This boy is about three we think, but we know nothing about him because he won't speak,' he said. Sok was in his thirties, with an exhausted chubby face. He was in charge of the camp's twenty-six lost children. The youngest was four and the oldest seventeen. They were refugees from the war-torn interior, who had been separated from their parents or watched them die.

A girl of about six took my hand. Her head was bent back as if she was staring up at the sky and she moved clumsily. 'This is Sheku Man. The rebels bent her neck back and now she can't walk properly,' Sok said. 'She's had a nervous breakdown.'

Sok was Ghanaian, but for the past three years he had been running a children's home in Freetown. On 6 January he had heard noises in the hills and realized the rebels were approaching. 'I knew I had to rescue the children,' he said. 'There were twenty-two of them and just two adults – me and the caretaker. We headed for the swamp but we missed the canoes that were carrying people across, so we had to cross on foot at low tide. We saw a lot of dead people that had been swallowed by the mud. The first night, we climbed into the mangrove trees and slept there. At daybreak, a fisherman ferried us to an island in his canoe. He made four trips to get us all across. We spent the second night on that island in the middle of mosquitoes and insects.' He shuddered at the memory. 'Oh! We didn't sleep that night.'

Sok and the children were on the run for three weeks, walking twenty miles every day, until they reached the comparative safety of Lungi airport. Two weeks later, they returned to Freetown and found the orphanage burnt down. They were transferred to the refugee camp, but Sok's compassion was at an end.

'I cannot stay here. I must return to my wife and children. The rebels are looking specifically for Nigerians and Ghanaians, because they are the fiercest soldiers in Ecomog. I know of eight Ghanaians in Freetown who have been killed so far. Two of them were teachers. One of them was my very good friend.' His bloodshot eyes filled with tears. 'This is not my country. There is a point when you can no longer risk your life for someone else's mess.'

The Ecomog soldiers felt the same way. Most were young men doing national service, who found themselves far from home fighting against an army of young boys high on drugs and home-brewed alcohol.

'It is not my war,' one young soldier staying at the Cape Sierra told me. 'Why should I die in a strange place for something I don't understand?' Yet America had decided this was a black problem and that blacks should sort it out. The Reverend Jesse Jackson had described the conflict as 'The longest, bloodiest and ugliest' of the decade, yet his country had deemed it worthy of war aid of only $15 million, compared with its down payment of $13 billion to Kosovo.

The Nigerians may have been shunned and despised by the international community for their human rights abuses, but they were the heroes of Freetown. We visited one of their senior officers at their barracks, just outside the city. As we entered, young soldiers leaned over the balconies that surrounded an inner courtyard and gave us cold stares. The officer had a room on the first floor. African music pulsated from a ghetto blaster drowning out his voice. His desk was covered in paper and his bookshelf filled with videos in plain white cases.

'They must entertain you,' Christopher said.

He gave us a supercilious stare. '*Actually*, they're for strategy.'

The officer was furious that some people felt they had not done enough to protect Freetown on 6 January. 'How were we supposed to stop the rebels? They came running into town, using women and children as human shields. It's pretty tough to shoot in that situation. Besides, if I had killed a civilian, I would have ended up in The Hague.'

Human rights organizations were keeping a close eye on the Nigerians to see that they did not avenge themselves

on captured child soldiers. 'But for Jesus's sake,' the officer
exclaimed. His handsome face was alight with indignation.
'My best friend, a brilliant soldier, was taken away just like
that by a twelve-year-old. He was a good man, he had a wife
and family. I am asking you – why should I not be allowed to
revenge him?'

Ecomog was especially contemptuous of the aid agencies.
Recently, they had expelled the International Red Cross from
the country, accusing them of supplying the rebels with radios
that they had used as spying tools. 'The IRC may not have
meant to give the rebels the radios, they were probably stolen,'
said the officer, sitting back in his wooden chair, feet on the
desk. 'But the point was, they came bumbling in with all this
talk about being impartial and helping everyone no matter what
side they are on. In this situation that is a very unhelpful attitude.'

He had a point. Unlike so many others, the war in Sierra
Leone was simple to understand. There were the good guys –
Kabbah's government and Ecomog, and there were the villains
in the form of the rebels, officially known as the Revolutionary
United Front led by Foday Sankoh, former wedding photographer and close friend of Africa's other master of despot-
ism, the President of Liberia, Charles Taylor, a man who
once cut off a rival's ears and then fed them to him. Six months
previously, Sankoh had been captured, tried and sentenced to
death for treason and murder. In jail, he drove other prisoners
to distraction by howling all night like a wolf. The temptation
to have him executed must have been overwhelming, but the
repercussions would have been devastating. Instead 'peace
talks' with him were scheduled for the following month in
Togo.

'The rebels say they want to liberate us,' Alghabi said. 'But
from what? We already had a democracy. They don't care for
the people. They just want to be rich.'

In Washington and London, the cocktail party circuit is full of earnest graduates who between mouthfuls of canapés will tell anyone who will listen that the RUF is fighting for democracy and the common man. They fail to mention the diamonds, the bauxite, the titanium and gold. And that although the RUF has murdered, cannibalized and maimed to gain control of their country's mines, they have yet to share the fabulous profits from these minerals with their struggling fellow brothers.

Of course, multinationals such as De Beers also want to control such mineral wealth. They want it so much that for years their staff have endured coups and tropical diseases to establish dozens of mines in the heart of the Sierra Leonean bush. But by 1997, these mines had been captured by the rebels. The multinationals were forced to flee. Their retreat was only temporary, however. Back in London and Frankfurt, they were urged by the exiled President Kabbah to call a British company, Sandline, which for $250,000 a week, plus expenses, despatched an army to Sierra Leone that restored Kabbah to power and the mines to their owners. It took them less than a week to fulfil their brief.

But then Sandline executives talked too much. They claimed that Kabbah had got their number from his very good friend and fellow exile, the British High Commissioner, Peter Penfold. To British companies such as Barclays Bank, who had been working in Sierra Leone for decades, this revelation was greeted with a shrug and a 'so what?'. But in Whitehall, there was panic. For the new Labour government the news was devastating. Backing mercenaries was strictly against its much-vaunted 'ethical' foreign policy, even if the mercenaries were helping the good guys. Tories jumped up and down with glee, ministers made embarrassed denials, the Foreign Secretary Robin Cook spluttered crumbs down his beard and

Penfold was recalled to London, where his knuckles were rapped severely.

In the corridors of the Foreign Office, Penfold was *persona non grata*. But in Freetown, he was a hero. The Sierra Leoneans granted him the honorary title of Komrabai – chief. They held a rally in his honour at the Siaka Stevens football stadium. Crowds greeted him as if he were a pop star. 'We love him, he saved us,' the soldier said simply. 'How can that be doing wrong?'

The following morning we were woken by the phone in our room at the Cape Sierra. 'Miss Llewellyn Smith? Peter Penfold here,' a voice said faintly. 'Would you care for a bite at the residence today?'

Komrabai Penfold lived at 'Runnymede' in Spur Road, a large white villa surrounded by high metal fences, a few minutes walk from the Hill Station Club. Close-protection men with walkie-talkies waved us through the gate. Sprinklers hissed on the lawn. Penfold's living room featured an extensive collection of glass and china hippos and a photo of him and his wife in traditional tribal dress. It was March, but a Christmas tree still sat in the hallway. Twelfth Night, of course, was the day the rebels came to town and Penfold had more to worry about than taking down the decorations. A bullet hole in the French windows had not yet been repaired. While we waited for him I picked up a leaflet called 'Things Britain is Good At'. It included: zoos, the national lottery and 'safety: we have the greatest proportion of people living to fifty or older in the world'. Such a world seemed very far off.

'Well, we *do* have a very good national lottery,' said Penfold defensively, when I mentioned this incongruity to him. As the Foreign Secretary's *bête noire*, Penfold was toeing the party line.

Peter Penfold looked more like a building society manager

than a hero of the people. He was fifty-four and of average height, with floppy grey hair, a beaky nose and bloodless lips. He had a nasal voice, a laconic manner and a CV that listed experience of two coups in Uganda, a revolution in Ethiopia and a war in Nigeria. In newspaper articles, he was frequently described as a figure from a Graham Greene novel largely because of his habit of wearing a tropical white suit. This was nonsense. A Greene character would have been riven by doubts, perpetually uncommitted. Penfold believed passionately in the future of Sierra Leone, so much so that when he was posted there, he decided to travel there by Land Rover from Senegal, one of the most perilous journeys imaginable. 'My feeling was that if I did it it would give the people new confidence. It's depressing being told you can't travel in your own country. I got a bit lost so I had to stop a policeman and say "Can you help me? I'm the new British High Commissioner." I had a spot of trouble crossing borders and there were a few problems in northern Guinea, but it was a nice way to arrive anyway.'

A servant offered us lamb chops from a platter and we drank Coca-Cola from crystal glasses. Then it was time for a drive. We set off in a convoy of two white Range Rovers, each with its own close-protection officer. As the Komrabai, Penfold was the rebels' first target.

We drove down the Kissy Road into the city's east end, a hopeless thoroughfare of broken concrete, weeds and burnt-out cars. People were camped in this ruin. Cardboard boxes had become walls, plastic sheets turned into roofs. This was the route that the rebels had taken into town. Penfold's young driver twisted round in his seat. He was tall and skinny, in an immaculate white shirt and shades. 'Once there were beautiful houses here, seventy or eighty years old. The rebels destroyed them systematically. Oh! Their coming was not an easy one.

Often they burned the houses after locking a whole family inside.'

Penfold had arranged for Foday Sankoh, the captured rebels' leader, to be driven along the road. 'It had quite an impact on him,' he said happily. I doubted this. This was the man who had decided that routine mutilation and rape was an excellent way of recruiting peasants, who would then hope to be spared such a fate. The international community was insisting that Kabbah should negotiate with Sankoh. Penfold was withering on the subject, although since our conversation was off the record, I can only paraphrase his views. 'It's a complete insult to democracy. We apply completely different standards here than we would at home. There, if we elect John Major, he is Prime Minister, no questions asked. We don't say "Well, now we must negotiate with the opposition and perhaps give them some seats in Parliament."'

We stopped at the Approved School on the edges of the city. The rebels were camped only two miles from here. Three months ago, it had been a private boys' school. In the headmaster's study there was an honours board. Gold letters glinted on a black background. Best-Behaved House: Aggrey; Best House in Sports: Crowther; Best-Kept House: Patterson. Next to it was a blackboard with writing in faded chalk: 'The change from solid to liquid is referred to as melting.'

Today nearly a thousand people were living here, existing on meagre rations of rice. Men and women were shitting on the playing fields. The air stank of death. People were dying daily of malaria, having preferred to risk the mosquitoes outside to a night crammed ten to a clammy broom cupboard. Above us, vultures circled. 'When the rains come, so will typhoid and pneumonia,' said Mattias who was showing us around. He was dressed all in black. 'Things are desperate. Every day we hear more and more bad news.' He pointed at a man, who was trailing limply behind him. 'He is the manager of the camp but he cannot work today. He escaped with his seventeen children but he has just heard that his village has been burned down. All his tribe has been killed.'

In the crowd Komrabai Penfold was in his element. Naked children with snotty noses clutched at his hand. Women brushed his face with skeletal hands. He stood in the centre of the screaming crowd holding a bundle of clothes above his head. 'These are a gift from the people of Wales,' he shouted above the bedlam. 'We get three dozen people a week at the High Commission asking for our help,' he said as he climbed back into the air-conditioned comfort of the Range Rover. There was a large sweat stain in the armpit of his blue-and-white striped shirt. 'But that's what the role of a chief is all about. It's the extended family ethos. If you pay seventy people a month, you are keeping a thousand alive. Otherwise no one could survive.'

Penfold was absent from Freetown for only a week after 6 January. The British High Commission opened a month before the American Embassy. In those scary days when the city was regularly bathed in the orange light of an explosion, the close-protection team had faced one particular difficulty. 'Peter's parrots,' an officer said. 'He had two of them and one escaped. He was desperate to get it back before his wife found out. In the end, we put a message out over the radio saying, "The big chief's parrot is missing." Within a day, it had been returned.'

V

That night at the Cape Sierra everyone was on edge. The rebels were closing in again. Aid agencies were drawing up evacuation plans. The talk was all the same: we are doomed, the helicopters are running out of fuel, we have to get to Conakry. Little had changed since Father Rank told Scobie: 'Not that you can believe a single thing you hear in this place.'

I was propping up the bar with Tejan, Fred Marafono – a Fijian-born, former SAS man turned mercenary – and Jaffal, a young aide of Kabbah's. Mosquitoes hung in the air like Zeppelins, too gorged to dart about.

'Freetown is full of rumours,' said Tejan. 'Don't be taken in by them. If you do you are giving the rebels what they want. They want to provoke instability and that is exactly what they are doing. All they have to do is send a message out on the Internet that they are on their way back and all those pussy aid workers are on the next helicopter. That's when the place falls apart.'

Fred was a wild-eyed man, fifty-eight, with a lumpy nose, dirty blond hair down to his shoulders and a magnificent moustache. He had spent the day flying the only government helicopter, a M117 called Bokkie, resupplying soldiers in the bush with food and ammunition.

'Without you, Ecomog would never have recaptured the city,' Tejan said, slapping his friend on the back. He turned to me: 'You know he should have been earning $2000 an hour, but for seven months now he hasn't been paid.'

'It doesn't matter,' said Fred. He had a twangy South African accent. 'Nothing in the world can justify what is happening here. There is no way on earth we can give up on these people. They are my people now. I am one with them.'

Initially, Jaffal confused me. He spoke like a Sierra Leonean and dressed like one in grubby floor-length white robes, but his skin was white under a black beard. He was a member of the Lebanese community, who had long been the most powerful minority in Sierra Leone. In Greene's day, the Lebanese, or Syrians as they were called, occupied an uneasy midground between Europeans and Africans. Their role was to 'make money. They run all of the stores up country and most of the stores here. Run diamonds too.' The villain of *The Heart of the Matter* is Yusef the Syrian shopkeeper, who lends Scobie money to send his wife abroad and then blackmails him over his affair with Helen. 'To give help to a Syrian was only one degree more dangerous than to receive help,' Greene wrote.

In those days, there had been 40,000 Syrians in Sierra Leone, but today only a quarter that number remained. Several of their women had been raped by the rebels, and most families now sent their children to school abroad. When the economy was at a virtual halt, those who remained still found ways to import Oreo cookies, make pitta bread and run bush airlines. Behind sheet-metal shutters, with their own electricity generators, they stayed on through coups, juntas and peace deals. In town, they ran the Crown Bakery, where just a week after the coup ex-pats could eat greasy fried chicken and chips in spotless, air-conditioned surroundings. Thanks to the Lebanese, for half an hour, you could forget the dust and rot of West Africa. As lunchtime regulars Christopher and I were exceedingly grateful to them.

'My family came here in 1977, when I was a small boy,' Jaffal said. 'We were running from the war. The jungles and the beaches felt free. We Lebanese have always had a reputation of being bold, of going into the danger zones. If you take risks, you make money, Now, my family has a penthouse in Beirut, a beach house nearby, but I prefer it here. I feel more at home.'

'Because you can get even fucking richer here, that's why,' said Fred, spitting out his words as if they were pieces of bad meat.

A low-voiced argument began between the two men. 'Fred

loves this country, he works for us for free and he hates to see the Lebanese ripping us off,' Tejan whispered to me. 'After the rebels left, they were the first to open their shops again but they were charging five times the normal price. They invest all their money outside the country. They take and they never give.'

Fred's face was tomato red. With a series of oaths that I suspected you would not find in Krio for Beginners, he grabbed Jaffal by the shoulders and shook him like a pillow. Then he marched out of the room.

Tejan grabbed Jaffal's arm. 'I want a word with you outside.' He hustled him on to the terrace, where he could be seen gesticulating furiously in the moonlight. Ten minutes later, they returned smiling. Some kind of deal had been done. Tejan winked at me as he ordered another round of Star beers. 'Sorry to have abandoned you, darling. But business never stops here.'

VI

Worryingly, I was beginning to enjoy myself in Freetown. By day, I could play the brave and compassionate war correspondent. At night I experienced the intense exhilaration that came with still being alive. Scary situations provoke intense camaraderie. Within a few days we seemed to know everyone in town. Life was a never-ending cocktail party fuelled by the hilarity that comes from a daily brush with mortality.

Why do I love this place so much? Scobie asks himself.

Is it because human nature here hasn't had time to disguise itself? Nobody here could ever talk about a heaven on earth. Heaven remained rigidly in its proper place, on the other side of death, and on this side flourished the injustices, the cruelty, the meanness that elsewhere people so cleverly hushed up. Here you could love human beings nearly as God loved them, knowing the worst: you didn't love a pose, a pretty dress, a sentiment artfully assumed.

Today such a sentiment rang even more true. Everything in Sierra Leone had been stripped to its rawest essentials but this had only served to enhance the beauty of what remained. The cities had been destroyed, but there were still the 'great green swollen hills', the empty beaches. The people who had lost everything maintained a dignity under pressure that moved me like nothing I had witnessed before.

I loved Sierra Leone and the Sierra Leoneans because they were forgotten by the rest of the world. It was the same kind of love that Scobie felt for friendless Helen Rolt. 'He had no sense of responsibility towards the beautiful and the graceful and the intelligent. They could find their own way. It was the face for which nobody would go out of his way . . . that demanded his allegiance.'

'Everyone likes it here,' said Paul, the Australian midwife. We were visiting his makeshift labour ward in the Siaka Stevens football stadium. 'That's why the Sierra Leoneans keep getting done over. They're just too fucking laid back.'

Hundreds of families were living in the stadium, camped out on the stands, their poor frayed clothing drying over the backs of seats. The pitch, however, was an immaculate smooth green. 'They couldn't sleep on that, it would be an insult to the Sierra Leone Lions,' Paul said. 'Mind you, the whole team left during the last military government and when they came back they had their arms cut off.'

Paul was considerably chirpier than the first time we had seen him, contemplating death at Conakry airport. But he was desperate for funds. 'No one cares about us, they only have time for Kosovo. I wish we had some starving people here. The world might finally be interested.'

It was true that Sierra Leone confused you. This was supposed to be the poorest country on earth but it didn't look it. The walking wounded were everywhere, like a Bosch painting come to life, but they were dressed in Tommy Hilfiger sweatshirts and baseball caps, while the stalls that lined the roadside were laden with garlic, loaves and green bananas. The statistics told a different story. Infant mortality was a staggering 187 for every 1,000 live births. Life expectancy was thirty-nine for men, forty-three for women. Literacy was 30 per cent.

'Freetown isn't Sierra Leone,' Paul said, digging a needle into the arm of a curly headed baby. 'In the bush they are still living in the Dark Ages. There is an absence of everything there, no employment, no police, no local government, no doctors. If you get sick you either survive or you die.'

Sierra Leone had been founded by the British under George III for the best of reasons: as a home for freed slaves and for captives rescued by the Royal Navy from slave ships. These Krio people based themselves in the capital and soon began to dominate the Temne 'natives' of the interior. 'They aren't even real niggers,' says the young civil servant Harris of the Krio. 'Just West Indians and they rule the coast.' The rebels shared this contemptuous view, declaring an aim to return the country to 'truly black' rule. 'People in Freetown don't associate themselves with people in the bush,' said Paul. 'That was why it was such a shock when the rebels came here. For the first time the people in the capital understood what the peasants had been going through.'

It was impossible for us to see for ourselves. Only Ecomog troops could travel into the bush. There people were starving out of sight of the cameras. Alghabi was even reluctant to take us down the coast to Lakka, a camp for former child soldiers.

'Only for 10,000 more leones,' he said cheerfully. That was around $3. 'Otherwise not worth my while. The road is too bad.'

He was right. The road was terrible. We bounced along a dusty red laterite path through what Greene described as 'bush villages of mud and thatch'. The scene was just as it was during those untroubled days: '. . . a girl with small crescent breasts . . . carrying a pail of water on her head; a child naked except for a red-bead necklace around the waist played in a little dust-paved yard among the chickens; labourers carrying hatchets came across the bridge'. To our right was the ocean, to our left jungle where leopards prowled and the rebels camped.

At Lakka beach there was an empty hotel called the Cotton Club. Now weeds oozed through the plasterwork. The Boutique de Paris, where holidaymakers once haggled for souvenirs, was locked, its window panes long gone. The swimming pool was drained out, with only a puddle of stagnant water at the base to recall the days of ease.

In the house next door Kwasi Adarkwah was living with forty-one former child soldiers aged between nine and seventeen and another thirty camp followers, of whom the youngest was four. The children had been placed there by Ecomog. Kwasi, another Ghanaian, had a tired, angry face. Every day he was risking his life to rehabilitate them.

'They are impossible to control,' he said, as we sat in his dark office. 'They do everything with force. For them a gun is everything. It's all gimme this and gimme that. They sleep where they want to sleep. Only the other week they beat up the cook because she asked them to water the garden. You have to be careful. I used to sleep elsewhere at night, but now I have realized that I must always be here.'

Kwasi took us down the road to the local school. Children in white shirts and royal blue shorts were skipping in the yard, playing elaborate clapping games. One child ran among them clutching an exercise book, showing pictures of clock faces. 'I am learning how to tell the time,' he said shyly.

Mohammed Kamara was ten, the kind of little boy you wanted to devour. He had a round face and pudgy legs. Thick eyelashes fringed his chocolate-drop eyes. Mohammed had been a captain in the rebel army. 'I had five bodyguards and many troops. You see, my mother died and my father had disappeared. The rebels took me and trained me in how to kill. My job was to burn houses and to chop off hands. I was promoted because I did really well.' He could have been an old colonel reminiscing from his armchair in the golf club.

'How did your mother die?' Kwasi asked him.

'I killed her. When the rebels captured me they said "Kill her and your brothers and sisters or we will kill you." I had to set fire to our home. I saw them dying inside.'

It was all so matter-of-fact. It was impossible to know what Mohammed felt now. He showed no emotion. He said he regretted his deeds, that he hoped for peace but without sincerity. 'Mohammed looks like an angel but he is a lot of trouble,' Kwasi said after his retreating chubby form. 'You can't get him to stay in one place. He is so wild. He uses force to get whatever he wants.'

Yet Mohammed still radiated a milky innocence. I was struck by another child, not much taller, but with a narrow, knowing face. While Mohammed giggled and ran about, this child traced military formations in the dust with a stick. 'Double up,' he barked at some younger boys. 'Everybody in line. Quick march.' When the other children giggled at the sight of me, this child stood apart and gave me a salacious wink.

We returned to the Cotton Club, to wait until the other children had finished school. I decided to go for a swim. Kwasi lent me some baggy shorts and a shirt. This was, after all, the most beautiful beach I had ever seen. The waves were big enough to play in but not frightening. The white sand merged into dense green coconut jungle. Unsurprisingly, there was not another person in sight. I wallowed happily in the surf.

A child was waving at me from the sand. He had a skinny body and a wide melon smile. I waved back. What friendly people the Sierra Leoneans were. The child picked up my sandals and walked down to the water's edge, holding them out to me. I waded towards him, teetering in the swell. Then I recognized him. It was the boy with the knowing face who had been organizing the marching.

Christopher appeared behind him, his face a strange blend of amusement and sadness.

'You're looking at a mass murderer,' he said.

Back on the terrace, Christopher and Alghabi had been talking to the child. His name was Saidu Kargbo. They thought I ought to hear his story. Salt water was dripping down my shoulders, as I settled in a hammock. Saidu nuzzled on Alghabi's knee, pushing a toy car up and down his leg. Occasionally, he reached over to touch my hair.

Saidu was twelve years old, but already he had enjoyed a distinguished career. 'By the time I was ten I had killed two hundred people – maybe two hundred and ten,' he said in his high child's voice. 'That figure includes two Catholic priests. They called me "Corporal Highway".' He had earned his nickname because for years he had controlled a rebel check-point on one of the country's main roads. 'We burned hundreds of vehicles,' he said. 'It was good being a corporal. The adults had to salute me.'

Saidu was five when he was snatched from his home at gunpoint to be brought up by the country's rebel army. 'They taught me how to use an AK47,' he recalled. 'They injected cocaine into my forehead or into my arm. It made me feel powerful.'

As Saidu spoke, Alghabi groaned and put his head in his hands. 'I know who this boy is,' he said. 'He used to broadcast on the rebel radio station, urging the other children to come to war. I can't believe they are trying to rehabilitate him. He is evil, pure evil.'

Yet Saidu was still a child, and it was impossible to treat him as anything else: 'A naked woman used to train us,' he said. 'We were naked too, but if our pricks went hard the other boys would beat us.'

Kwasi took us to the carpentry workshop to meet Basheru Pokawa. He was fifteen with the by now familiar expressionless features. At Kwasi's request he lifted up his T-shirt to show the initials RUF carved into his back. 'I ran away once and when I came back, they branded me,' he said. There was sweat on his brow. 'He can't travel anywhere, because if the soldiers at a roadblock saw this, they would kill him,' Kwasi said.

Basheru was twelve years old when he was made a sergeant. He went on to become one of Sankoh's bodyguards. 'We used to attack and loot villages but I never killed anyone,' he said. Kwasi gave him a stern look. 'How do you become promoted to sergeant without killing anyone?' he asked.

There were girls at the camp too. Kadiata Allieu was seventeen with a face as sad as a Byzantine Madonna. Kadiata mothered the younger children. She had not seen her family for eight years. 'The rebels came to my village in the south and killed my father,' she said, staring at her toes painted with orange polish.

'I was nine years old. My mother and sister decided to go to Freetown, but on the way we were attacked. Many people were killed and our vehicle was burned. I was caught and taken into the bush. The chief commander of the officer training corps said: "If you cry we will kill you and if you try to escape and you are caught we will kill you." I did the cooking, the housework, the sweeping. They taught me how to shoot a gun. If they were angry with me they beat me over the back of my head with a rifle. I was frightened all the time because we were constantly being attacked by the Sierra Leonean army.

'They put me in charge of the wounded soldiers and then they told me I must marry one of them. I didn't want to, but they said if I refused they would shoot me. Eventually, two years ago we came to Freetown for the coup. We were demobbed and I begged my husband to lay down his arms and learn a trade. At first, he agreed and began to study welding, but then when Kabbah was returned he decided to go back to the rebels. He took me with him but I could not bear it any more, so I ran away back to Freetown. My suffering had become too great.'

'What do you think of the war now?' I asked.

'I don't even want to think about it. I just scream when I am reminded of the agonies. It gives me nightmares, I just want to see my family again. My mother is still alive, but the road to her is blocked. My sister is married to a soldier. I don't know if I will ever see them again.'

There are still 2000 children in the rebel army. The Kamajors – who support Kabbah – use them too. 'They never question orders, they are nimble, they make excellent scouts,' said Kwasi. 'And they are being born in the bush now. They will never know another life except killing and fear.'

The leap of faith that Kwasi was making in caring for these children was extraordinary. 'They're so cunning,' he said. 'They say they want peace to get an education, but there's no guarantee that given the chance they won't run back to the rebels.'

The rebels' method was a bastardization of the Jesuits' boast that given a child before he was seven they would make him a devout Catholic for life.

It seemed an impossible task to try to recapture these children's lost innocence. Even if their families were alive, many refused to take them back. 'We've traced Mohammed's father but he doesn't want him,' Kwasi said. 'He's frightened for his safety. If he were to return home now, there would be a lynch mob waiting at his door.'

The last bout of fighting had seen dozens of amputee refugees arrive at the Cotton Club. Emaciated women sat in the red dirt yard stirring a cooking pot with one arm, while their naked children ran about. 'Can you imagine the irony of it?' Kwasi said. 'They have lost everything to these children and then they come here and see us trying to help them. It makes things very awkward.

'The other day, a Nigerian came here from Ecomog. He spotted one of our children and started screaming at him. He was saying, "The last time I saw you, you had a gun pointed at my head. I had to manoeuvre to save my life." I had to beg him to leave the boy alone.

'I had to take another of the boys to Connaught hospital in Freetown. A four-year-old was sitting in bed with his arm missing. He shouted, "Daddy, daddy, there's the boy who did this to me." We had to run for it or there would have been mob justice.'

The rebels had stolen a generation of children's pasts and by doing so poisoned their country's hopes for a future. I couldn't see how Saidu and Mohammed could ever be healed, because that would involve a full comprehension of what they had done. How could they survive that? 'These children are so traumatized,' Kwasi said. 'How can they be expected to run the country alongside people who lost their arms and legs to them? How can anything good happen here for at least another twenty years?' Later, I realized that in all the time we had spent with him, he had not smiled once.

VII

Since Greene's time, the expat community of Freetown had changed significantly. Once, they were railway engineers and clerks transplanted 3000 miles to a 'fetid White Man's grave'. Today, of course, the empire builders had retired to bungalows in Salthaven and in their place were sanitation engineers from ICRC, child protection officers from Unicef, doctors from MSF and supervisors from USAid. They had taken over their 'bungalows of Cape Station', given them a new coat of whitewash and an electric fence and employed an old Krio to snooze in a watchman's hammock all day, guarding the Land Cruisers and Mercedes.

Greene loathed the expats' provincial mentality. In *Journey Without Maps*, he called his chapter about Freetown 'A Home from Home' and railed against its rulers 'who had to reproduce English conditions, if they were to be happy at all'. Greene had come to Africa to look for his spiritual origins, to find what man might have been like before the corruptions of materialism set in. He was revolted by his fellow Englishmen's inability to do the same. Their conversations about children – whom Greene loathed – wives, golf and library books all reminded him of the England of *Brighton Rock*, an England he found sterile and limiting.

I wondered what Greene would have made of the unhappy British travel agent Bill's home, a villa out on Lumley Beach

with a view of the golf course with Beatrix Potter stickers on
the bathroom walls and a bar covered with fake fur that was
growing mildew in the heat. At the bottom of a wardrobe, I
found piles of mouldy copies of *Steam Railways* magazine,
while in the living room under the squashy brown sofa the
colour of a hotdog, I found a two-month-old copy of the
Daily Express.

Christopher and I were staying at Bill's house as guests of
his tenants Eamon and Fiona, an Irish couple working for an
Irish charity. They had met in Angola, done a spell in the Sudan
and were clearly bored stupid with each other. The nights had
always been long for the white men in Freetown. Today, curfew had made them an eternity. It was not even possible to enjoy
Greene's favourite time of day – sunset – when the clay roads
were transformed into a 'delicate flower-like pink'. From dusk
till dawn, you were trapped in your compound with little to
do but drink and seethe. Greene's young civil servants Harris
and Wilson had entertained themselves in their room at the
Bedford Hotel with cockroach killing competitions. James
and Suzanne from Oxfam played the board game Twister all
night, contorting themselves across a brightly coloured board
according to the instructions of a spinning wheel.

'What with just two of you?'

'Well, there's nothing else to do. The video is broken.'

James and Suzanne from Oxfam invited us to stay, but by
then we had already accepted Eamon and Fiona's invitation.
We spent our first evening with them, sitting on the veranda,
eating our take-away supper from Paddy's off our knees. The
gossip was as intense as it had been in the days when Scobie
wooed Helen Rolt. The only thing that had changed was
the number of acronyms. 'Emma from STC and John from
UNHCR are looking very close. She's a naughty girl. She's
got a boyfriend in Rwanda. He's ICRC.'

Eamon was tall and stocky, with red hair and a freckled bully-boy face. I didn't like Eamon and he didn't like me. Or any woman come to that. He ignored Fiona completely, unless it was to criticize her. She was sweet but cowed. Or so I thought.

On our second night the couple went to visit their next-door neighbour, an Irish priest, to talk about borrowing some office furniture from him. Even during curfew it was possible to move around between checkpoints. Christopher and I were left on the veranda making conversation with the other house guest, Martin, a Scottish aid worker and photographer.

Martin was a war bore. 'Yeah, I've been to every conflict zone in the world,' he droned, rolling a cigarette. 'Chechnya was pretty heavy for most people I guess, but then they weren't friends with the Liberation Army like I was. Somalia was great. Sierra Leone I don't know much about, except it's the only country in the world where the mountains rise next to the sea.'

'Um, I think you'll find that there are mountains next to the sea in Scotland even.'

'No. It says in my guide book that it's the only country in the world . . .' We dug out a Lonely Planet. 'Oh, well in southern Africa.'

Even Christopher, normally the most courteous of men, was obviously finding it hard to be polite to Martin. I was desperate to go to bed. It was only eight o'clock. On the cliffs behind us the starving pye dogs that kept Greene awake all night were howling at the moon. The lights went off and the thunderous air-conditioning sputtered out. 'Power cut,' said Martin smugly. 'Well, what do you expect from a war zone? In Afghanistan one time . . .'

In the dark, I inched down the staircase to the kitchen and fumbled in the cupboards for candles. All around us there was a roar as the generators of the surrounding houses kicked in.

'Do you know where the generator is here?' asked Martin.

'No.'

We sat in the dark. From downstairs came a crash. Rebels. My heart stopped. Then I heard: 'Oh . . . fuckin' . . . fuck!'

Our hosts were back. They reeled on to the veranda. 'Fuckin' . . . fuck . . . does anyone know how to work the generator?' said Eamon.

'How are we all?' said Fiona, pulling herself on to a high stool. 'I sink itsh time for a good ole sing song.'

She began to sing. 'All sings bright and beautiful. All creatures great and shmall. All sings wise and won-derful . . .'

She had a truly terrible voice. 'All sings wise and wonderful. Zhe Lord God . . .' I tried to catch Christopher's eye but it was too dark. I yearned for Martin's war stories.

'Very good,' said Martin as she finished. 'Now why don't you sing a traditional Irish folk song?'

Fiona ignored him. 'All sings bright and bee-yoo-tee-ful . . .'

She sang it six times in a row. We tried to interrupt her. Now I was glad of the darkness. It concealed my embarrassment. 'An Irish song?' Martin pleaded. Perhaps he wasn't so bad after all.

'Yeah, OK.'

She was off again. 'Come all ye young rebels and list while I sing. For the love of one's country is a terrible thing. It banishes fear like the speed of a flame. And it makes us all part of the Patriot Game. My Name is O'Hanlon I just turned sixteen. My home is Monaghan where I was weaned. I've learned all my life cruel England's to blame. So now I am part of the Patriot Game.'

Eamon who had been catatonic in an armchair stirred.

'I'm Scottish,' said Martin smugly.

'So am I,' I said. 'On my mother's side.' Christopher was silent.

Fiona's impromptu concert ended with an 'Oh, fuck'. She leapt off her stool. We heard her stumbling wildly through the dark.

She never returned. The relief was tangible. Christopher, Martin and I chatted softly in the moonlight while Eamon groaned. Then Martin excused himself. He was gone for a long time. So long I went to look for him. I bumped into him in the corridor. He reeked of Dettol.

'Don't use the bathroom,' he said urgently. 'Fiona's been sick all over the place. I went in and slipped in the vomit. I've had to wash all my clothes in the bath in the dark.'

There was no more war talk from Martin that night. I refused to enter the bathroom. I ended up peeing in the sink in the laundry room next door.

'We should have stayed with Oxfam,' Christopher said.

Oxfam, in fact, were a little hurt that we had turned them down. 'And surprised,' said James. 'Eamon and Fiona's house is the most vulnerable in Freetown. It's the only NGO house with no satellite equipment. In fact, they haven't even had their land line installed yet. If the rebels came, you would be completely helpless. That's why I thought you'd be better off staying with us.' A few months after our visit, Foday Sankoh moved into a villa a few hundred yards up the road from Eamon and Fiona, in his new un-brokered role as Vice President with 'minerals portfolio'. A peaceful demonstration outside ended in gunmen opening fire and killing dozens of civilians.

VIII

On our last day in Freetown we visited the place where *The Heart of the Matter* began, the Bedford Hotel in Bond Street, where Wilson sat on his balcony and watched Scobie go by as

'the Cathedral bell clanged for matins'. Its real name was the
City Hotel. In Greene's days, it had been a centre for the
expat community. 'The City is usually more crowded and
noisy [than the Grand] because there's a billiard table; people
are rather dashing, get a little drunk and tell indecent stories.'
It had been one of the few buildings in Freetown to escape
the rebels' holocaust but neglect was destroying it anyway. Its
white stucco frontage had developed psoriasis, and exotic
weeds sprouted from Wilson's balcony. The faded green railings were draped with frayed towels. By the gate, a Nigerian
soldier was slumped on a bench. Next to him a woman in a
brown and green robe was eating hungrily from a yellow
plastic pot.

'It is a hotel for refugees now,' said Ali, the flat-faced boy
who had 'volunteered' to show us round. 'They pay 6000
leones ($2) a night to stay here.'

It was an outrageous price, given that a policeman was paid
8000 a month. No wonder few of the rooms had been taken.
Ali ushered us up a creaking, decaying staircase. A sign on the
wall reminded you of the hotel's former days: 'No more than
two (2) guests are allowed in a room at any time . . . No guest
is allowed to rent his/her room out'. From the back windows,
there was a view of the courtyard. Half a dozen families were
camping there. Bob Marley wailed from a ghetto blaster.

'This used to be a very nice place,' Ali sighed. 'Then Freddie
died. He was the owner. The manager escaped to Guinea.
Then, I am afraid to say, it became a place for ladies of the
night. But now there is no work for them. Who can spare the
time and money?'

We stood on Wilson's balcony, with a fine view of the
burnt-out casino opposite. The vultures still circled overhead.
These days, they were well fed. The God that Scobie and
Greene had struggled to find in Freetown seemed more absent

than ever before. Ali sighed: 'Freetown used to be such a beautiful city. Why has the rest of the world forgotten us?' He clutched at my elbow. 'When you return to your country you will tell your Mr Blair to help us – and help will come.'

In 1949, in Sierra Leone, Greene's melancholia evaporated like dew on a summer morning. Sitting on that same balcony, he wrote to Catherine Walston: 'It's very very hot & sticky & I love Freetown.'

I asked Ali if he had read *The Heart of the Matter*.

'Of course,' he said. 'But really I don't think a novel like that has anything to say about Freetown today. You know the book I think of when I think of our city? I think of *The Omen*. What else could it be? We are all heading fast towards doomsday.'

3. Vietnam

He would have to learn for himself the real background that
held you like a smell does . . . The gold of the rice fields under
a flat late sun . . . those silk-trousered figures moving with
grace through the humid noon.

THE QUIET AMERICAN

I

Another day in the Socialist Republic of Vietnam. I woke up
at dawn in my room at the American Hotel. My sleep had
been fitful, thanks to the blue flashing of a neon Pepsi sign
penetrating the thin nylon curtains and lighting up my room
like a disco. Then there was the serenade of a million mopeds
setting off for work. When it was clear that I was going to
sleep no longer, I got dressed and went downstairs to the
lobby where Mr Than, the hotel proprietor, was processing a
credit card transaction. A Take That cassette was playing in
the background and his son Houm was yawning after another
late night at the Apocalypse Now bar. A group of executives
from British Petroleum were checking out.

Not for the first time since I arrived in Vietnam, I was
confused. 'Is Vietnam still a Communist country?' I asked Mr
Than.

'Oh yes,' he bellowed, over the screech of next door's
power drill. 'Vietnam is socialist republic – with hundred per

cent capitalist freedom. You know what they say? We can buy or sell what we want. We just can have no opinions.'

II

People fall in love with Vietnam. Graham Greene did. He first visited in 1951, at the height of the war to overthrow the French colonists, and liked it so much he spent four consecutive winters there. He loved the opium dens, the brothels, the beauty of his surroundings and the frisson of living in a land at war. 'In Indo China I drained a magic potion, a loving cup which I have shared since with many retired *colons* and officials of the French Foreign Legion whose eyes light up at the mention of Saigon and Hanoi,' he wrote in *Ways of Escape*.

Not long after Greene's last visit, the Communists took charge and for a decade Vietnam was closed to the outside world. But today everyone is fighting for a little piece of Vietnam. Businessmen predict it will be the next 'Asian tiger'. Tourists boast of having visited the new Thailand. 'Get there before everyone else does,' they urge each other in the transit lounge at Kuala Lumpur.

Today's Vietnam still seems much the one Greene knew before the war. There are colonial cities with shaded streets and green-shuttered villas, dense jungle and sleepy rivers, peasants in cone hats goading skinny water buffaloes, gleaming rice paddies and modest smiling girls.

From the moment I arrived in Saigon – no one calls it Ho Chi Minh City – I loved it too. The sun was shining. Mr Than was waiting for us at the airport in a new white Peugeot. Our room looked out over a building site, but there was a welcome bowl of lychees on the bedside table and Mrs Than brought us glasses of steaming fragrant tea. That night my friend Victoria and I drank cocktails on the roof of the Majestic Hotel 'with a wind from the Saigon River', just as Greene did whenever he was in town. We dined on crunchy spring rolls and raw beef salad at the Blue Ginger restaurant. At the end of the meal we hailed two cyclo drivers who pedalled us back on the rickshaws down wide and silent boulevards.

Like Greene, I discovered the best thing about Vietnam was the way it tempered the exotic with the familiar. 'Hadn't I on my first walk up Rue Catinat noticed first the shop with the Guerlain perfume and comforted myself with the thought that, after all, Europe was only a distant thirty hours?' said Fowler, the protagonist of *The Quiet American*. I felt the same when the next morning we visited that very same street – the only change being its new name, Dong Khoi – the city's main drag leading from the 'hideous pink' twin-spired Notre Dame cathedral to the Saigon river. We ate fresh croissants in the Paris Deli, before going shopping in Catinat Fashions – which stocked the latest styles from Moschino and Inès de la Fressange. All I needed was a pair of jodhpurs and a crisp white shirt and I was Catherine Deneuve in *Indochine*, gently reprimanding the servants for not cooling the wine properly.

The luxury was appreciated all the more after the ordeal of our journey. The cheapest possible flight to Saigon had been with Aeroflot via Moscow, with a stopover in Novosibirsk. Our grey seats had a deep hollow in the middle, worn out from years of abuse from Russian bottoms. The arm of my seat kept giving me an electric shock.

Our fellow passengers were a group of young men and women who appeared to be embarking on the Russian equivalent of Club 18–30. They had pushed down the seats around them to form a large table, on which they had spread a picnic of jars of pickled onions and raw red peppers. A vodka bottle was being passed around. Everyone was smoking. A ghetto blaster played pulsating house music. A bleached blonde stood straddled across a man who was naked from the waist down. They kissed enthusiastically. We began taxiing up the runway. The stewardesses chatted to each other in the galley. I had never listened to a safety demonstration in my life, but now I decided that I might quite like one. The party continued unabated.

There were to be fourteen more hours of this. The sound system was playing 'Mr Dick' by E-Rotic. Victoria was flicking through a copy of *Moscow News*. 'Why Do Russians Die So Young?' read the headline. Glancing at the party behind, I had a pretty good idea. I unbuckled my seat belt and attempted to climb over my friend.

'Where are you going?' she asked.

'To the loo.'

Victoria was outraged. 'You can't do that!' she shrieked. 'They haven't turned the seat belt sign off yet.'

III

After the torpor of Russia, arriving in Saigon was like finding yourself in a Fellini film played at top volume on amphetamines. All life in the city takes place on the street. On the narrow pavements, a group of boys were chalking a game of noughts and crosses, a young woman flailed the life out of someone else's laundry, beggars on crutches pulled at my arms and old men sat on miniature stools slurping from their bowls of watery noodles. A gym had flung its doors open revealing a room the size of a Western bathroom full of men lifting dumb-bells. The transvestite fortune-tellers, just like the ones witnessed by Greene, still squatted at the side of the road. Beside them, barbers wielded their sheepshears on the heads of customers who watched themselves in scraps of mirrors nailed to trees. In the evenings, beautiful girls, their backs as straight as flagpoles, still cycled in long, white *ao dai* tunics and trousers down the Rue Catinat.

After dark, Cholon, the Chinese quarter, still came to life like a 'pantomime set'. The merchants who had buried their gold in the ground when the Viet Cong moved in had dug it up once more and the 'wings' of dark alleyways where Communist agents once plotted were now being used as drug-processing plants to refine the opium smuggled across the border from Laos. Carpenters chipped at chairs and tables, tailors turned out made-to-measure suits in twenty-four hours and grannies made up baguettes full of pâté and coriander from street-corner stalls. Today, even Greene had become a marketable commodity. Every time you sat down outside a café a five-year-old child would materialize waving a bulky photocopy of *The Quiet American* – or should English not be your first language, *L'Américain bien tranquille*.

'A few years ago, I would have been frightened to buy a new pair of trousers in case my neighbours reported me to the police for having too much money,' said Mr Than. 'Now they say "Where do you buy them? Are they Levi's?"'

In Saigon the unemployed not only got on their bikes, they loaded them with saleable goods. There were five million people in the city, and at any time it seemed that most of them were on the streets. Motorbikes, bicycles and cyclos crowded the laneless boulevards fifteen abreast. All were carrying impossibly large cargoes. One cyclist was ferrying what appeared to be an entire dining room set, another bore a live pig. They looked like ants carrying grasshoppers. The drivers of the hopelessly outnumbered cars honked their horns constantly. Crossing the road seemed about as wise as wandering around downtown Kabul in a bikini. Like riding a horse, you had to show no fear. 'Remember to make no sudden moves,' the guidebook advised. The theory was that you stepped straight into the buzzing maelstrom and the bikes would swerve to avoid you. In practice Victoria and I lost at least an hour a day cowering on the pavement, until some bystander would take pity on us and usher us through the traffic like a kindly lollipop lady.

Since Greene had been to Saigon, everything had changed, yet nothing had altered. Expatriates who lived in Vietnam before the war regard *The Quiet American* as the most poignant evocation of a country they adored. The novel tells the story of Fowler, a cynical English journalist and Pyle, a naive American, both living in Saigon. Pyle falls in love with Fowler's Vietnamese mistress, Phuong (pronounced Fung), and eventually persuades her to leave Fowler, with promises of taking her to America. The French colonists are fighting Ho Chi Minh's Communist army in the north, the Americans, who want neither side to dominate such a strategically important region, are desperately searching for a 'third force' that can replace them both. Pyle sees potential in General Thé, the leader of the Cao Dai religious sect, but his trust is to prove mistaken when the General uses American money to detonate a bicycle bomb in the city centre that kills dozens of innocent civilians. Fowler, who has previously held a neutral stance, is so disgusted by what he sees, that he turns Pyle over to the Viet Minh. Pyle's body is found floating in a sewer in the slums and Phuong returns to Fowler.

Greene's novel was remarkable because it predicted the disastrous consequences if Americans continued to muddle in Vietnamese affairs. In the end, they found their 'third force' in the corrupt and weak Catholic president of South Vietnam, Ngo Dinh Diem. Their disastrous choice of ally resulted in three million Vietnamese – most of whom were civilians –

dying in the 'American War'. So did 57,600 Americans. Many regretted that their policy-makers had not taken Greene more seriously.

The Communist forces of Hanoi marched into Saigon, banning gambling, whoring and opium smoking – in other words all the things the city was famous for, and for the next decade the country was closed. Finally in 1986, severe famine forced the Vietnamese government to bow to the conditions of the World Bank and introduce *doi moi* – its version of perestroika – and embark on a series of 'Joint Ventures' with foreign companies. The Saigonese, who had never wanted to be communist in the first place, reacted to the changes with the force of a catapult held taut for eleven years. Within a few weeks the city was throbbing with all its old mercantile zest. Several landmarks had been demolished by the tide of progress. Number 104 Rue Catinat, the address of Greene's friend René Berval, the editor of *France Asie*, and his girlfriend Phuong, on which Greene based Fowler's home, was now a pile of rubble earmarked for rebuilding by Ocean Place Developments.

Other haunts of Greene's had been stamped out by Party puritanism. He spent much of his time in Saigon in opium dens, describing his first experience in some detail in *Ways of Escape*. 'I could smell the opium as I came up the stairs. It was like the first sight of a beautiful woman with whom one realizes a relationship is possible: somebody whose memory will not be dimmed by a night's sleep.' It was an apt metaphor. Greene was depressed by the current state of his relationship with Catherine Walston and was looking for a way to numb his emotions and escape from thoughts of women. The drugs helped: 'For the traveller who does not want the unimportant act (to give his gold piece in a brothel) it helps enormously,' he wrote in an undated entry in his journal.

Sometimes, however, 'the unimportant act' was still necessary. For this, Saigon was the right place to be; hundreds of brothels were crammed together in the narrow streets of Cholon, including the House of Five Hundred Girls, with its immense open-air courtyard surrounded by cubicles (in fact it was the House of Four Hundred Girls), which Fowler, Pyle and the vulgar American journalist Granger visit. Today the brothels still existed of course, but up furtive flights of stairs in obscure backstreets. Other favourite haunts of Fowler had also gone underground. Opium dens – which I tried desperately to visit – were, I was told, the province only of junkies and a place where I would surely be killed. Gambling dens, such as the Grand Monde in Cholon where Fowler first met Phuong, had been banned. The Continental Hotel, where Greene liked to drink in the evening, still stood in its prime position over the former Place Garnier, but the outdoor terrace, where Saigon's elite once congregated for a pastis and a gossip, which Greene used for the setting of Fowler's first encounter with Pyle, had gone. 'The Party decided it was going to stop selling in the street,' a waiter told me. 'In Vietnam, it is about as crazy as throwing an ice cube into a furnace. Nobody paid any attention, but we had no choice. We are owned by the government you see, and they said we could not serve drinks on a terrace and must knock it down. It has killed the soul of our hotel.' And indeed, the indoor bar of the Continental was empty – save for a few bored tourists listening to the only ugly Vietnamese girl in existence playing Karen Carpenter's 'Clouds' on the cello.

Saigon's rich and beautiful had moved to the Q Bar, a hundred yards away behind the opera house, which was being redeveloped. There they played hip hop on the stereo, there were Caravaggio murals on the walls and an ebony sofa in the Ladies. It was always heaving, but the journalists of Greene's day had all gone – confined by the Party to the capital, Hanoi.

Instead, the tables were filled with French Telecom engineers, New Zealand hoteliers and American language teachers, all here to toast Vietnam's commitment to 'Joint Venture' with a glass of cognac and a young local girl.

'Christ, those girls depress me,' exclaimed Carol, an Australian lawyer we were meeting for a drink. She was tall and strapping, the exact opposite of the Vietnamese girls.

The girls depressed me, too. After a day in Saigon's heat, I was pink-faced and lank-haired. My white legs were covered in mosquito bites. The Vietnamese women around me were as immaculate and graceful as they had always been. Greene, whose interest in women rarely rose above the superficial, found them quite marvellous. The plot of *The Quiet American* pivots around Fowler and Pyle's fight for the beautiful and gormless Phuong. 'She looks so small and breakable and unlike our women,' Fowler tells Pyle, before adding in a rare moment of self-awareness. 'But don't think of her – as an ornament.'

You saw couples like Phuong and Fowler all over Saigon. She wore too much make-up and a poker face. He was '. . . a man of middle age, with eyes a little bloodshot, beginning to put on weight.' They sat in a glum muteness born out of their lack of a common tongue. At least that was how it seemed to me. Fowler saw it differently: 'We sat in silence content to be together,' he said, and no doubt his modern-day equivalents would agree.

To many foreigners, raised on a diet of *Rambo* and *The Deer Hunter*, these girls are what 'Nam is all about, along with landscapes wrecked by Agent Orange and jukeboxes that play perpetual Jimi Hendrix. In the backpacker cafés of Pham Ngu Lao street – where, according to Mr Than, Vietnamese families like to go at weekends 'to laugh at the hippies' – goateed Americans too young to remember John Travolta the first time he was famous compare 'genuine' Zippo lighters and agonize over their country's misdeeds.

'The Vietnamese are, like, so forgiving,' Travis Bolton, from Geneva, Illinois, told me over his banana pancake. 'No one blames me for being American. It makes me feel so humble.' His countrymen nodded in grave agreement.

Unfortunately, it doesn't quite work like that. The truth is that even if Travis wore nothing but Stars and Stripes Y-fronts and marched about singing 'The Star-Spangled Banner', the Vietnamese would be unmoved so long as he gave them his dollars. No one in Vietnam could care less about the war. After all, they have never seen *Apocalypse Now*. 'Qua roi,' they say when you ask them about it. It means: 'past enough'. Vietnam is a young country. More than 60 per cent of the population was born after 1975. They are far too busy preparing for an uncertain future to dwell on a past they never knew.

I was too young to remember myself, and war films had always bored me − nonetheless I thought I ought to make some effort at 'Nam tourism. It wasn't easy, though. The bomb craters had been filled in, the cities rebuilt and the Vietnamese soil was so fertile that the countryside devastated by Agent Orange now dazzled with its richness. We ended up like every other tourist at the War Crimes Museum in Saigon, enjoying the guilty frisson that comes from looking at foetuses deformed by Agent Orange in bottles and scouring photographs of Westerners demonstrating against the war, hoping to glimpse our fathers in loon pants and bandannas.

The following day we made the hour's journey in a minibus to the Cu Chi tunnels, 200 miles of underground passage-ways dug three storeys deep, running directly under the biggest American air base the world had ever seen. Vietnamese guerrillas lived there, hiding like moles by day and at night slipping out to infiltrate and attack. The US Air Force dropped half a million bombs on Cu Chi, turning it into a lunar wasteland of craters, but the explosives didn't exterminate the Communists.

The tourist board had done their best to make Cu Chi a fun day out. We travelled there in a tourist minibus, posed for photos next to life-sized dummies of Vietcong fighters, let off a few rounds from an AK47 at a firing range and shopped for model jet fighters crafted from Coke cans. The highlight was the crawl through a 200 metre tunnel section that has been specially widened for lardy Western bodies. After ten minutes I was sweaty and breathless. My thighs ached from waddling along on my haunches. The Vietcong lived inside these tunnels for six months at a time. They were surrounded by bats, rats, snakes and scorpions. When they came out they often suffered temporary blindness. Afterwards, we watched a video about Cu Chi's history. Dozens of men and women dug happily in jerky black and white. When they realized they were being filmed they stopped – like a bunch of day trippers – and waved at the camera.

'See the little girl in the field?' commented a squeaky female voice, with the Vietnamese habit of shedding all word endings so her phrases ran together in a shrill bark. 'By day, she is sweet and gentle. At night, she become American . . . Killer . . . Hero.'

Our group of Dutch and Danes exchanged anxious glances.

'Americans come,' the woman continued. 'They kill women, they kill children, they even kill . . . *chickens!*'

I think the video was meant to make me admire the Vietnamese; instead, for the first time, I began to feel sorry for the chicken-killing Americans who vainly poured gas and lobbed grenades down the tunnels. You messed with this lot, as a series of gruesome booby traps showed, at your peril.

Our guide looked on approvingly. 'The last time my country had sustained peace was in the 18th century,' she told us, twisting round in the front seat as we swerved and hooted all the way back to Saigon. 'The Chinese invaded, then the Mongols, then the French. Then there was the American War, then we fought Cambodia. But you know something? We Vietnamese repelled them *all*.'

IV

It was difficult to get to know the Vietnamese. For a start there was the language barrier. Vietnamese is a tonal language. Take the word *Ba*. Pronounced alto it means *three*. Soprano it means *grandmother*. Bass – *poisoned food*, Mezzo-soprano – *any*. Heaven knows what Victoria and I ended up asking for every time we ordered the local 333 beer.

Greene loved the beauty of Vietnam, its food, its girls, its intrigue, but – as with most countries he visited – he showed little interest in the locals. Phuong was nothing more than a 'twittering bird'. The Vietnamese Fowler meets socially are '. . . small, neat, aloof' people who are never 'prey to untidy passions'. The peasants who masterminded the tunnels at Cu Chi want nothing more from life than to work as rice farmers with 'one day much the same as another'.

This inscrutable image suits the Hanoi government. Visitors are welcome to enjoy the beaches and the sights, but the people, official brochures imply, are unknowable. But the truth is that the Vietnamese are desperate to talk to anybody who will listen.

The day after going to Cu Chi, we met a middle-aged man I'll call Mr Dai, who had been assigned to show us Greene's room at the Continental Hotel. It was situated on the corner of the second floor and had pink walls, red velvet curtains and mahogany furniture. There were two balconies, one over-looking the Place Garnier, which Greene used as the setting for the bicycle bomb explosion, today dominated by a giant red Fuji sign and Cindy Crawford wearing an Omega watch. Mr Dai ushered us on to the other one with a view of Rue Catinat and the Givral patisserie, the 'milk bar' where Phuong enjoyed her daily chocolate malt, its window full of wedding cakes and chocolate éclairs.

'I love it here,' sighed Victoria, leaning happily on the rail.

Mr Dai looked as if we had just told him the world was flat.

'No! Vietnam very bad!' He had a sad face and nervous manner.

'We think it is very beautiful.'

'No! Very ugly!'

'The people are very kind.'

'Very savage!'

'Well . . . the food is delicious.'

Another incredulous look. 'Chinese food much better.'

Mr Dai beckoned us closer. The traffic howled so loudly, we could barely hear him speak.

'Listen,' he said. 'I want to tell you how it is for me in Vietnam. I was born in Saigon. Until 1975, I worked for an American company. That is why I speak English so well. Then we lost the war. The Americans left, the North Vietnamese came. Things were very bad. They sent me to a re-education camp. I stayed there two years. In that time I saw my mother only once. I have two brothers. They worked for the local government. One was in a re-education camp for ten years. The other eleven. My mother died without ever seeing them again. When my brothers were released they went to America.

One brother is very ill because of what they did to him in the camp. The other is very old. We all hate Vietnam.'

It was much later I realized that on the balcony this conversation would be undetectable to bugging devices.

V

In the throbbing surroundings of Saigon, it was hard to make sense of such dramatic confessions. No one else referred to the government. They were all too busy buying and selling, buzzing around on mopeds, eating in ice cream parlours and laughing at my attempts to speak Vietnamese.

But then many things in Saigon didn't make sense. According to the Economist Intelligence Unit, 70 per cent of Vietnam was living in 'absolute poverty'. The country had suffered a civil war that was just as bitter and more protracted than that in Sierra Leone; its average income was only $230 a year – $140 less than Haiti's, and its population was only marginally less dense. But those other places were dumps and Vietnam was wonderful. I didn't understand. Was Saigon an optical illusion? Were people going without food to pay their mobile phone bills?

'No,' said Carol. 'What those statistics don't include are the millions of dollars that pour into the country every year from the overseas Vietnamese and that are quickly turned into sapphires and diamonds and gold. Some people are very rich indeed. But they are careful not to flaunt it. The family next door to me live in an air-conditioned mansion built from cash sent from their family in California, but they still squat on the street and eat their noodles with everyone else.'

We were sitting on a train, heading north from Saigon towards the beach resort of Nha Trang. From the window you could see the shanty towns – acres and acres of leaking rattan huts. Naked children ran about covered in sores. Old people sat slumped like discarded sacks. It was in a place like this that Pyle was murdered by the Vietminh.

'In the countryside, just a few miles from here, the peasants have been rioting,' Carol said. 'They are hungry and the government has been ripping them off over the price of grain. That's what everyone is talking about when they drink their cups of tea in the street in the morning. But you will never read a word about it anywhere.'

The misery that thousands of peasants had fought to abolish – and that Greene and other ex-pats largely ignored – is as terrible as ever, if perhaps not so visible. *Doi moi* and 'Joint Venture' have created a gap between the richest and the poorest in Vietnam that is greater than that in the United States or even India. 'The irony of Vietnam today is that those who gave and suffered the most, and were promised the greatest benefits, have gained the least. The Communists are abandoning them to the inherently precarious future of a market economy which increasingly resembles the system the US supported during the war,' wrote the anti-war activist Gabriel Kolko.

But then the Vietnamese were never true Marxists. Rather, like the Cubans, they were fierce nationalists and it was for this that Greene admired them, rather than for their left-wing ideology. In a post-colonial world, he vigorously supported their right to self-determination. 'They want enough rice,' Fowler says. 'They don't want to be shot at. They want one day to be much the same as another. They don't want our white skins around telling them what they want.' If survival meant dropping capitalism for communism, then so be it. Today, the situation had merely reversed.

On the beach at Nha Trang, we met Tu, a cheerful young

man with long fingernails. He offered Victoria a massage for $5 and threw in an analysis of the current economic situation for free. 'Russia is very weak,' he explained. 'We want to be very strong.'

Nha Trang is a trainee version of Thailand, a quiet place with pastel houses, streets lined with frangipani, a golden beach and a limpid aquamarine sea. There was little to do there except lie on the beach or take a 'cruise' with stops for snorkelling and lunch, after which everyone floated in the sea in lifebelts and the skipper passed around glasses of red wine and a joint. 'Most people I massage very fat. And very old,' Tu said.

'How old?' I asked from my lounger.

'Oh thirty, thirty-two.'

Victoria was thirty-five. He must have felt her muscles tense. 'Maybe thirty-eight, forty-four,' he added hastily.

'Many Americans come to Nha Trang,' he continued. 'Many men. They go to disco but they don't want to dance with girls. They like to dance with boys. They go to restaurants with boys. I don't know why. One man takes my friend with him to Hanoi. He buys him many T-shirts. I don't understand why he so kind.' It was impossible to tell if he was being heavily sarcastic or totally naive.

I thought I could never tire of Vietnamese food, but that evening we decided we had had enough of noodles. We headed for an American-style diner with hamburgers on the menu. Its owner was a stoned Kiwi called Neil.

At the table next to us there were six Americans – five men – one of whom was black, and one woman. They were quite unlike all the other Americans we had seen whose shorts and T-shirts were peppered by joint burns and who clutched their Lonely Planets to their chests like shields. These men had crew-cuts and skin pitted with acne. The woman had permed bleached blonde hair and wore blue eyeshadow. They looked as if they had been plucked from a shopping mall in Kansas. Yet their conversation was all helicopters, reconnaissances, interpreters and X-rays.

'Who are they?' we asked Neil.

'Shhh,' he whispered. 'They don't like to be talked about. They're an MIA team. They're having some R&R after a jungle mission.'

MIAs – soldiers missing in action – are central to America's continuing grudge against Vietnam. More than 2000 American soldiers are still unaccounted for in South East Asia. Of them, 1400 are believed to have died, the rest to have been taken prisoner. Today, a substantial number of Americans think they are still being held alive and want their men home. Of course, a substantial number of Americans also believe that Elvis is living on the moon, but no one has bothered to inform them that 78,000 Americans are still missing from the Second World War and 8000 from the Korean War. Instead, Washington has done everything in its power to exploit this urban myth. It used it as an excuse to wait until 1993 before removing its block on international aid to Vietnam. It did not end its trade embargo until 1994 and only sent an ambassador to Hanoi – who happened to be a former POW – in 1995. In return for normalizing relations with Vietnam, they have demanded access to top-secret war files, which they claim will help them find the missing men. The Vietnamese see it as an outrageous breach of sovereignty, but if they want the dollars they have no choice.

We were dying to talk to this squad but Neil would not let us. 'What do they do all day?' Victoria asked. 'Surely there can't be anything left to track down any more.'

'Oh yes there is,' Neil said. 'Every year they come back with something. Even if they just find an eyelet from a boot, they have the technology to track down what boot and what batch it was issued in and who it was issued to.'

'And then they can tick another one off the list.'

'Exactly.'

'But what about the ones who aren't dead?' I asked excitedly. 'Haven't they found any living in the jungle, married to Vietnamese girls?'

Neil gave me a pitying look. 'Julia, the MIAs all died thirty years ago. The Vietnamese know that. The American government know that. These guys know it best of all. But they don't want to let anyone into their secret. If they did, it would be time to stop playing Rambo and come home.'

VI

Vietnam was Greene's political Damascus. Initially, he – like Fowler – had taken a neutral view of the conflict between the French and the Vietminh, regarding both sides with faint suspicion. By now, his religious certainty had gone, if indeed it had ever existed. He reserved a special contempt for politicians. The Second World War had made him despair of human nature. 'Nothing nowadays is fabulous and nothing rises from its ashes,' Fowler says.

Yet by the time of his fourth visit, Greene, again like Fowler, began to see that he had no choice but to become involved. He was disgusted by Americans, whom he saw as naively intent on imposing their culture on the rest of the world and was scornful of their argument that they must protect the rest of the Far East from the Marxist bogeyman. Pyle tries to make America's case. 'If Indo China goes . . .' Fowler interrupts. 'I know the record. Siam goes, Malaysia goes. Indonesia goes. What does "go" mean?'

'Sooner or later,' the Vietminh agent Heng tells Fowler, 'one has to take sides.' Greene plumped for socialism not so much out of belief in its potential but more, as he told an interviewer in 1979, because he had decided to go to any length to 'put my feeble twig in the spokes of American foreign policy'. When *The Quiet American* was published in 1955, the British praised it, the Russians exalted it (*Pravda* called it 'The most remarkable event' of recent British literary history) and the Americans trashed it. To Greene's fury, when the inevitable film was made, Pyle was transformed into a brave hero and Fowler became the unwitting dupe of the Communists.

But the longer I stayed in Vietnam, the clearer it became that although America had acted catastrophically, Ho Chi Minh's successors had equally betrayed their people. The further we travelled north towards the seat of government, the louder were the dissenting voices.

From Nha Trang, we went to Da Nang, where the GIs had gathered for I&I – intercourse and intoxication – at China Beach before being choppered back to the combat zone. From there we took the train to Hué, the imperial capital of Vietnam. This is supposed to be one of the most beautiful journeys in the world. 'Sit on the right-hand side of the train,' said the guidebook. It failed to add: 'Facing the engine'. As we chugged over the Hai Van Pass, a place so allegedly stunning that it impressed even Paul Theroux, we could see nothing but the bottom of a fat Bulgarian who was leaning out of the window and snapping happily. When I stood up and craned for a better look two French backpackers shouted me down.

A balding man in a Hawaiian shirt stood up and graciously gestured at his window seat. 'For you, Madame.'

Ignoring Victoria's poisonous looks, I took it. Far below I

could see a scimitar of shining beach and a bay full of fishing boats. 'Where you from?' said the man.

My heart sank. I wanted to look at the view now and talk later. 'England,' I replied, staring out of the window.

'England! Very good! Manchester United.'

'Yes.'

'Tottenham Hotspur.'

Clearly, I was supposed to make an effort. 'Vietnam is very nice, too,' I said.

Once more, that shocked look. 'No! Very bad.'

I'll call him Nguyen. He was travelling to the Swedish Embassy in Hanoi. He was going to be interviewed about his visa application that would allow him to join his wife who worked in a Chinese restaurant in Stockholm.

'My wife was my girlfriend in high school, long time ago,' he said. 'But after 1975, it is no good for the Chinese in Vietnam. She left for Sweden. But she was always betrothed to me and at last, three months ago, we married. Now I hope they will let me join her.'

He showed us the wedding photographs. Nguyen was sweating and proud. She was radiant and obese with crossed eyes and sticking-out teeth. They were embracing in a restaurant while their families applauded. He was cradling the microphone in a karaoke bar while she looked on adoringly. They were cuddling in front of a fountain in the park. Then they were standing in front of Saigon railway station, surrounded by suitcases and looking bereft. 'This is the day she goes back to Sweden,' Nguyen said.

Nguyen had left Vietnam once before. 'I am boat person,' he said proudly. 'In 1990, I left Vietnam for Hong Kong. We were twenty people on a boat twelve metres by three metres. We sailed for twelve days.' He shuddered. 'It was terrible. The sea was calm but at night the sky was so black.'

In Hong Kong, he spent five years in a refugee camp. 'It was bad, crazy, horrible. At least, I have a job. I am a translator, so I can leave the camp each day. My friends didn't go outside for five years. At the end, they sent us all back to Vietnam. It was the project of my life and it was for nothing.'

Nguyen was lucky though. More than a million boat people left Vietnam. One third of them are thought to have died at sea – the victims of pirates, storms and fevers.

But he was unlucky too. More than 90 per cent of the 'first wave' of boat people who left Vietnam before 1979 were granted refugee status and foreign passports. Nguyen was part of the second wave, by which time foreign governments had lost patience and were demanding instant repatriation.

'Why did you want to leave Vietnam?'

'My family is Chinese. We are rich people and my father was a very rich man. But in 1976, when I am fifteen, the army comes and takes all my father's gold away. He died three days later. It was shock. My mother cry and cry. She is a young woman, only forty, but she never marry again. My family is ruined. Today the government treats the Chinese better. But still I want to leave. I cannot forgive my country. I want to have many children. Here, the party punishes you if you have more than two. Besides, the world is so big and I want to see it. Besides, I cannot stand the weather. In the north, it rain every day. In the south, always sun.'

'In Sweden there is a lot of snow,' I said.

'Only in winter,' Nguyen retorted. 'In summer it is hot. They have seasons in Sweden. That is my dream, to see the spring turn into summer.'

Nguyen was right about Vietnamese weather. The Hai Van Pass acted as the 49th Parallel dividing the country into communist and capitalist. It also acts as an invisible weather vane decreeing that while the south shall be bathed in brilliant sun, the north shall be perpetually cold and damp. If the Eskimos have more than fifty words for snow, then the inhabitants of Hué must have just as many to describe the varying degrees of drizzle that wrap their city in a permanent dank shroud.

In Hué, for the first time you felt yourself to be in a Marxist state. The women no longer wore white *ao dais* but shapeless dun anoraks fresh off the plane from Bucharest. Their faces were flatter and darker than in the south and less smiling. There were Party posters everywhere of workers gazing fixedly into the middle distance like strangers in a lift.

The guidebook said that Le Loi, the former government guesthouse had a 'certain antique charm'. We instructed the cyclo drivers to take us there. To protect us from the rain, they draped their vehicles in a brown plastic sack so that we could see nothing at all.

'Why you go Le Loi?' mine wailed. 'It is very bad. It belongs to government. You no go there. You go to private hotel. Much better. Much cheaper.'

But the *Rough Guide* never lied, we thought. This is how we came to find ourselves staying in a living museum of Marxism. Our room was a clammy shoebox at the back of a crumbling villa, with blue nylon curtains that refused to close properly. When I pulled them back I could see two cows grazing on the lawn. The loo blocked immediately and attempts to tackle it with a plunger sent a jet of brown liquid all over the bathroom floor.

The staff were so imbecilic that they could only have been selected on the basis of being distant cousins of minor Party officials. The receptionist had a severe squint, the porter a pronounced limp. The doorman, a lanky young man, in a beige polyester uniform, sat in front of the television all day and night with his tongue hanging out of the corner of his mouth.

The room was $20 a night, and payment was required upfront. The hotel the cyclo drivers had promised us was $10. The receptionist took our money.

'So tomorrow, you will check out at six in the morning.'

'What?'

'Six in the morning. We have a big party of businessmen. They come from Hanoi. We need your room.'

'But in the room it says checkout is at noon.'

'So-rree. I say six.'

After a fruitless argument on this subject I needed a leisurely tour of Hué to calm down. Set on the banks of the Perfume River, Hué is to Saigon what Boston is to Disneyworld. On the wide boulevards, there was not a Honda in sight. Pigs snuffled in the middle of the road and petals dropped softly from the tamarind trees. We hired bicycles, pulled on our cagoules and spent a day looking like rejects from the Famous Five.

For a century and a half Hué was the imperial capital of Vietnam, home to the Nguyen Dynasty who established themselves in the city at the beginning of the 1800s. The old people in the city could remember the funeral of the Emperor Khai Dinh. Two elephants and 160 porters were needed to lift his giant bier. The wide grey Perfume River was still full of floating sampans, where fishermen slept under cone hats, their heads tilted back, their mouths wide open. Only when you approached them could you hear their motors roaring and only when you took one out could you see the chimneys of the power plant tucked around a bend in the river.

Perhaps, I decided, I should regard the hotel's failure to grasp the principles of good relations with its guests as charming and old-fashioned, rather than merely useless. I returned to Le Loi in a benevolent mood. It lasted until precisely half an hour after I had gone to bed. The hotel had decided that the best way of getting us up at six was to make sure we never slept at all. We turned the lights out. Instantly, there was loud knocking on the door.

'Laun-dree!'

I disentangled myself from my mosquito net and opened the door. A woman was standing there, proudly, flourishing one pair of grey knickers and a pair of socks. Mosquitoes drilled into my bare flesh.

'I'm sure they're malarial here,' said Victoria cheerfully.

I turned off the lights again. A few rooms away, someone was watching television at top volume. From another, a woman with a voice like the three little pigs on helium kept up a breathless monologue. A telephone rang continually. On the threshold of the room next door a man was loudly paying off a prostitute. I lay awake all night fantasizing about McDonald's, MTV and Holiday Inns.

There was no room on the train to Hanoi, at least not until we had bribed the station attendant more than double her monthly wage to find us two first-class berths. There were dirty tiles on the floor and cockroaches nestling around the light fittings. Foreigners always slept on the top bunk. The petite Vietnamese disliked being so far from the ground. We travelled at a steady 30 m.p.h., stopping at every station where vendors crowded round the windows selling cuttlefish and dried seahorses. The rules of the Vietnam State Railways were printed on the back of our tickets: 'Passengers are prohibited to carry on board dangerous items such as explosive, inflammable, radio-active or dead body, nauseating items, live stock or other commodities.'

In our compartment there was an Englishman. His name was Alex, he wore round wire glasses, had a bland face and he was a journalist for an international news agency in Hanoi.

We exclaimed at the coincidence and exchanged 'Do you know's. Alex told us where to stay in Hanoi, and I said that he must enjoy living in Vietnam.

He gave us an odd look. 'Hardly.'

Just like the Vietnamese, Alex could not believe that anyone liked this country. 'It's an evil, corrupt dump,' he said. 'And life for foreign journalists is practically impossible. The Party makes our lives a misery. Every Saturday morning they hold a meeting and discuss how we have been behaving. If we do something that they don't like, it's not us that gets it in the neck – it's our Vietnamese staff. They threatened one girl with the death penalty recently because her boss at the news agency had been critical of the regime. We have to submit everything for censorship and give five days notice before we travel.

'Come to the pub tomorrow night,' Alex offered. 'Meet some of my friends. See what life in Hanoi is really like.'

VII

Hanoi and Saigon are as far apart as London and Rome and in every way as different. Tourists usually like Hanoi best. They rave about the peeling French villas and crooked alleyways, the sleepy expanse of Hoan Kiem lake and the restored splendour of the Opera House. It's like preferring the latest Salman Rushdie novel to a fat Jackie Collins. But guiltily, I yearned for Saigon. I missed the brashness and verve, the cacophony and the smiles. Greene felt the same way too: 'It was cold after dark in Hanoi,' he wrote. 'The lights were lower than those of Saigon.'

When he visited the city in 1955, Greene described a place of 'sadness and decay' that derived from 'the mere lack of relaxation: nothing in the cinemas but propaganda films, the only restaurants prohibitive in price, no cafés in which to while away the hours watching people pass.'

Post war, however, all that should have reversed. Hanoi should have assumed the victor's mantle and appropriated its rival's buzz. Yet despite – or rather because of – the fact that this is the Party headquarters – Hanoi has remained the country cousin, morally superior but secretly coveting the savoir faire of its flashy southern relatives.

I remembered what Alex had said. 'It's terrible for the Hanoians. They know they rule the country but as soon as they step off the plane in Ho Chi Minh, they are reminded of what bumpkins they really are.'

If I found it hard to be moved by the city's legendary beauty, perhaps it was because legendary is all it is now. The ochre villas that survived the American bombs are now falling victim to Korean property developers intent on replacing them with the ugliest office blocks ever conceived.

'In public, the Party shakes its head at these architectural monstrosities,' Alex said. 'But in private, it's accepting as many bribes as it can from speculators who want to build golf courses.'

We were sitting in the bar of the butter-coloured Metropole Hotel where Greene always stayed when he was in town. Today, it belonged to the French chain Sofitel, and had a business centre, an outdoor pool and an authentic English pub, where ex-pats played darts, banks of television monitors showed silent CNN and the nightly buffet offered *raclette*.

'Life here has improved so much,' said Pat, a New Zealand lawyer whose hair was too long for her fading face. 'When I arrived four years ago there were no traffic lights, let alone any decent restaurants. Now we have a Tex Mex, an Irish pub. We have a proper *cave* that can find you any wine you want. We even have a sandwich bar. It's called "No Noodles". It does a marvellous chicken tikka baguette.'

Pat was a friend of Alex's, all of whom seemed to be women. Jenny, a hatchet-faced Swede; Jessica, an intense Jewish New Yorker; and Sarah, a beautiful Englishwoman, who managed a news agency and had a boyfriend in Hong Kong.

'Over to mine this weekend,' said Pat. 'I have a fantastic cook. He makes proper Kiwi grub. Are you coming Sarah? Oh no, I suppose you'll be jetting off to see Richard. Well, all right for some. The rest of you must come over to mine and get pissed.'

We dined at the Press Club on lamb with pesto sauce, at $35 a dish. Everyone was very excited about the wine list. 'Australian wine,' cried Jenny. It was the first sign of life she had showed all evening. The Vietnamese *sommelier* told us it had a grapefruity aftertaste. 'Oh, good boy,' said Sarah. 'You can actually talk us through a wine list. Aren't you clever? Well done.'

They seemed amazed that the Vietnamese could do anything right. 'Well, we don't expect them to treat us well,' said Sarah. 'I was crossing the road recently and someone drove his car straight at me. It's my blonde hair. They take as much money as they can from us, but they despise us because they think we're superficial.'

There was no answer to that.

Yet there was no doubt that corruption made Hanoi a depressing place to live. Despite the promise of free medical care for all, the sick still had to pay extra for the most basic treatments. If a child was to pass exams, then teachers had to be paid for 'private tuition'. If you wanted to move house, change jobs, or leave the country, someone was always waiting with an outstretched hand.

'Even the Swedish embassy can't describe their revulsion for the Vietnamese,' Jenny said. 'The Party has betrayed the people's dreams.'

'You know it shocks me,' slurred Jessica. 'I come from an impeccably liberal background. My earliest memories are of sitting on my father's shoulders during anti-war marches. But you know what I think now? I think America was right to invade. And I tell you another thing. I think it's a shame we didn't win.'

The Vietnamese Communist Party was founded by Ho Chi Minh, former pastry chef at the London Carlton Hotel. In 1955, in what was to be the first of a series of adulatory encounters with left-wing leaders, Greene interviewed him for *The Sunday Times* and confessed to succumbing to hero-worship. Uncle Ho had a wispy beard, rubber sandals and wore a frayed uniform. To Greene, he was the embodiment of the archetypal English schoolmaster Mr Chips: 'Wise, kind, just . . . prepared to inflict sharp punishment without undue remorse . . . capable of inspiring love', and left convinced that Vietnam was better off red.

Uncle Ho died before the country's final victory over America. Today his body lies in a vast Stalinist mausoleum overlooking a wide empty square, quite out of place in the twisty streets of Hanoi. White-gloved attendants ushered us past his glass case two by two along a red carpet. The pace was so brisk it was impossible to get more than a moment's glimpse of a face the colour of weak tea, a wispy beard and two wax hands cupped on a black sheet. Most of Ho's body was covered by a rubber sheet. Rumour had it that since perestroika Russia was no longer prepared to preserve the corpse of its old ally, and that under the sheet there was nothing but crumbling bones.

Afterwards, we visited the wooden house built on stilts

above a fish pond, which Uncle Ho expropriated from the French governor and referred to as his *grand château*. It had plain polished floors and bare wooden furnishing. The idea was to emphasize Ho's asceticism, but today the result was pure Elle Deco. 'And where is the bathroom?' said the French woman next to me, scandalized.

What I took to be a multi-storey car park next door turned out to be the Ho Chi Minh museum. The gift shop was full of jade Buddhas and lacquer portraits of the Madonna and Child, a fitting tribute to the founder of a modern secular state. On the ground floor was a sad little exhibition, documenting Uncle Ho's legacy to modern Vietnam, consisting of two porcelain washbasins and a photo of the escalator at Than Son Nhat airport. Upstairs the tone was more grandiose. Giant portraits of Einstein, Charlie Chaplin and Lenin were reflected never-endingly in a series of mirrors, and symbolized the era into which Uncle Ho was born. A pile of bricks topped with some wooden sticks represented a volcano or 'How greatly the revolution under Ho Chi Minh's name encourages other struggles for national liberation in Asia, Africa and Latin America in their wake.' A set of giant chairs around a giant table topped by a giant plaster lemon, pineapple and two bananas was the embodiment of 'Uncle Ho's expectation that young people shoulder the responsibility for the protection and preservation of peace and the environment.'

Uncle Ho was a modest man. His wish was to be cremated and his ashes be placed in simple shelters in the north, south, east and west of Vietnam. He would have hated his mausoleum, just as he would have hated *doi moi*, the metered taxis, the burgeoning skyscrapers and being leered at by American coach parties. In the garden with its lawns covered in plastic laughing frogs, I got chatting to a couple from New York who had just disembarked from their cruise ship.

'You're travelling around Vietnam by yourself?' the man asked incredulously.

'Yes, it's very easy.'

'You're eating the local food?'

'Yes, it's delicious.'

He tried to decide if this was a joke. 'You're English huh?' There was a long pause. 'It figures.' I thought of Pyle and his sandwiches spread with Vit-Health sent by his mother from the States because he dared not touch meat prepared by the Cao Dai – 'You have to be careful in this heat.'

Most of all, though, Uncle Ho would have hated the fact that despite the overt signs of progress, Vietnam was failing. Newspaper headlines told a story that directly contradicted the gold-rush vitality of the streets: 'Hundreds laid off as car sector stalls', 'Writing's on the wall for struggling ad man', 'Hotel investment plan fails at 11th hour'. The whole of the Far East had gone into economic meltdown, and Vietnam with its old-fashioned insistence on employee protection was helpless in the face of the *laissez-faire* approach of Thailand, Burma and Singapore. Foreign companies were being charged a premium for everything, including water and housing. Advertising rates were six times those of their local competitors. When Post-It notes opened a factory they were charged 40 per cent duty for being 'office products' rather than the 10 per cent imposed on 'adhesive-backed paper' making the locally produced notes far more expensive than identical ones brought in by smugglers from Thailand. Coca-Cola and Procter & Gamble were both getting involved in nasty public battles with insolvent Joint Venture partners. A Taiwanese investor was so frustrated by corrupt customs officials who failed to do what they had been bribed to do that it tried to sue one of them for breach of contract.

'The foreigners are all packing their bags and running,'

Alex said. 'The Party simply can't bring itself to help outside investors. The fact is, whatever the IMF tells them, outsiders have never done this country much good.'

The Party remained omnipotent and inviolate. Any imaginative young politician faced certain promotion to the ministry of lavatory cleaners. The Vietnamese had little love for their leaders but most were too busy earning a living to protest in any organized fashion. Instead, they wilfully ignored the authorities and channelled the energies once used to dig Cu Chi into corruption and clock watching.

This might have been a very bad thing for the Vietnamese but for me it was hard to be sorry that things had not yet taken off. The old Vietnam refused to budge up for the new, so for now they were co-existing as awkwardly as a houseproud mother and her sluttish daughter-in-law. On Highway 1, the country's main road that ran all the way from Saigon to Hanoi, buffalo carts monopolized the outside lane at 10 m.p.h. A BMW was parked in the central reservation while its occupants picnicked on the bonnet. At night everyone gathered around the television to watch melodramas about ancient knights on horseback saving princesses from dragons. From the lobby of a twenty-storey glass and marble skyscraper, I watched an old woman struggle along the street bent by the weight of a bamboo yoke across her shoulder. One pail was filled with Pepsi bottles, the other with Coke.

On the pavements, vendors sold live armadillos and cobras in jars. There had, however, been a clampdown on cat restaurants, because the countryside was being overrun by a plague of rats.

A horrible thought crossed my mind. 'What cat restaurants?' I asked Alex.

'Oh, any place that has "tiger" in the title,' he told me cheerfully. Dog meat, of course, was on sale everywhere in the north. 'But you won't eat it,' Alex assured us. 'It's a delicacy. You'd spot it on the menu because it would be so ridiculously expensive.'

VIII

In the countryside, the pace of change was even slower. Fowler predicted: 'In 500 years there may be no New York or London, but they'll still be growing paddy in these fields, they'll be carrying their produce to market on long poles wearing their pointed hats. The small boys will still be sitting on their buffaloes . . .' and sure enough, just twenty minutes outside Hanoi you found yourself in a timeless green land-scape, where peasants wearing lampshade hats planted rice shoots and buffaloes waded fetlock-deep through the paddies.

Few tourists visited this corner of the northern Delta. We were on our way to Phat Diem, a small village with a cathedral that is the focus of the Vietnamese Catholic community. In *The Quiet American*, Fowler watches a battle between the French and the Vietminh from the cathedral's belltower, just as Greene himself did in 1951.

Catholicism came to Vietnam with the Portuguese in the 16th century, but gradually the religion grew away from its European origins. By the time of the Franco-Vietminh war, the Catholics were seen as one of the country's third forces, separate from either side and mistrusted by both. The Bishop of Phat Diem even had his own army. 'In its strange medieval way under the shadow and protection of the Prince Bishop, it had been the most living town in all the country,' Greene wrote.

Our driver, a handsome young man with a mobile phone and an alarming talent for nodding off at the wheel, was half impressed, half worried by our desire to visit Phat Diem. 'These people are all Catholics, you know. The government says you must not talk to them.'

There were eight million practising Catholics in Vietnam – around 10 per cent of the population – but only 2000 priests to serve their needs. Several planned visits from the Pope had been banned. The Party believed, with some justification, that the fall of Communism was the fault of the Roman Catholic Church, along with Mikhail Gorbachev.

Since Greene's visit the village of Phat Diem had barely changed: 'A long, narrow street of wooden stalls, cut up every hundred yards by a canal, a church and a bridge.' The only additions were a couple of karaoke parlours and the ubiquitous pool hall. On the canals grim-faced women rowed barges the shape of watermelon slices. Two small boys fought each other with wooden swords. A woman thatching a haystack stopped to inspect a mosquito bite on her arm.

The cathedral had done everything it could to pretend to be a Buddhist pagoda. The stone tips of its roofs turned up like a Teddy boy's quiff and in front was a lake filled with *koi* carp. Only the statue of Jesus in the middle, standing 'with sugary outspread arms', as Greene put it, and the small cross on the roof, betrayed its true orientation.

The only other visitors to the cathedral were a honey-mooning couple who had hired a photographer to accompany them. The groom had a floppy mop of hair, which he rearranged constantly with a comb and pocket mirror, before hiding it under his green baseball cap. His bride, a hunched woman in a dark green jacket and purple nylon flares, watched dumbly as he ran across the courtyard to request that Victoria and I appear in their souvenir photograph. The photographer fussed with his tripod and flash gun, while the groom – whose head came up to my shoulder – fervently squeezed my waist.

Then, with a bark of triumph, he spotted a motorbike parked in the street outside. Tugging at my arm, he pulled me over and gestured that I should sit on it behind him. His wife looked on resignedly, as he whipped a pair of dark glasses from his anorak pocket and gave her his hat to hold. Somewhere, to this day, in a parlour in the northern delta, a photo will exist of the bridegroom in a moody James Dean pose, with a foreigner grinning sheepishly on the pillion.

'We don't see many foreigners,' explained our guide benevolently.

He was the head of the seminary, an old man in a pinstripe jacket and black skullcap. His face was creased with exhaustion, his French self-taught from a book. Like virtually every priest in Vietnam, he had been in a re-education camp. Most of the priests in the Hanoi diocese were in their seventies. A new archbishop had only been recently appointed after a five-year wait and there have been no cardinals since 1990. 'Every Sunday this church is packed,' he said, digging in his pockets for the key to the belltower. 'There are two thousand people in the cathedral and another thousand outside in the courtyard. But then there are ten thousand people in the district and seven thousand are Catholic. It is impossible to attend to everyone.'

We climbed the winding steps of the belltower, followed by a group of giggling young men. 'They want to be priests,' he explained. 'They have been waiting maybe five years to join the seminary, but a new class can only be admitted every two years. Every applicant must be interviewed by the local government to ensure that as well as being a good Catholic he is a good Socialist. Sometimes people wait decades before they are ordained. Sometimes it never happens. *La vie est dure.*'

From the tower you could see church spires as far as the horizon, looming out of the flat, green land that reminded

Greene of Holland. 'Rice shoots and golden harvests take the place of tulips and churches of windmills,' he observed. At ground level, hundreds of green and scarlet crosses in the gaudy colours of a pagoda marked graves. The Vietnamese have always buried their dead amongst their crops, so the soul of their ancestors will enter the rice and be passed down to the next generation. From this point, Greene had witnessed the Vietminh win one of the most important victories of the war. At a distance, the battle seemed "picturesque"; it was only later when he toured the town with the French army that he found the canals 'full of bodies', like 'an Irish stew containing too much meat'. Atrocities such as these did little for the reputation of the French army, and much to convince the people of Phat Diem that they were better off backing the Communists. 'We'll never know if we made the right decision or not,' our guide said wryly.

As usual, he wanted to know what we thought of Vietnam.

'*C'est un très beau pays*,' I said, although by now I knew that my compliments would be rejected.

The guide sighed. '*Oui*,' he said eventually. '*C'est beau, mais c'est très pauvre*.'

IX

We flew back to Saigon on a shiny new Vietnam Airways Boeing with a British pilot. We were going to visit the headquarters of another religion and another third force, the Cao Dais, whose temple was an hour's drive from Saigon at Tay Ninh.

Two million Vietnamese are Cao Daists – not bad for a religion that was only founded in 1926 by a civil servant whose aim was to create the ideal religion by fusing Christianity,

Buddhism and Islam. It has a Pope and female cardinals and contacts the spirits through a planchette, a wooden board with a pencil attached. Its saints, who direct the priest's hands to inscribe their messages, include Louis Pasteur, Lenin, Victor Hugo, Winston Churchill and William Shakespeare, although the last we learned had not made contact since 1935.

Greene described the temple as: 'A Walt Disney fantasia of the east, dragons and snakes in technicolour.' The roof is supported by pink pillars circled with cute snub-nosed dragons. The baby-blue ceiling is scattered with silver stars. It is like worshipping in a giant nursery.

There was nothing mystical or private about a Cao Dai act of worship. So long as you took your shoes off when you entered the cathedral, anything went. We watched the service from the balcony. As the priests chanted some kind of liturgy, a group of British backpackers were loudly comparing hangovers. Skimpily dressed Swedes walked in and out, and an old bearded man carrying a clipboard tapped us on our shoulders and asked us our nationality. No one attempted to explain what Cao Dai might actually be all about.

The service was phenomenally boring. The congregation of 200-odd endlessly prostrated themselves before the altar, while a chorus chanted a tuneless dirge. After about five minutes, the tourists began to leave. After about twenty, when it was clear that there was to be no change, we followed. Outside, there was no shelter from the midday sun or protection from the six-year-olds selling chewing gum. 'It always seemed hotter in Tanyin than anywhere else in the Southern Delta,' Greene wrote, 'perhaps it was the absence of water, perhaps it was the interminable ceremonies which made one sweat vicariously.'

If the Cao Daists were to survive they had to be nice to the tourists. During the war, they had represented a 'third force', with 'a private army of 25,000 men armed with mortars made out of the exhaust pipes of old cars'. After the war, of course, they were in deep trouble. Their cathedral was closed for nearly a decade. Only after intense pressure from the United Nations was it allowed to reopen in 1983. Since then, they had been doing everything possible to lure the tourists, knowing that the more people visited the harder it would be to close them down again.

But the Cao Daists have always been masters of PR. In Greene's day, they invited anybody who was anyone in Saigon to the temple for a spot of corporate hospitality. 'The Pope invited members of the government (who would turn up if the Cao Daists at the moment held office), the Diplomatic Corps (who would send a few Second Secretaries with their wives or girls) and the French Commander-in-Chief, who would detail a two-star general from an office job to represent him.'

Fowler – and by extension Greene – distrusted these attempts at ingratiation. 'This was not the Indo China I loved ... this was play-acting ... trickery.' But Americans, like Pyle, were impressed by the Cao Dai, believing that they offered the best alternative to the threat of the Vietminh. Greene merged fiction with historical fact in his account of the fictional Pyle giving plastic explosives to the real Cao Daist, General Thé. In the novel, Thé explodes a bomb in the Place Garnier, outside the Continental Hotel. In reality, two such bombs exploded in the centre of Saigon in 1952, killing ten innocent civilians and injuring thirty-two. Initially, the Americans blamed the Vietminh for the devastation. Greene, however, was convinced that CIA money was behind it. 'There was certainly evidence of contacts between the American services and General Thé,' he wrote in *Ways of Escape* and he believed this until the end of his days.

X

It was good to be back in the south, to feel the sun on our necks, to be greeted by smiles, however insincere, and to sip mandarin juice on the roof terrace of the Rex Hotel, surrounded by bonsai trees, statues of prancing elephants and a crown-shaped marquee that lit up the Asian night like something out of Las Vegas.

I felt guilty that I was so taken with Saigon. The poverty, the dictatorship, the human rights abuse, faded into insignificance. Like Greene, I had been seduced by 'the tall elegant girls in white silk trousers, by the pewter evening light on flat paddy fields, where the water buffaloes trudged fetlock-deep with a slow primeval gait, by the French perfumeries in the Rue Catinat, the Chinese gambling houses in Cholon'.

But it was in Vietnam that Greene lost his political virginity. From this point, he was committed, albeit tentatively, to the Left, a commitment which would deepen when he visited pre- and post-Communist Cuba.

Yet Greene was too cynical about human nature ever to put his faith completely in an ideology. Were he to return to Saigon today, he would be saddened rather than surprised at such sights as the Apocalypse Now bar, where young girls still ran their fingers over the heads of shorn-haired Americans, quiet or otherwise, who were reclaiming the city as their rightful territory.

It was our last evening. We went to the Q Bar. The red-faced Fowlers were still sitting with their delicate Phuongs. The only single man in the room looked like one of Pablo Escobar's bodyguards. Whenever I caught his eye, he winked and ran his tongue around his lips. I felt like an Essex girl on the pull. I fixed my gaze firmly on the selection of grey sleeveless T-shirts pinned to the wall. They were very chic and bore a discreet grey 'Q' logo.

'How much?' I asked.

'Eight dollars,' said the barmaid. She had the body of a Western ten-year-old.

'Can we get two in large.'

'No large sizes,' she smirked. 'Only medium.'

We looked at each other dubiously. 'Well, medium should be OK,' Victoria said. 'They must sell most of them to Western women.'

Back at the hotel, I discovered I could barely squeeze my head through the neck hole. Having pulled it on, I looked in the mirror. I looked like I had just been placed last in a wet T-shirt contest. There was no way I could ever be seen in public in this garment. Victoria had already bundled hers into a ball at the back of her suitcase. Once again the foreigners had been enticed by a Vietnamese promise. Once more, they had been left deceived.

4. Cuba

'This is only my second trip to Cuba. Gay spot they tell me,'
he said, blowing down his pipe and laying it aside for lunch.
'It can be,' Wormold said. 'If you like roulette and
brothels.'

OUR MAN IN HAVANA

I

When I bought my ticket to Havana with Cubana airlines, the travel agent told me to check in at least three hours in advance. 'The flights are always a hundred per cent over-booked,' he said. 'If you don't get there early, you won't get on. You may have to wait days for another flight. Don't say I didn't warn you.'

The problem is that everyone wants to go to Cuba these days. The first time I visited the island, in 1992, my fellow Cubana passengers were all twenty-something social workers and schoolteachers from north London who smoked roll-ups and took the rigours of our eighteen-hour journey via Lisbon and Newfoundland in their sandalled stride. The guests at my hotel, the Lincoln, were exchange students from Zimbabwe, with whom I spent many happy hours stuck in the lift, dis-cussing the marital problems of Charles and Diana.

In those days, Cuba was an oddity to be visited out of solidarity with your socialist brothers. In the intervening years, everything has changed. Today, every travel brochure offers Cuba all in for £599, every holiday programme includes a visit to a cigar factory, every glossy magazine features cocktails and colonial architecture. Today, the departure lounge at Gatwick was full of suburban mums in velour tracksuits reading Maeve Binchy novels and elderly couples immersed in the *Daily Telegraph Book of Quick Crosswords*.

Cuba is almost as fashionable now as it was when Greene first went there in 1955, four years before Castro's glorious revolution, when Havana was the most glamorous resort in the world. Tourists like Greene were not bothered by the fact that the country was suffering under the corrupt and brutal dictatorship of General Fulgencio Batista, a puppet of the Americans. 'I enjoyed the louche atmosphere of Batista's city,' he wrote in *Ways of Escape*, 'and I never stayed long enough to become aware of the sad political background of arbitrary imprisonment and torture. I came there . . . for the brothel life, the roulette in every hotel, the fruit machines spilling out jackpots of silver dollars, the Shanghai theatre where for one dollar 25 cents one could see a nude cabaret of extreme obscenity.'

On his first visit, Greene played roulette, smoked marijuana, watched a lesbian performance at the Blue Moon and scored cocaine from his driver. 'Nothing apparently was easier.' But the white powder had no effect and Greene realized he had been sold boracic powder. When he returned in 1957 he found the driver, who confessed to his deception.

Greene got there only just in time. Havana was in moral and physical decay, teetering on a profound abyss of change. Che Guevara's rebel army was gathering in the hills. *Our Man in Havana* was published in 1958, a year before the revolution transformed America's playground into Russia's bedfellow. 'Tourists were sadly reduced nowadays in numbers, because the President's regime was creaking dangerously towards its end,' Greene says at the beginning of his novel, but scarcely touches on the political situation from then on. In fact, as Greene later explained, his idea for the comic tale of a bungling spy was based on his experiences in Sierra Leone and was originally to be set in Tallinn, the capital of Estonia, in 1938, until he realized that Europe on the eve of war was an unsuitable venue for a comedy. Havana, it struck him, was a far better choice. 'Here in this extraordinary city, where every vice was permissible and every trade possible, lay the true background to my comedy.'

If Greene was making a political point in his novel it was to poke fun at the looming threat of the Cold War, rather than to expose the iniquities of the Batista regime. His story's main character is Wormold, a British vacuum cleaner salesman in Havana. His wife has left him and he is bringing up their acquisitive daughter, Milly, alone. To cater to her needs, he agrees to spy for the British government. Unable to discover any real intelligence, he invents his reports and is horrified when they begin to come true.

The Cuban government is corrupt, the British secret service is inept. The God of Greene's earlier novels is absent. To survive, Wormold becomes an anarchist acting for nobody but himself. 'If I love or if I hate, let me love and hate as an individual,' he says. 'I will not be 59200/5 in anyone's global war.' Eventually, his deceptions are found out but the embarrassed British authorities, frightened of exposure, award him an OBE nevertheless.

Yet Greene's tale was to have an eerie epilogue. Wormold sends his employers drawings of vacuum cleaners, which they interpret as plans for an enemy missile base. When the Cuban missile crisis erupted just three years later many wondered at the author's prescience.

Politics may not have featured in his novel, but on a personal level, Greene's experiences in Cuba confirmed the idea he had first flirted with in Vietnam – that Communism might give us something bigger to believe in. His encounters with Ho Chi Minh had turned him into something of a groupie of left-wing revolutionaries and he was keen to meet the Cuban rebels' young leader, Fidel Castro. In 1957, Greene was given an opportunity when he was asked to carry some warm clothes for the rebels on a flight from Havana to Santiago in the south. It was, as his biographer, Michael Shelden, pointed out, hardly a death-defying mission but it endeared him to Castro, who declared him a friend for life.

Cuba, along with Vietnam, became one of Greene's commitments. In 1962, when America was urging Nato countries to help suppress Castro's Cuba, Greene wrote a letter to *The Times* questioning American accounts of a 'despotic and unjust' regime. Castro was suitably grateful for such support and when Greene returned to Cuba in 1963, 1966 and 1983, there was always a chauffeur-driven car and military plane at his disposal.

'Fidel admired him greatly,' my Cuban friend Alvaro recalled. 'I remember him saying that Greene was a very fit man and that he thought he must do a great deal of exercise, but then he discovered that he drank a bottle of rum every morning.'

The feeling was mutual. Although on the later visits Greene felt some nostalgia for the old Havana, 'that great open city for the bachelor on the loose', he was impressed by the social transformations that he witnessed.

In 1963, reporting for the *Sunday Telegraph*, he noted with approval the 'homes of the millionaires' now being used as schools for peasants, the freedom of the church and the 'cheerful Bank Holiday crowd' who gathered to listen to one of

Castro's three-hour speeches, which was 'not the regimented or hypnotized crowd that used to greet Hitler'.

In 1966, when he returned again for the *Telegraph*, his reaction was more sombre. The American blockade and Hurricane Flora had exacted a toll. Rations were tight, queues were long and, he suspected, forced labour camps were being used as dumping grounds for 'homosexuals, layabouts and priests'.

Yet, Greene was touched by the public's still tangible enthusiasm for the revolution. 'This is a revolution of the young, not of men grown old in the British Museum reading room,' he wrote. A man so riven by ambiguities would never have admitted outward support for Castro, yet to the end he defended him, telling an interviewer in 1988 that his authoritarianism was only the result of the implacable attitude of the United States – and in any case was not as ugly as Pinochet's in Chile.

Yet if Greene returned to Cuba today he would struggle to remain supportive. More than forty years after Che and Castro stormed the Moncada barracks, the Cubans are as poor and exploited as they were at the height of Batista's power. Havana is as decadent as when Greene knew it. 'No, more,' Alvaro insisted. 'Because when he was here, the buildings were still standing. Today Havana has collapsed. The only structures intact today are those that cater for tourists or the American dollar.'

II

In 1999, forty years after Castro came to power, I set off again for Havana with my cousin Frances. The flight took off three hours late, thanks to unspecified 'technical problems' and we were seated next to the lavatories which broke down two hours into the flight. At least, unlike the last time, there was a drinks trolley.

'Ooh,' said Frances, a Scot. 'I'll have a Bloody Mary.'

'No vodka.'

'OK, a tomato juice.'

'No tomato juice. Only Coke or Diet Coke.'

I distracted myself by reading the inflight magazine, *Sol y Son*. There was an article about the new red and white terminal building at Havana's José Martí airport. 'Among the terminal's installations are: two final waiting rooms and one for remote positions.'

There was also, much to my surprise, an article about a shopping mall, Plaza de Carlos III, that had recently opened in Havana and was already taking in $100,000 a day. 'Carlos III is a novelty for the city's inhabitants,' I read. It was a novelty for me, too. The last time I visited Cuba was just after the collapse of the Soviet Union in what became known as the 'special period'. There were long power cuts and no traffic on the roads. The shops and the bars stocked nothing. Fidel had promised everyone enough to eat, yet in 1992 the people of Havana were making hamburger meat out of banana peel and steaks out of grapefruit rinds. Some were raising *jutias* – native, rodent-like creatures – for consumption, while others were simply eating rats. Black marketeers were melting the rubber from condoms to masquerade as cheese in sandwiches.

Cuba did not have an Aids problem, because anyone with HIV was put in an isolation camp. When people found out that at least you got enough to eat there, they began injecting themselves with the virus.

The people were happy, though. They told me so. 'Why should we want to live in America?' one teenage boy asked me.

'Because they have food to eat there?' I ventured.

'Yes,' he said witheringly. 'But they have violence also. If you have no money in America you live on the street. You must pay to go to hospital, to go to school.'

'Well . . .'

'We Cubans are spiritual people. We do not listen to rock music. We do not need to eat. We have our education. We have our health. We know what is important in life.'

At the time, I was impressed by this response. It was only later, much later, that I found that all Cuban schoolchildren are taught to reel off this argument like the national anthem or the iron ore statistics for the state of Pinar del Río.

III

Maybe things really were different, I thought as we disembarked. Terminal 3 of José Martí airport had over-enthusiastic air-conditioning and banks of televisions showing pop videos. Just as in Vietnam, the Cuban government had been forced to adapt. The tourists who before had been merely tolerated were now the saviours of an economy bereft of Soviet aid and wooed with an ardour once reserved for Romanian trade delegations.

In 1992, you could only buy one guide to the country – the *Travellers Survival Kit: Cuba*. It informed me that: 'Tourism is planned to quadruple over the next five years, but most observers feel this to be hopelessly over-optimistic.'

The third edition, printed six years later in competition with more than a dozen similar titles, said: 'In 1995, tourism grossed $1 billion, ten times as much as in 1990.' It added that tourism had just overtaken the sugar trade as Cuba's main hard currency earner. In other words, things were back to just how they had been before the revolution.

Yet although foreigners were now welcomed in Cuba, this did not mean they were loved. 'Fidel is desperately digging for oil off the coast,' Jan, a German photographer who lived in Havana, told me. 'As soon as he finds it, the tourists can get lost.'

However, on this occasion the immigration officer stamped my tourist card – detachable from my passport so capitalist countries need never know where I had been spending my dollars – smiled and said: 'Have a good stay in Cuba.'

We got into a taxi. It had a meter. The driver switched it on without being asked. He stuck to the 70 k.p.h. speed limit, did not touch his horn once and made no attempt either to cadge a Western cigarette or to light up some noxious local brand.

Once the empty highway to Havana was lined with billboards of uplifting slogans: '*Socialismo o Muerte!*' '*Hasta la Victoria Siempre*'. Today they have been replaced by advertisements for Bic biros, Omo soap and Mercedes Benz.

Something had definitely changed in Cuba. When we arrived at the Hotel Inglaterra, there was a receptionist who spoke English. She had a record of our booking. She even smiled. The lift arrived in less than five minutes. Our room had a high ceiling, a tiled floor, tall shuttered windows looking out on to the narrow Calle San Rafael (once the principal shopping street), and a television with twenty-four channels – including MTV and CNN. In the bathroom, there was a hairdryer – albeit cunningly disguised as a colonic irrigator. There was even a telephone, although when I picked it up I was greeted by the kind of hollow crackle that suggested the aliens had landed.

The Inglaterra was the oldest hotel in Havana and, in my opinion, the loveliest. It had the elegant façade of a French château, a red neon sign of a Mid-Western diner and a cool, tiled lobby like a Moorish palace. Federico García Lorca had stayed there, so had the correspondents sent to cover the fall of the Batista regime and so had Wormold's secretary, Beatrice, on her first night in Havana.

We took the lift to the rooftop bar and leant over the balustrade. Below us rows of Cadillacs and Oldsmobiles sat waiting for a fare. The streets were eerily quiet, save for the odd tring of a bicycle bell. Here we were on the same level as the carved muses who topped the neighbouring Gran Teatro, offering a stone wreath to the starry sky. Beyond them, the great dome of the Capitolio – modelled on Washington's Capitol – glowed in floodlights. It was an utterly seductive scene. Perhaps the Cubans had worked this tourism thing out after all.

IV

To realize how naive this thought was, I had only to wait until morning and the delights of the Inglaterra's breakfast buffet. Under the chandeliers of the green-and-white tiled dining room sat a sad selection of some glistening tongue sandwiches, one rotting banana and a Cuban Swiss roll, the jam replaced with radioactive-green pickle. We sat at a table with a dirty white cloth. A tall, black waiter in a tuxedo poured coffee-coloured liquid into our cups.

Frances and I stepped out of the Inglaterra to a welcome not heard since Manchester United came home with the triple. The Italians wolf whistle, the Moroccans pinch your bottom, but for sheer persistent hassle no one can beat the Cubans. It is just as well Americans can't travel there. Ten minutes in the streets of Havana and every man in the country would be facing a grand jury on charges of sexual harassment.

Our every step was greeted with rapturous kissing noises, a
'Psst, *amiga*' or a 'Jesus Christ! I love you'. We felt like
Wormold's Milly, whose approach could be detected: 'Like
that of a police car, from a long way off. Whistles instead of
sirens warned him of her coming . . . silence would have
seemed like an insult to her now.'

Milly, however, was fifteen, with 'Hair the colour of pale
honey, dark eyebrows and her pony tail was shaped by the
best barber in town.' Frances and I were almost twice that age
with chalk-white bodies and sweat-sodden locks.

We were also competing with the sexiest women in the
world. Cuban women wear tight denim shorts and platform heels. They bare their midriffs and unbutton their shirts.
When they walk their bottoms sway from side to side
like a pendulum, when they stand it is with their hips thrust
forward. This is the only country in the world where the
question 'Does my bum look big in this?' demands the answer
'Yes'.

The last time I had been here, the atmosphere was even
steamier. In a time of extreme hardship, sex was the only thing
not on the ration books. Not only that, but I had been
travelling with my friend Jo, a sex bomb from Wigan.

I had been at Cambridge with Jo, and my abiding memory
of her comes from the first term, when I was sitting on
someone's bedroom floor desperate to go to sleep but equally
eager to make friends. I was listening to a pompous under-
graduate discussion about where we would most like to be
in the world. 'I,' said one pimpled student, 'would like to
be watching the Pyramids at sunrise, like I did in my gap
year.'

'I,' another chimed in, 'would like to be canoeing down
the Orinoco like I did in my summer holidays.'

It was Jo's turn. 'I,' she said, 'would like to be lying on a surfboard on Blackpool beach having my nipples licked really slowly.'

Jo and I had been in Havana for slightly less than five minutes when a bearded cyclist with bloodshot eyes whispered: 'Hey, *linda*, where you from?'

I stalked on, head up, eyes averted. Jo turned round and gave the man a big smile. 'Wigan, England,' she said. 'Perhaps you would like to show us round?'

The consequence was that by the end of the day Jo and William, her boyfriend, were snogging. By the end of the week they had checked into a 'Love Motel', where free Japanese condoms were distributed and beds were rented by the hour.

Meanwhile, I had a rather sad holiday, either wandering Havana alone – unless you counted the pack of men at my heels shouting: 'Sexy, where you from?' – or joining the happy couple for meals in which William would order dozens of beers and lobster, I would have to pick up half the tab, and the evening's conversation would progress along these lines:

'*Tu amiga es muy linda.*'

'*Si,*' yawn. '*Muy linda.*'

'*Y muy sexy.*'

'Yes, she is very sexy.' She is also my friend and I would occasionally like to have a meal alone with her.

Luckily for me William had a friend called Pepe, who, inevitably, was keen that we should make up a cosy foursome. In the afternoon, we would congregate at the one-bedroom flat William shared with his mother and four siblings. He and Jo would slow dance to Tracy Chapman and Pepe and I would argue.

'No, Pepe. I will *not* kiss you.'

'Why not? Jo is kissing.'

'I have a boyfriend in England.'

'So? He will never know. Kiss me. Come on.'

'No.' And so on. One day Pepe bullied me into exchanging some dollars with him for utterly useless Cuban pesos. He stuffed them into the pocket of his Bulgarian jeans, leaving no room for his identity card. He gave it to me to put in my money belt.

Shortly afterwards, I left him and returned to the hotel. I was lying on my bed when there was a banging on the door.

'Police! Open please!'

Shortly after I had left, the police had stopped and searched Pepe. They found him to be carrying dollars but not his identity card. Both were serious crimes. I gave his card back but he was still sent straight to jail and for all I know is still there. A drastic way of getting rid of a pesky admirer, but effective.

William, however, had staying power. At the airport he and Jo clung together, but as soon as she boarded the plane she admitted there was no chance she would ever see him again. Then, about six months later, my phone rang at work.

'Miss Llewellyn Smith? It's Heathrow immigration here. We have a William X in custody. He has arrived in Britain on what appears to be a false visa, although we are waiting for confirmation from the British Embassy in Havana on that. He has two numbers in Britain, yours and a Miss Joanna Brown's but we gather from Miss Brown's office that she is on a business trip to Poland.'

William, it transpired, had stowed away on a plane from Havana to Madrid. From there he had made it to London, with a visa, which the British Embassy in Havana was to confirm was false.

It took them a week to check this, however, during which time William was allowed out of detention to spend a week with Jo who, on returning from Poland, had been stopped at immigration and informed: 'Your Cuban lover is waiting for you in the cells.' Her boss, travelling with her, was unamused. Jo lived in Basingstoke. At the end of their seven days together she was legally bound to return William to the airport, which she did.

'How did he smuggle himself on to a plane and fake a visa?' I asked.

'I haven't the faintest idea.'

'What did he make of Basingstoke?'

'I don't know. I didn't ask.'

V

In those days it had been difficult to sense anything of Greene's Havana, but seven years later the city was beginning strut its stuff once more. We were sweating down the Prado, the famous street that led from the Inglaterra down to the seafront. In the centre was an oak-shaded paved walkway, lined with alcoves containing carved marble benches. Dark-green, wrought-iron lamp-posts shaped like griffins held big light globes. When Wormold walked along it, it was a gauntlet of hustlers. 'At every corner there were men who called taxi . . . every few yards the pimps accosted him', and today their sons were equally busy besieging us with offers of cigars and rum and inviting us to stay in a friend's house or eat in their brother's private restaurant.

Despite years of socialist training, the Cubans, like their Vietnamese comrades, are still some of the most persistent salesmen on earth. But while the Vietnamese open noodle stalls or whizz up silk shirts in fifteen minutes, the Cubans tend to prefer the role of middleman. After all, why bother to make something when it is so much less effort to procure.

Yet, gradually, things were beginning to change. Old men in vests chomped cigars as they rode along on three-wheeled butchers' bikes pulling trailers of sunflowers. Girls sold slices of hot, doughy pizza through narrow window slits. We walked on, along the wide seafront boulevard, the Malecón. In the virtual absence of traffic, there was no sound but the tring of bicycle bells and the sound of the 'jalousies above the colonnades creaking in the small wind from the sea'. Above the arcade rose mini-mansions, three storeys high, each one cheerfully different from the next. Some had art deco murals in faded blues and gold, others bore the dim outlines of caryatids; some had Moorish pointy windows of stained glass. Greene wrote:

The pink, grey, yellow pillars of what had once been the aristocratic quarter were eroded like rocks; an ancient coat of arms, smudged and featureless, was set over the doorway of a shabby hotel.

Even in his day, the city had been crumbling as the middle classes began to abandon the inquisitorial alleys of the old city for the airy mansions in the 'white rich suburb' of Vedado. Wormold sensed a 'slow erosion of Havana', and that erosion had been propelled into fast forward by Castro's government, which had diverted all its resources away from the bourgeois city and into the countryside.

We headed back along the Malecón, past the fortress that guarded the port and through the Plaza de Armas, a palm-shaded square with a second-hand book market full of medical textbooks and coffee-table tomes called *Treasures of the Hermitage*, useless souvenirs of former solidarity exchanges to Leningrad. Two blocks south we were in Calle Lamparilla.

The colonial houses that lined it were now leprous shells. Their bright blues and greens had been bleached to the colour of knickers put through too many boil washes. Few had window panes, almost none had doors. Even the odd scaffold pole looked as if it had been rotting there for twenty years.

Number 37, where Wormold and Milly lived, had been demolished. In the space where it once stood there was now a tiny park with a tatty fountain dominated by a hideous socialist statue of a man with arms uplifted, presumably in victory. A few mothers watched their babies stagger around in baggy nappies, while half-a-dozen representatives of Havana's enormous dog population nosed hungrily in the dust.

For a country that boasted no unemployment there were a surprising number of people in Havana slouching on doorsteps and lounging on street corners. This was not the happy idling of a Lilt commercial. The women gave us hard stares. The men hissed at us through their teeth. Frances and I walked through the dilapidated Plaza de Cristo, where Wormold was 'swallowed up among the pimps and lottery sellers of the Havana noon'. Two teenage boys were kicking a deflated football in the dust.

'Oh, poor things,' cried Frances, sweet-natured as ever. 'It breaks my heart. I'd love to buy them a new ball.'

The boys shouted after us. 'What are they saying?' my cousin asked eagerly.

I translated. 'They're saying "Hey darling, I'd love to take you up the arse."'

In the surrounding buildings people were living five to a room, sharing the bathroom and kitchen with two or three other families. Every week a couple of these structures collapsed, often with people still inside them. Dozens of doctors and teachers had been seconded from their jobs and recruited into 'special worker brigades' to rebuild the city. They were told that they would only be needed for six months, but some had done nine years already. You could spot the construction sites where these brigades were employed by the downed tools outside and the groups of special workers sitting around smoking and making kissing noises at their female colleagues. If you peered up into the scaffolding you could see rows of rag dolls, suspended from a rope between the poles like voodoo figurines. 'We hang one for each year we have lost from our lives so far,' one builder told me. 'I have wasted seven.' In his former life, he had been a biochemist.

In the eighteenth century, Havana had been the most glorious city in the world. When you came across a patch that had been restored with UNESCO funds, you saw how beautiful it must have been. Rows of formal colonial mansions in pink, yellow and green shimmered in the sun. Every nail-studded door and wrought-iron balcony was surrounded by tourists gabbling excitedly and snapping. In the Plaza de la Catedral, the doors and shutters of the colonial mansions had been newly painted agate blue. The paving stones were buffed to the texture of an ice rink. The lone blind beggar whom Wormold saw on the steps of the baroque cathedral had now multiplied into a whole troupe of picturesque cripples, rattling their tins. A skinny old lady in pedal-pushers and with her hair in curlers sat chewing a cigar in a doorway demanding $5 a picture. The statue of Columbus that looked 'as though it had been formed through the centuries under water, like a coral reef, by the actions of insects' had been removed as a relic of colonialism and there were no longer 'negro dolls' in the curio shops, but there were still gourds and rattles for sale, along with a few shoddy metal keyrings in the shape of Che's head. The crafts were terrible, but there was no doubt about their authenticity. This was the work of university lecturers or economists; or, at least, people who had never travelled and had no idea what a quality souvenir should look like yet were desperate for greenbacks.

We paid to enter the two-storey building facing the cathedral, once owned by Havana Club rum where Wormold and the sadistic Captain Segura, whom Greene modelled on Batista's dreaded henchman, Major Esteban Ventura, played draughts and drank free shots of rum. Today, it was the Museum of Colonial Art, full of heavy Spanish furniture and Baccarat crystal. Blue-uniformed attendants followed us from room to room, whispering: 'Psst, *amiga*. Candy? Soap?'

The ban on Cubans possessing dollars, which had put Pepe in jail, was lifted in 1994 in response to rioting in the streets of Havana – the first open act of defiance against Castro. Today, Cubans are even allowed bank accounts into which their American relatives can deposit as much hard currency as they like. In Havana, 80 per cent of the population is estimated to have access to hard currency, although in the countryside almost no one does.

Despite his political sympathies, Greene missed the old Havana. Today everyone wants to see Cuba before Castro goes. Greene encouraged his friends to make the most of Havana before Castro arrived. 'When communism starts, puritanism immediately follows. You ought to see what is on offer here before it goes,' he wrote to one. When he returned in 1963, he noted that the Mambo, 'the brothel which greeted the incoming tourist on the road from the airport is a restaurant now: the Blue Moon is closed: the discreet superior establishment on the Malecón also'. He would have been delighted by today's Havana where sex is as easy to find as a decent daiquiri. Frances and I sat down for lunch at La Julia, a *paladar*, or private restaurant, in Calle O'Reilly. Christmas lights flashed behind the tiny bar and a budgerigar sat morosely in its cage. At the table next door, two impossibly sexy black girls, no older than eighteen, were giggling and chattering with their dates in pidgin Italian. One man had a heavy moustache, while the other wore a T-shirt that read 'Every day of my life I add another name to the list of people who piss me off'.

The waitress plonked vast dishes of beans and fried chicken on the lace tablecloth. The flirting stopped. The girls ate with fierce concentration, stopping only to pile more on to their plates. The men fondled them under the tablecloth and smiled at each other, unable to believe their good luck.

'It's just the way it is,' said the waitress, as the giggling couples departed. She was a formidable Hispanic woman in a knee-length blue dress covered by a white lacy apron. 'Officially it's illegal, but how else are you supposed to make money. My neighbour makes around a thousand dollars a week, after bribes, by running a guest house where foreigners can bring their Cuban friends to stay the night. If I was a young woman now, who's to say I wouldn't be doing the same? The girls aren't prostitutes, you see. They want these men to marry them.'

VI

In the afternoon, the quest for Greene's Havana continued. As with everywhere in Greeneland, Greene's geography was extremely precise. What was wrong were the names he had given some of his locations. The Prado may bear the name El Paseo del Martí in books, but it is never called that in real life. Nor is the Malecón ever known by its more formal title: Avenida de Maceo. When it came to reconstructing the city in his imagination, Greene had clearly preferred to rely on printed maps not remembered conversations. We were looking for the Wonder Bar on the Prado, where Wormold and his friend Dr Hasselbacher used to enjoy their mid-morning daiquiris. There was no sign, but an old man, sitting on a bench, directed us to the door of a dirty pink building with a brown iron gate. The door was opened by a middle-aged Hispanic man, who listened in amusement to my stumbling introduction. His name, he said, was Eduardo and we were not the first Greene tourists. He ushered us inside. All that remained of the bar was a peeling mural of traditional Spanish dancers. Crumbling whitewash revealed the former colour scheme of green, yellow and red paint. The floor was stone, the furniture cheap and shabby, set off by garish vases and a collection of dolls.

Eduardo had lived in the Wonder Bar for more than thirty years. 'After the revolution, the owner went to Florida, and it was closed,' he said. 'Nine years later, while I was working for a taxi company, I met the owner and he told me the place was empty and asked if I wanted to move in. Where we lived was very crowded so I took up his offer. It was very eerie, as it had been closed for so long. There was a picture of Nat King Cole on the wall, which was so vivid it looked real. It scared me silly, so I took it down. Sometimes the place still gives me the shivers — it's as if it's haunted by ghosts. There were many people who had a violent end here.' Including Dr Hasselbacher, who was shot dead here by the Secret Services.

He introduced us to his wife, Clara, a stocky woman in a faded housecoat. 'I never went into the bar when I was a young woman — it was a bad place. There were often fights on the street outside. I just remember walking past it and how it was always packed. Everyone wore very elegant shoes,' she said.

There were no daiquiris on offer now; instead Frances and I nipped round the corner to the dollar supermarket to buy imported beer. On our return, we sat on the green plastic sofa, while Eduardo set himself to work decoding Greene's Havana for us. 'Sloppy Joe's!' he cried, spotting the name of the bar where Wormold was recruited to MI6. 'That was just across the street. Let's go and have a look.'

Sloppy Joe's was closed, too, although its name was still visible on the pavement in fading mosaic tiles. Eduardo borrowed a chair for us to stand on from a yawning bootblack sitting under the yellow colonnades, so we could peep through the rusting metal shutters. In the darkness, we could just make out a dusty mahogany bar with the cobwebbed optics behind it. It was like gazing at the wreck of the *Titanic*. 'No Havana resident ever went to Sloppy Joe's', Greene wrote, 'because it was the rendezvous of tourists.' Eduardo agreed. 'They used to cram in here. It had a huge bar with seats all along it and the daiquiris were supposed to be the best in Cuba.'

Eduardo put us in a taxi, to take us the short distance to Chinatown, where we could find the site of the old Shanghai theatre. Wormold and Beatrice came here to speak to one of his agents – Teresa the go-go dancer.

The Shanghai was in a narrow street off Zanja surrounded by deep bars. A board advertised *Posiciónes*, and the tickets for some reason were sold on the pavement outside. Perhaps because there was no room for a box-office, as the foyer was occupied by a pornographic bookshop.

Today, all the bars had gone and the space where the Shanghai stood was a patch of scrubby grass, where children were playing baseball. 'Before the revolution there were lots and lots of bars and clubs here,' said our driver. 'The streets were full of people, I remember stepping over people lying drunk in the gutter. Prostitutes were everywhere. My mother used to tell me not to look.'

He was a middle-aged Hispanic, dressed in Ray-Bans and Levi's. His car had air-conditioning and electric windows and he looked sleek and healthy, like his cousins in Miami. 'I used to be a schoolteacher, but I packed it in,' he said. 'Then I was earning $12 a month. Now I make $100 a week. Sometimes I feel a bit guilty, but my wife would hardly have thanked me otherwise.'

Much of Havana might be collapsing, but at least Communism had saved sites such as the Shanghai's from being taken over by shopping malls and flashing McDonald's signs. Much of the time you were in Havana you felt as if you were walking through a 50s time warp, past faded signs for Singer, Hotpoint and National Bank of Boston; high-finned Chevvies and chrome-plated Dodges.

Slowly the government was realizing that it might be profitable to exploit its shameful past. We put our heads round the door of the Floridita bar, considered by Greene to be 'one of the great restaurants of the world' and where Wormold proposed to Milly's mother. The chrome and red velvet banquettes were packed with coach parties sipping daiquiris at $6 a piece. For the third time that day we wandered back down the Prado to the Hotel Sevilla, *née* the Seville Biltmore, home to Greene's MI6 agent Hawthorne. In the lobby, the tiled walls were decorated with photographs of its gangster owners, while a picture of revolutionary students smashing up the casino was made to look like a happy holiday snap. A cha-cha-cha dancer shimmied and a couple in sunglasses pouted into the lens. In such jolly company, the balding man with a wall of books behind him and haughty exophthalmic eyes looked out of place. 'Mr Graham Greene the distinguished English author who mentioned the Hotel Sevilla's Room 510 in his novel *Our Man in Havana*,' read the caption.

In fact, Wormold had had his rendezvous with Hawthorne

in room 501. It was easy to slip into the lifts and make my way up to the fifth floor. The rooms were '. . . built as prison-cells round a rectangular balcony'. I knocked on the door, planning some excuse about honeymoons and wanting to look at the room. It was opened by a confused Italian woman. Clearly, she had been enjoying a wonderful dream. She snapped at me, I muttered something and retreated hastily down the stairs. Wormold would have sympathized with my ineptitude.

It was time for a swim. We hailed a bright yellow motorized beach buggy driven by a young woman in Lycra hot pants, who introduced herself as Rosa. With much honking of her horn, she manoeuvred us through the hot streets of Central Havana, where the buildings were modern and their decay therefore simply ugly. Every time we passed a traffic policeman, Rosa blew fervent kisses and honked. 'Wankers,' she said, grinning perilously at us over her shoulder. 'But it never hurts to keep them sweet.'

We were going to the Hotel Nacional, an imposing building overlooking the sea flanked by two sandblasted Moorish minarets. It was in the dining room that Wormold narrowly escaped being poisoned by his Secret Service enemies. Today, the bar was adorned with black-and-white photographs of guests from the Batista era: Fred Astaire, Marlon Brando, Frank Sinatra, Ava Gardner, Betty Grable, Nat King Cole and John Wayne. Post-Batista, the guest list veered dramatically away from Hollywood into the realms of radical chic as Danielle Mitterrand, Jean-Paul Sartre and Gabriel García Márquez hurried to investigate this socialist paradise.

It was only in 1997 that true glamour returned to the newly cool republic, with the arrival of Kate Moss and Naomi Campbell, who held a press conference with Fidel Castro. He granted them a private audience of half an hour – twenty minutes more than he gave the Pope, and was apparently very taken with Naomi. I wondered how the Cubans who salivated over Frances and me would have responded to those two.

When the Nacional opened in 1930, it was allegedly the grandest hotel in the world. Even now, it had splashing fountains and peacocks strutting on the lawns. Blue-uniformed maids swept leaves off the paths. We sat by the pool watching a plain thirty-something English redhead we had spotted that morning at the Inglaterra. She was accompanied by a younger, fitter, better-looking black Cuban boy who was rubbing cream into her peeling back and stroking her droopy white buttocks which were nudging out of the sides of her bikini bottoms. Occasionally, she would hand over a wodge of cash. He would return with cigarettes and beer. While he was gone she flicked through her copy of *Spanish for Travellers*, her eyes full of anxiety. His expression was blank and bored.

We were in heaven.

'Hello, beautiful ladies,' said a voice behind us. 'I am here to talk to you about the beautiful Hotel Nacional. I will join you now. That is OK?'

We turned to see a tall and portly man, with a vulpine grin made more sinister by his mirrored wrap-around shades. His name, he said, pumping our hands, was Pedro. He spoke in an American monotone that suggested long hours with a Linguaphone cassette and brooked no deviations from the script.

He pulled up a chair and leaned forward confidingly. 'And so ladies, I must ask what country you are from?'

'England.'

'Scotland.'

'Ah, England. I am sure of that already. All the most beautiful ladies come from England.'

Frances wiped some spittle from her shoulder and smiled politely. 'Scotland,' she insisted. *'Escocia.'*

'Ah, Scotland. All the beautiful ladies are from Scotland, too. And so ladies, I invite you tonight to dinner in the restaurant of the Hotel Nacional. It is very good, very cheap. Only $25 per person. Plus wine.'

He turned to Frances with a rictus that suggested a sudden flash of inspiration. 'We have very good Scottish wine. You will love it!' Seeing her look of disbelief, he continued. 'No, I assure you! Very good Scottish wine. And after you will come to our nightclub, the Paris. I invite you. It is so very good, all our guests come to me and say, "Thank you, Pedro, for the recommendation." You will come tonight?'

'Thank you, but tonight we're going to the Tropicana,' I said.

Pedro ignored this treacherous news. 'So I will call you and tell you more about my hotel!' he concluded. 'You tell me. Which hotel do you stay in?'

There was a small pause. 'The Sevilla,' I said.

'The Sevilla is a very bad hotel. You are much better at the Nacional,' he said, scribbling the name on a piece of paper. 'Which room, ladies?'

The shades meant that it was impossible to make eye contact. If we had, I would have laughed. 'Room 501,' I said.

VII

I wasn't lying when I told Pedro that we were going to the Tropicana, the nightclub under the stars and another relic of Cuba's notorious past. We had booked our tickets that morning from a busty lady at the tour desk of the Inglaterra. They were restricted-view seats at $55 each. 'Be in the lobby at 8 p.m.,' she instructed us. And at 7.55 p.m., wearing our prettiest dresses, we were there.

At 8.30 p.m., we were still there and thirsty, not daring to order a beer in case the bus arrived. Around us, other well-dressed couples checked their watches. Periodically someone would go outside to check there was no other, hidden, muster point.

At 8.45 p.m., Frances approached reception.

'Excuse me, when will the bus for the Tropicana arrive?'

The woman did not bother to hide her yawn. 'Yes. You wait in the lobby.'

'But when will the bus come? They said 8 p.m. It is now 8.45.'

Another, wider yawn. 'Usually it comes at 9.15. Maybe 9.45.'

'So why did you tell us 8 p.m?'

'Usually it comes at 9.15,' said the receptionist. She returned to her crossword, then looked up again. 'In Cuba is normal.'

The bus arrived at 9.40 and we were briskly herded on to it. It set off down the Malecón and then left up La Rampa, the sloping avenue dominated by the Habana Libre, formerly the Havana Hilton, and the Coppelia Ice Cream parlour where the peso queue took several hours and the dollar queue no time at all. We drove through Vedado, where Greene saw 'little cream and white houses owned by rich men'. Today, the colours have flaked away, the gardens are overgrown and large families sit on the front steps tapping their feet to ghetto blasters.

We must be nearly there, I thought, marvelling at how far the city spread. Then I did a double take. On my left, again, were the skyscrapers of the new town, 'like icicles in the moonlight'. To the right was the Coppelia queue, which had maybe advanced three places. Here again was the Malecón, sprinkled with embracing couples. We were going round in circles. 'Ahem, excuse me,' said the elderly English gentleman in front of me. 'What do you think is going on?'

'We forget something,' snapped our guide. The bus pulled up in front of the Nacional. There was an altercation between the guide and a doorman. Then we set off again on our third tour of Havana by Night.

Irritation whipped down the bus like lightning.

'What exactly did you forget,' demanded a Spanish woman.

'We forgot seven guests. But it's OK. They have gone to the Tropicana in a taxi.'

The Tropicana sat under a cloudy sky, its huge stage surrounded by banks of closely packed tables. The setting was the same as when Wormold took Milly here for her seventeenth birthday, when 'chorus girls paraded 20 feet up among the great palm trees, while pink and mauve searchlights swept the floor'. The arena was filled with video-toting tourists (cameras $25 extra) and raucous Cubans who received the tickets as an annual bonus from their unions. We were shown to the last empty table, directly behind a mammoth pillar that almost completely blocked our view of the stage. A waiter served us with a 'Welcome Drink'. Before the addition of three dozen ice cubes, it might have borne some relation to Coca-Cola. We sipped them slowly, in the knowledge that the next round would cost us $20 each.

By Cuban standards, the show was remarkably slick. If I strained to the left I could see a long line of girls dressed in old Quality Street wrappers. To the right, a buxom old woman and what passed in a dim light for Julio Iglesias's younger brother were warbling a duet. My eyes returned to the girls. 'To live in Havana was to live in a city that turned out human beauty on a conveyor belt,' Greene wrote, and if this was a factory, then these girls were top-of-the-range, with bottoms like cantaloupes wrapped in tin foil and cheekbones like geometry. In comparison, Kate and Naomi were anaemic grasshoppers.

Yet the evening's climax was even more impressive. The goddesses launched themselves into the audience, trailing their ruffled sleeves over our heads and looking for a victim to dance with them on stage. English men and women would have stared into their drinks or hurried to the loo, but the Cubans jostled for attention like the class swot. They were middle-aged, paunchy and dressed in Bulgarian lounge suits, but on stage, grinding their hips and gyrating their buttocks they were transformed into socialism's answer to John Travolta. The pale, gawky, porky tourists gaped enviously. Here was proof that if God gave with one hand, He took away with another. For all our dollars, we would never be able to acquire an ounce of their grace. 'The stars look down and bless our love,' sang the fat lady singer and the audience erupted into rows of happy gyrating Conga lines.

VIII

Music is everywhere in Cuba. It booms out of every unpaned window, it sneaks into your dreams and it rouses you soon after dawn. Every meal is accompanied by black beans, rice and a pack of ungifted guitar players who know one song, 'Guantanamera'. The lyrics are: '*Guantanamera, Guajira, Guantanamera. Guantaname-e-ra. Guajira, Guantanamera.*' All tourists can sing it and none has a clue what it means.

Fidel did a clever thing in allowing his people to sing and dance so freely. It confused the enemy who knew that a true communist state must be cold, grey, utilitarian and miserable. Cuba was warm, bright, sophisticated and outwardly happy. 'The Cubans have such an enduring spirit,' solidarity campaigners tell you. 'They don't let the fascist American embargo get them down, they have their music and salsa.'

'What patronizing nonsense,' said my Cuban friend Alvaro. 'Yes, the Cubans like to party. But why does that make us happy people? We do it to forget our misery. Do you know that Cuba has the highest rate of suicide in the Western hemisphere. Do you know that we have one of the highest rates of alcoholism in the world?'

We were drinking beer on the terrace of the Inglaterra, but I felt as if I was in the monkey house at the zoo. Hemmed in by a low wall of wooden plant stands, we sat on one side with our drinks and club sandwiches, while on the other side half of Havana jostled for our attentions. One man was busily making atrocious sketches of the tourists. An old woman held out her hand and kept up a cry of 'soap please, soap!'. Another in a blue and white dress, her grey hair held back by a red clip, just gazed at us longingly like a child in front of Hamleys' Christmas windows.

The waiters at the Inglaterra had perfected the art of avoiding eye contact when you wanted the bill, but they were masters at ejecting undesirables. Every time they disappeared into the kitchens, two black girls – one in a tight polka-dotted sundress, the other in a striped Lycra body suit – would make a run for the lobby. A few seconds later they would be returned to the pavement. A whey-faced Dane was bashfully entertaining his 'girlfriend' with coffee and Marlboros. He was confused and indignant when the waiters also asked them to leave.

I laughed at these men, yet at the same time I was paying for Alvaro's beers and cigarettes. The truth was that in Cuba even friendship had a price in dollars. You paid, they took, and no one ever said 'thank you'. Sometimes, I couldn't help being irritated by this, although mostly it made me feel less guilty about playing the *seigneur*.

Alvaro was a photographer friend of a friend. He had the

long face of an abandoned bloodhound. His greying hair was tied back in a plait and his ribs stuck out through his chest like an X-ray. He dressed younger than his forty years but his face was older. Alvaro had never left Cuba. 'My foreign friends tell me that I would like New York City,' he would say dreamily. 'What do you think?' I thought it would terrify him.

Alvaro's profound intelligence combined with his limited surroundings had left him deeply frustrated intellectually. He would talk for hours in perfect English about Milton and Shakespeare and then suddenly say: 'I hear the Ritz in London has the most beautiful bar in the world. Is that really so?'

Travel was impossible for Alvaro and for all Cubans without a letter of invitation from a foreign friend, followed by endless permits and visas. 'Before I buy my ticket I have worked out that I must pay $390 just in bureaucrat's fees,' he said. 'Then my ticket is $700. It is impossible. How much did you pay for your ticket?'

The storm that punctuated every Havana afternoon was arriving. Large drops of rain ricocheted off the pavement. Men and women rushed for cover, their heads covered with plastic bags. The gale rocked the palm trees in the Parque Central and churned up the dust. Lightning cracked over the Hotel Plaza.

Suddenly my expectations of gratitude seemed churlish. 'About $700.'

IX

Night was the best time in Havana. Friends chatted on the sea wall of the Malecón and old ladies sat in their rocking chairs on the pavement. In the day it was too hot to walk more than a couple of blocks at a time. No sooner had you left the shower than it was time to go back for another one. The heat and the lack of rain had ruined the sugar crop, which meant it was going to be another hard winter.

'Ai-ee,' shouted Rosana, our landlady. '*Qué calor!* Such a heat is impossible. How can a woman can be elegant in this? Always, you are perspiring.'

After our obligatory three pre-paid nights at the Inglaterra, it was time to economize. Frances and I needed to find a *casa particular* – the Cuban equivalent of bed and breakfast. We ended up a few blocks behind the Inglaterra at Rosana's.

Rosana was a well-connected Cuban who, most unusually, had travelled in Europe. Her bathroom was full of Boots Number 7 body scrubs and Pantene deep conditioners. She knew that guests disliked cockroaches and preferred if not hot, then at least permanent, running water. Consequently, she was making a fortune.

As with all Cuban attempts to liberalize the economy, the B&B revolution was being stifled before it could even draw its first breaths. 'I have to pay the state $100 a month for every room that I rent out – even if I have no visitors,' Rosana told us. 'In addition, there is a tax on each room depending on its size. So I tell the state that I have only two rooms available, when in fact I have seven and I am building more. If anyone asks you, you say the same. OK?'

Given the vigilance of Rosana's neighbours, it was extra-ordinary that she had managed to dupe the authorities at all. At any hour of the day or night, at least three old women were hanging out of the windows of the houses opposite, observing every coming and going.

Greene's secret policeman Captain Segura with his cigar case made from human skin had been replaced by the men and women of the Dirección General de Inteligencia, a unit closely modelled on the KGB. On the street, it was represented by the ubiquitous CDRs, Comitées para la Defensa de la Revolución, an organization with a role somewhere between that of Neighbourhood Watch and the Gestapo. Members were encouraged to inform on 'counter-revolutionary neighbours', whose children would then have difficulties finding jobs. 'They hate me,' said Rosana. 'But I promise them cleaning jobs with lots of dollar tips and that seems to shut them up.'

The guests at Rosana's included Cristina, a Greek woman who had dreamed all her life of coming to Cuba to take photographs. On her second evening in Havana, she was mugged and her camera stolen. Her attacker dragged her along the street by her hair until she let it go. She lifted up her T-shirt and showed me the scars on her back. 'What upset me most was that dozens of people were watching, but no one did a thing to help me,' she said.

It was a common story, despite the tourist brochure boasts that Cuba was 'free from crime'. Last year, two Italians had been shot dead on a beach outside Havana and the body of another tourist had been lying for months in the city mortuary, because no one could identify it. But if the tiny foreign press corps were to report such incidents, they would be immediately deported.

A boy no older than ten tried to mug Frances in broad daylight on the Malecón. He ran up silently behind her and grabbed her bag. A tug of war ensued, which she won. He walked slowly and arrogantly into the traffic, smirking at us over his shoulder. A rickshaw driver, who I later realized was the accomplice, watched the whole scene impassively.

'Was the boy black?' Alvaro asked. He was. 'They are all criminals,' he said. It was a jarring remark coming from a man with a ponytail who listened to Pink Floyd, but political correctness had not yet reached Cuba.

'This is a racist country,' Alvaro said. 'When I was growing up in the provinces, we would walk up and down the *paseo* every Saturday night, meeting friends and chatting up girls. The blacks always walked on one side of the street and the whites on the other. My father said that when he was a boy before the revolution there was actually a tape down the middle to keep the two races apart.' No wonder that the blacks were still loyal to Fidel. Yet forty years after the revolution, there were still few senior black faces in the leadership. Blacks still cut the sugar cane and rolled cigars, just as in Batista's day. 'Now we're saying that to exist here you have to have *fe*. It's the word for faith, but it also stands for *familia exterior*. Because only if you have relatives in Florida can you beat the system.'

X

The peasants had no family in Florida, but still they adored Fidel. 'It is only in Havana we hate him. In the country they know nothing about the world, so they can make no comparisons,' Alvaro said. Recently, he had visited the eastern provinces where tobacco was grown, and had returned with a case of amoebic dysentery. 'The people there are living like animals,' he raged. 'They have no shoes on their feet, they have no possessions except a bed with a ragged mattress. I went to a union meeting and they were asking for clothes. Their bosses said they couldn't have any. Their lives are so empty, they have nothing to occupy themselves with but gossip and petty feuds.

'I asked a man if he was better or worse off since the revolution. He told me worse because before the revolution no one was starving. The children there have rickets. They are going blind from lack of protein. They live on nothing but raw beans, because they have no oil to cook with.'

Despite the state of affairs in the countryside, it was still a relief to leave the stickiness of Havana and take the empty four-laned highway that cut vertically across the island to Cienfuegos on the south coast.

Wormold had made this same journey in his old Hillman. Frances and I took the bus. Outside the city, sugar cane swayed at the side of the road. Turkey vultures swooped overhead and bony cattle grazed on the verge. Occasionally, we passed through a village of single-storey wooden shacks. On the outskirts, there was usually a billboard with slogans: '25,000 children die each day of a curable disease. *Not one of them is Cuban.*' 'Thousands of children are homeless. *Not one of them is Cuban.*'

In the eighteenth century Cienfuegos was the richest city in the world, thanks to the vast quantities of sugar cane passing through its port. By the 1950s it was in decline. In a letter to his sister in Northampton, Wormold describes it as 'one of the quietest ports in the world. Just the pink and yellow streets and a few cantinas and the big chimney of a sugar refinery'.

Arriving on a Sunday, such a description sounded positively racy. The tidy streets of Cienfuegos were deserted in the afternoon glare. There were no taxis to meet the bus, in fact there were no vehicles at all, just a few overladen Chinese bicycles. After Havana, it was blessedly clean and eerily silent.

We were staying with the Cardoso family, relatives of a friend of Alvaro's. They lived in one of the pastel, neo-classical buildings off the Prado, the main pedestrianized avenue. Their home was built around a central courtyard on one storey. You entered directly into a dark sitting room. The ceiling was high, the floor tiled, the pink walls mottled with damp. One corner had been partitioned off into a bedroom. Four rocking chairs sat facing each other in a square. At night, the family would sit in them, just as Greene had noticed: '. . . rocking towards each other and rocking away, making little currents of air'. In the corner was a large Sanyo television and video. On the sideboard, a CD player was blasting out the greatest hits of Celine Dion. 'I think you like to hear English music?' smiled Sara, the daughter of the house.

Sara was in her mid-thirties and a scientist – a job that had given her the occasional chance to travel abroad to Mexico, Canada and Russia. 'Those were the happiest days of my life,' she said. She had a plump, open face and a bright smile that masked an intense dissatisfaction with her lot.

She had a nine-year-old son Rafael, a handsome, spoilt boy with a stack of *Star Wars* videos. Her mother, Celia, was a sharp-featured, plump woman in a faded cotton housecoat, while her father, Manuel, had a wide toothless grin and walked around bare chested, revealing a deep scar running from his breastbone to his navel.

Frances asked Sara what had happened.

'He fought in Angola,' she said.

Celia had prepared us a dinner of 'Chinese chicken', a mountain of rice concealing the odd morsel of meat. We ate in the kitchen off a table draped in a lacy cloth. We filled up on avocados the size of melons and bananas, which the family ate like sausages with their knives and forks. The family terrier, Lassie, brushed against our legs.

After dinner, it was time to go out. Sara replaced her grubby pink housecoat with a pair of stonewashed denims and a stripy top. Rafael sat in a rocking chair with Lassie on his lap as his mother tied his shoelaces. Celia slumped in a chair fanning herself.

In the background, the television news was playing. The main story concerned Castro, who was giving a press confer-

ence in the Dominican Republic. There were shots of a
rentacrowd chanting: 'Fi-del, Fi-del'. A brown-suited journalist asked an oleaginous question. Castro's reply lasted for
about fifteen minutes. A sidekick watched him with adoring,
upturned eyes. Frances and I were the only ones watching. As
with all icons, it was a shock to discover that Fidel moved and
talked. His voice was surprisingly soft and whispery. 'I've
never heard Fidel speak before,' I said to Sara. She gave me a
suspicious look. 'Really?' she said, raising an eyebrow. To a
Cuban, a world where Castro was no more than an image on
a poster on a bedsit wall was unimaginable.

At night, Cienfuegos, like Havana, took on new life. The
Prado was crowded with promenading families. A surprising
number of people were blonde and blue-eyed – a relic of their
French ancestors who settled in the port in the nineteenth
century. There were relics everywhere of that former pros-
perity. I thought of Greene's description of the town – one of
the most lyrical he ever wrote.

The light here is wonderful just before the sun goes down: a long
trickle of gold and the seabirds are dark patches on the pewter swell.
The big white statue on the Paseo which looks in daylight like
Queen Victoria is a lump of ectoplasm now. The bootblacks have
all packed up their boxes under the arm-chairs in the pink colon-
nade: you sit high above the pavement as if on library-steps and rest
your feet on the back of two little sea-horses in bronze that might
have been brought here by a Phoenician.

Forty years later, the bootblacks were still polishing shoes and
Queen Victoria – in fact a memorial to an actress at the local
Teatro Tomas Terry – still dominated the Paseo. The open
doors of the stuccoed houses revealed candlelit vignettes of
elderly men playing dominoes. To us it was enchanting, but

not to Sara. 'Why do they have no light?' she demanded. 'I think we are about to have another energy shortage.'

Sara knew everyone and stopped frequently to exchange kisses and pleasantries. To us, she whispered: 'If anyone asks, you are friends I met in Mexico. Otherwise, things could get nasty.'

Materially, travel had been good for Sara. During each trip abroad, she had hoarded her government living allowance and spent it at the end on the video, the television, the CD player. But the memories of her travels chafed. As we walked down Avenida 54, the Oxford Street of Cienfuegos, her brown eyes were full of resentment.

'It's impossible to live in this country,' she said as we peered into a shop window full of computers. 'Guess how much I earn? 400 pesos a month. That's $20. Guess how much a litre of milk costs? Five pesos.' Frances and I started wrestling with some mental arithmetic. Later, we agreed that this was like asking a nurse on $12,000 a year to pay $12.50 a litre.

'Do you know how much a pound of pork is?' Sara continued. 'I'll tell you. Fifteen pesos. Do you know how much my father's monthly pension is? 130 pesos. This is a man who would have died for his country in Africa. He will never say so, but he is so disappointed in the revolution. I think it has broken his heart.'

In any case, these miserly wages were almost useless. Almost nothing could be bought with pesos. In the peso department store, the formica-topped showcases were empty. We looked in the window of a government dollar shop opposite. Washing machines, cookers and fridges glowed in the fluorescent light. There was even a little red vacuum cleaner – straight out of the boot of Wormold's Hillman – priced at $198. 'Why would I want one of those?' Sara snorted. 'All our floors are tiled.'

Life was difficult for the Cardosos. Running water was only

available between noon and 4 p.m. and then only in a cold trickle. During those hours the shower was left permanently running and water collected in plastic oil drums. The house was infested by cockroaches, which one invariably stepped on returning from the bathroom in the middle of the night. And always there was the question of food.

Every morning, Manuel was up hours before us, hunting for our breakfast – a meal that no Cuban eats. 'The bread is not too hard today,' he would cry exultantly as we sat down to enjoy the fruits of his expeditions. One morning Sara asked us if we liked eggs for breakfast. 'I saw in Canada that this was what people ate,' she said.

Thoughtlessly, we said we did. From then on, each morning we were presented with a two-egg omelette. We were about to leave for the beach when I saw Manuel's tatty ration book lying on the kitchen table. Furtively, I leafed through it. One bread roll per person per day; 6 lb of rice, 3 lb of sugar and less than 1 lb of black beans a month. The egg ration was two a week. In a few days, Frances and I had carelessly consumed his and Celia's monthly allowance.

We tried to make it up to them, by pressing a wad of cash on Sara when we left, and by funding a series of day trips. Once we went to Trinidad, the so-called jewel of Cuba, a colonial town, which, thanks to the embargo, remained picturesquely intact.

We were driven there by Sara's uncle Juan in his Lada Moskvich. Juan taught engineering at the university and the car had been a reward from the Party for years of good membership. He had immediately turned it to good use as a taxi and since then had visited the faculty perhaps once a month. He wore tinted glasses, a black vest and jeans that were a little tight. His left arm was burnt orange from hours spend leaning it out of the car window. When we stopped, he waited for us in the shade and read his book: *Ideological Cuba*. Like all the Cardosos, except Sara, he spoke little English, but his Russian was good after a few years in Azerbaijan. 'Too cold, but plenty to eat,' was his verdict on that experience.

The road to Trinidad wound through spinach-green countryside. We overtook cowboys in straw stetsons on horse-back and were overtaken by speeding, open-top Jeeps filled with screaming Italians in Ray-Bans. Butterflies fluttered in through the windows. Sara and Juan chatted and smoked in the front, and in the back Rafael sat sandwiched between me and Frances, playing intently on an inferior type of Gameboy.

At every crossroads, a crowd of as many as forty people stood in the sun, smoking and chatting. Another ten were huddled under a corrugated iron shelter. 'Who are they?' we asked.

Sara gave us another chilling look of disbelief. 'They are hitchhikers,' she said. 'They are waiting for someone to pick them up. You see the man with the ribbon around his waist? He is a marshal. His job is to make sure nobody jumps the queue.'

'But how long do they wait for?'

'Three hours, maybe four. I hitch every day to the university. But everyone in Cienfuegos knows me, so I have no problem getting a lift.'

In Trinidad, the sun slapped you in the face. The cobbled, sloping streets were deserted, the tourists all sheltered huddled in bars drinking Coca-Cola. Sara marched us around the town like a chain gang. 'This is the main square, this is the church, this is a museum. Do you want to visit it? No? OK, then we will go to the beach.'

Finally, we were in tourist-brochure Cuba. Twenty minutes outside Trinidad, we found talcum-powder sand and the limpid Caribbean. Within seconds, Rafael was in the water. A group of Canadians were playing volleyball to loud, distorted music. A French woman lay under her umbrella, absorbed in her copy of *Bien Maigrir*. A few hundred yards away at the hotel Germans wiggled flabby bottoms in a salsa class. Officially this beach was open to everyone, in reality the $5 fee for using the sun loungers meant it was off limits to virtually all Cubans.

We lay on white plastic loungers under a palm tree. Juan stripped down to his boxer shorts. Sara took some of our sun cream. 'Only now can I love my country,' she said.

In Canada, Sara had had a boyfriend called Eric. She showed us a photo of a round-faced Pole, with milky skin and smiling eyes behind thick, square glasses. 'Eric loves Cuba, he has been here many times,' she said. 'He says to me: "I am Cuban." I say to him: "Come and live like a Cuban and then see if you like it."'

Sara longed for Eric to ask her to marry him. 'I love him,' she giggled. 'But I am very careful never to ask him for anything. I don't want him to think I am like the other Cuban girls, so I always refuse his presents. He mustn't think I just want him for his money.'

Thanks to Rafael, the government was happy to let Sara travel freely. 'They know I will never defect when my son is here,' she said. 'If I married Eric, he could come to Canada with me. But then my parents would have to come, too. I couldn't leave them behind. And even if I do marry Eric, the wedding has to be in Cuba and I wouldn't be allowed to join him for another year.'

Rafael was the result of Sara's first marriage to Carlos, whom she met when she was studying in Moscow. 'He was also from Cienfuegos, in fact he was in my brother's class at school, but we only met in Russia. We married there, but a year after we returned we divorced.'

Everyone in Cuba divorced, it seemed. 'Yes, it is impossible to stay married here,' Sara said. 'There are no houses so a couple must live with the bride's parents. It never works. Always, the stress becomes intolerable.'

We ate fried chicken and soggy chips and drank numerous beers on a terrace overlooking the sea. Rafael picked at a *'Jam and Cheeese Sanwish'*. We laughed and clinked glasses and asked the waiter to take our photo. The bill came to $41, twice Sara's monthly salary. It was sunset by the time we set off home, the sky was Ribena red and there was a fingernail of a moon. Rafael lolled against my shoulder.

'When I am a man,' he said dreamily. 'I will be able to look at girls like Frances in the street and say *psst, psst, psst.*'

'No, you mustn't,' Frances retorted, shocked. 'It's horrible. Girls hate it.'

Sara twisted round. 'But he must! He is *Cuban.*'

XI

The following day, we visited a beach for Cubans. Playa Rancho Luna was about twenty minutes from Cienfuegos. The sand was a gritty grey. Bottles floated in the sea. We lay on a patch of mud surrounded by wasp-ridden rotting mangoes. A child in the tree above us shook the branches threatening to brain us with the unripe fruit. His mother bellowed at him to stop. To stay in the shade we had to move every few minutes. Sara was embarrassed and grew defensive.

'This is a Cuban beach,' she said. 'You must see how we live. Anyway, I think the sand here is cleaner than at Trinidad.'

This was a patent untruth, but we assured her we were happy. We went to the bar, where a fat German in his sixties sat on a high stool swigging rum from a bottle. One girl ran her fingers through his chest hair, another caressed his knee. We bought Cokes and Sprites, but no food was available for dollars. Frances and I had no pesos. 'I invite you,' said Juan, a little over-magnanimously, considering we were paying him $45 a day. After a long wait, we were presented with a plastic container containing a lump of gristle on dirty rice.

'I've never seen such a fine advertisement for E-Coli in my life,' Frances whispered.

Our host was looking at us expectantly. We took as small a nibble as we could. When Juan was distracted, I stuffed great chunks of it into the mouth of my Coke can. About forty-eight hours later, Frances's predictions were proved correct.

No one was sorry to leave the beach, except for Rafael, who had spent the morning collecting rubbish from the sea. He placed it in a tidy pile on the sand just below the high-tide mark, thus ensuring some other little boy could get the same pleasure tomorrow. We returned home sandy, hot and sticky-haired. The water had just been switched off.

XII

On the way back from Cienfuegos, we guiltily stopped for the night in Varadero, the most popular resort in Cuba, visited by hundreds of thousands of foreigners every year. Varadero represented the best of Cuba in that the beach is idyllic, the food in the restaurants edible, and the worst in that you could be anywhere in the world. The only Cubans in Varadero are necessary staff. Others are deterred by $5 'fee' to pass through the toll gates that guard the peninsula.

In our hotel bar we met Jan, a German photographer who had been living in Cuba for five years. He was pale and wild-eyed like an escaped convict. He had been staying in

Varadero for five days, and had spent the time locked in his room watching CNN and ordering room service. Not once did he go to the beach. 'I can do that any time,' he said. 'I come to Varadero to have nothing to do with Cuba.'

'What's the worst thing about living here?'

'Bloody Minint,' he said without hesitation. 'Ministry of the Interior. They tap our phones and have us followed.' Minint was not listed in the phone book and its headquarters at the Plaza de la Revolución were distinguished only by its façade with its famous metal mural of Che's head. 'There are so many stories here – like the shanty towns that Fidel claims are non-existent, which surround the city. But one word or picture gets out and you're on the next plane home. Just the other day, a Swedish friend of mine was deported because she tried to write about corruption at the higher end of the Party. There's no way.'

'So what are you doing here, if it's so awful?'

'Waiting for Fidel to die,' Jan said, stirring his pina colada. 'When he does it will be the biggest news story in the world, but there will be a few days between his death and the foreign journalists arriving. That's when I am going to clean up. I'll be able to retire.'

'When do you think Fidel will die?'

He was plunged back into gloom. 'God knows. Soon, I really hope. At this rate, I think I am going to die first.'

XIII

Everybody in Cuba was waiting. They waited in queues for food, they waited slumped on the kerb at crowded bus stops, they waited at country crossroads for a lift into some torpid town. They were waiting for their foreign boyfriends to propose. But most of all they were waiting for Castro to die.

When Fidel came to power, he was the youngest leader in the world. Now, he was the longest serving. He was undoubtedly a great man, but he had a fatal flaw. He was incapable of confronting his own mortality. Now in his seventies, he still refused to appoint a successor. Ask anyone what would happen after he had gone, and they would just shrug.

At the British embassy I asked the second secretary what she thought would be the likely outcome. 'When Fidel dies we are hoping for a smooth transition to democracy,' she said. She had a dark, pretty, amused face. 'But in all likelihood, it will be apocalyptic. There may be a civil war, culminating in an American invasion. Then all the Cubans in Miami will return to claim their property. Put it this way, we have drawn up tight contingency plans for the evacuation of all British citizens from the island at any time after Fidel's death.'

The embassy was a comforting environment. There was picture of the Queen on the wall and four-day-old copies of the *Guardian* on the table. In the loo there was a Marks & Spencer hanger for trousers, size: medium.

In Greene's day, the embassy had been in Havana Vieja, but a few years ago it had moved to a salmon-pink building in the diplomatic enclave of Miramar. The streets were wider in Miramar, there were inviting-looking cafés and the banks had tellers who smiled when you changed a traveller's cheque and gave you your money in twenties and tens, rather than the uncashable hundreds they insisted on downtown. Frances and I didn't want to leave.

We only glimpsed Our Man, a man with a white beard in a pale green shirt, as he ascended the sweeping staircase lined with pictures of battleships. 'I trust they're looking after you,' he said. He must have thought we were some of the four or five British tourists who arrive there every day, penniless after being bumped off the Cubana flight home.

The British embassy was not the biggest in Cuba. That honour belonged to the Americans, despite their claim to have no representation in enemy territory. Instead, there was a 'Special Interests Section' in the Swiss embassy with a staff of 444. 'The 44 are American and they all work for the CIA and the 400 are Cubans, who all work for Minint,' Jan the German photographer had told me.

'Cuba is the most bizarre place to live,' confided the second secretary. 'Your only Cuban friends are informers and you know that every word you tell them is going straight back to the Party. They can be great fun and very charming and they love it when you take them out for a decent meal, but you would never achieve a true friendship with any of them.'

Part of Britain's role in Cuba was to keep an eye on the well-documented human rights abuses. 'But it can be tricky. People romanticize Cuba so much, they will not hear a word against it. At international conferences, the people who criticize Colombia or Guatemala go into orbit when you mention Cuba. They accuse you of being an imperialist and tell you how if there are any problems there, then it is all the fault of the American embargo.'

In fact, no proper study has ever been made into whether Cuba's disastrous economy is really the fault of the embargo. Some whispered that inefficient socialist planning had played the larger part. 'That's what we think,' the second secretary said. 'What the embargo has done is bolstered Fidel's popularity. Both at home and abroad he is seen as a heroic David figure, standing up to the mighty American Goliath.'

The benefits of the revolution had been over-exaggerated. 'You might get into a hospital, but you would have to bring your own food and sheets, and unless you were actually dying the doctors would probably tell you to go home.'

Why is Cuba important to Britain, I asked. The woman smiled. 'Well, in global terms, it isn't. But we have dependent territories in the Caribbean and we don't want them to be swamped with refugees when this place goes into meltdown. We try to promote human rights and to ensure a peaceful transition to democracy. But Fidel is so intransigent. He refuses to move with the times. He transformed Cuba once and he will not do it again.'

Yet the longer you spent in Cuba, the more you could not help admiring Fidel for his brilliant manipulation of the situation. Here was a man who had been living like some spoilt Notting Hill trustafarian sponging off his Soviet dad, who was happy to fund his way-out experiments in socialism, to the tune of $1 per person per day, because it angered his old enemy America. But then dad had died and Cuba had been exposed as a country whose industry had been destroyed, agriculture ruined and whose best brains had deserted it.

But Cubans did not see it that way. As far as they were concerned their country's collapse was all the fault of the Americans and their 'economic warfare'. The Americans, equally stupidly, could not see that as long as their embargo continued Fidel had an excuse for everything that was wrong with his irremediable society.

Fidel's charisma was extraordinary. I told Alvaro how much I disliked Margaret Thatcher. Yet on the one occasion I met her, her aura was so powerful that I nearly curtsied. 'It was just the same when I met Fidel,' he cried. 'I wanted to tell him that I hated him, but the words wouldn't come. It wasn't just fear. He radiates power. You just have to respect him.'

Fidel's control was absolute. He lived with his second wife and their two teenage children, but for security reasons this was never mentioned in either the Cuban or the foreign press. Any foreign journalist who wrote about it would be instantly expelled.

'Everything that happens to Fidel is turned to his advantage,' said Alvaro's friend Paco. We were sitting in his fourth-floor flat in central Havana. To reach it, you had to climb a stinking staircase with a wobbly balustrade in total darkness. The lightbulbs had all been stolen. The walls were covered in mildew. There was no glass in the window and no water at all – not even a bucket to flush the fetid lavatory.

'Take when Ceauşescu was executed in 1989. News of that was just beginning to trickle through here, when that very same week General Noriega had his come-uppance in Panama. So Fidel was able to direct all the coverage towards the fitting end of a right-wing dictator and ignore what had happened to his old communist buddy.

'In 1994, there were the riots. We were desperate in those days. Every day hundreds of people were setting out on rafts for America. Castro came out on to the Prado to calm the people and they started throwing stones at him. He was surrounded by bodyguards but they were outnumbered. I couldn't believe my eyes. I thought this would be the end. I was frightened, but I was also very excited that, finally, we were rebelling.

'But then Fidel did a brilliant thing. He said to the boat people: "Go then, we don't want you." They went and suddenly America had more boat people than it could cope with. Always, America has said it will welcome all Cubans because it does not recognize Cuba as a state. But now, President Clinton was forced to say "Stop" and by doing that he had to give Cuba official status. It was another brilliant victory for Fidel.'

Paco was an artist with a capital A. He was small with

shoulder-length curly hair, while his canvasses were huge melodramas of twisted figures bent by insanity, pain and desire. He and Alvaro were obsessed with astrology. Fidel, Clinton, Princess Diana, Hitler – they knew all their star signs and analysed them accordingly.

They insisted on drawing up our astrological charts and then charged us an outrageous sum of $40 each to be insulted and depressed. 'Hmm,' he said looking at mine. 'This shows that you like talking to yourself in the mirror.'

'No, she doesn't,' Frances said loyally.

Worse was to come, however. 'I think you will be very famous,' he said, peering at his hieroglyphics. 'It will be in connection with . . . how do you say the word? Fossils.' Frances meanwhile would never marry. I would but my marriage would be devoid of passion and I would never have children.

Life in this hopeless country had destroyed any sense of autonomy. The only way Paco and his friends could cope was by blaming everything on fate – or by trying to manipulate it. Alvaro had been told he would drown in this, his 40th, year and therefore turned down all our invitations to the beach.

The church has never been important in Cuba. Catholicism was the province of the now-exiled upper classes. The lower classes practise Santeria, a form of voodoo. Yet when Greene returned to Cuba in 1963, he spoke of a 'new voice in the Communist world' and marvelled at the freedom of the church there, although on later visits he noted the presence of priests in concentration camps.

In January 1998 the Pope came to Cuba. He was greeted with adulation. 'It was very exciting, not because it was the Pope but because for the first time ever someone was coming who was bigger than Fidel,' Alvaro said.

'So Cubans are not religious people?'
'No. But they are very superstitious.'

XIV

On our last day, we visited the Museo de la Revolución. Its displays included the sewing machine that made Castro's uniform, some tatty berets and a moth-eaten spacesuit, as a symbol of Cuba's contribution to world science. In the room dedicated to the horrors of the Batista regime was a photograph of a black woman in a skirt and bra, her back to the camera. 'Many women were obliged to become prostitutes to survive,' read the caption.

Downstairs, in the Rincón de los Cretinos – 'cretins' corner' – there were giant effigies of Reagan dressed in a cowboy outfit and Bush in a toga. 'Thank you cretin for helping us consolidate the revolution,' said the sign. In the museum café, the attendants were drinking Coke and crowding round the television to watch a Brazilian soap opera.

The place was a monument to failure. Alvaro, who had come with us, was horribly ashamed. 'You must understand,' he said. 'The revolution was necessary. We just need to move with the times.'

He accompanied us to the airport. Frances went to buy beers and was gone for half an hour. One barman was standing behind the counter doing nothing slowly, while a horde of thirsty travellers tried to grab his attention. In a back room, six of his colleagues were watching television and smoking.

We stood in the queue to pay the rip-off airport tax. In front of us was an elderly pot-bellied Englishman. His Cuban girlfriend, who could have been no more than nineteen, clung to him like a child. 'No, no,' he said gently, and prised her fingers from his arm. 'Be good now. I'll come back, I promise.'

The immigration official stamped our tourist cards. We kissed Alvaro goodbye. I gave him $20 for his taxi back into town. I knew he would take the bus and buy some meat with it. We pushed through a door and were in the air-conditioned no man's land of duty free. Wormold was right. More than ever, Havana was 'a city to visit, not a city to live in'.

5. Haiti

I

Haiti is only an hour's flight from Miami, a twenty minute hop from Jamaica, but nobody seems to know that. My friends and family couldn't quite place Haiti. My granny, who is known to endure sleepless fortnights when I announce I am off to Greece, was quite unmoved by the news that I was going to the poorest country in the Western hemisphere. 'Don't get sunburnt, darling,' she said. Later, I found out she thought I was going to Hawaii.

My taxi driver burst into song when I told him my destination. 'Happy talk, keep talking happy talk.' No, not Tahiti. Haiti.

Even the people who could find it on a map couldn't pronounce it. 'So, you're going to *High-ee-tee*,' said Cambridge graduates. No. I was going to the far less exotic Hate-ee. As in the verb to hate.

They may not have known where Haiti was, but they sure knew plenty about it. After all, wasn't Haiti the setting for *Live and Let Die*, in which James Bond goes voodoo in a black polo neck and Jane Seymour ends up tied to a post in a chiffon nightie, while pop-eyed witch doctors wave snakes in her face?

Thus prompted, the information began to snowball. Haiti, home of the Tontons Macoutes, killers in Ray-Bans, and their psychotic leader, Papa Doc. Haiti – world Aids capital. In fact in every league of horror – infant mortality, life expectancy, illiteracy, Haiti either topped or tailed the chart.

One in ten babies die at birth, two out of three people are unemployed and more than eight out of ten cannot read. In the cemeteries robbers dig up graves to steal handles from the coffins. In the neighbouring Dominican Republic, there are Haitians in prison because they sneaked over the border to steal the topsoil.

So I was not prepared to love Haiti. In fact, I was not prepared to do anything but weep as my American Airlines airbus for Port-au-Prince – Pee Pee they call it locally – flew over the Bahamas, those delicate strips of land fringed by azure waters.

Down there, the only risk tourists faced was doing their backs in after too much limbo dancing, or tooth decay from an excess of pina coladas. Where I was heading the local idea of fun was biting the head off a live rooster and crowning your enemy's head with a burning tyre.

Hand luggage restrictions do not apply on the Port-au-Prince flight. No Haitian is going to entrust his worldly goods to a Port-au-Prince baggage handler. There were 24-inch televisions strapped on to seats and fridges in the aisles. The woman next to me struggled to put a 12-foot long wind instrument in the overhead locker. The stewardesses, who had clearly seen it all before, yawned and intoned automatically into the microphone: 'The captain cannot prepare for take-off until all carry-on items have been stored.'

It is a rule of air travel that the grottier your destination, the better the service. Thus when you fly Paris to Geneva, a plate of foam-rubber vomit is shoved under your nose with a grunt. Everyone knows that you will be enjoying a fondue that evening – so why spoil your appetite?

On the Miami to Port-au-Prince hop, however, you enjoy every mouthful of your stir-fried chicken with cashew nuts and leeks, followed by pecan pie, Brie and biscuits. 'Enjoy,' smiles the hostess. 'In a few hours you will be gnawing on a scrawny goat's shin.' As the plane began its long descent over Haiti's arid mountains, longlife milk had never tasted more delicious.

As a man obsessed with degeneracy, Greene's obsession with Haiti is no surprise. By the 1960s when he wrote *The Comedians*, the world's bastions of evil were proving a bit of a let-down for him. Ho Chi Minh and Fidel Castro might have been generally considered as pariahs in the West, but to Greene they were a pair of friendly, well-educated blokes with fine intentions. But in Haiti, a country only twice the size of Yorkshire, Greene – who had spent some jolly holidays there in the 1950s – sensed he might find hell on earth.

He was not to be disappointed. In 1963, Greene returned to Haiti on assignment for *Paris Match*. He found an 'evil slum floating a few miles from Florida', a country where the President for Life, Papa Doc Duvalier, tried to converse with the heads of his dead enemies. One of Duvalier's rivals was beaten to death before the good doctor performed emergency brain surgery in an effort to revive him.

Like *The Quiet American*, much of *The Comedians* reads as straight reportage. The plot, however, could almost be a Greene parody: world-weary hotel owner Brown returns to Haiti and his mistress Martha. He gets involved with a group of freedom fighters and the louche 'comedian' Jones, a British opportunist with a shady past. Scared that Martha is falling for Jones, Brown helps him to join the revolutionaries. They escape across the border but on the way Jones dies a hero's death. Alienated from everyone, Brown ends up working as an undertaker in the Dominican Republic.

When *The Comedians* was published in 1966, Papa Doc was not amused. He published a pamphlet called 'Graham Greene: Finally Exposed', in which the author was reviled as a 'negrophobic, benzedrine addict', a 'conceited scribbler' and a 'habitué of lazar houses'. When the film, starring Elizabeth Taylor and Richard Burton and shot in the African republic of Benin, was released, Papa Doc sued in the French courts. He was awarded one franc in damages. For years anyone visiting Haiti who shared Greene's surname could expect a hard time at passport control and copies of *The Comedians* were routinely confiscated.

But Greene visited Haiti nearly forty years ago. Duvalier is long dead and his kleptomaniac son, Baby Doc, who sounds like a reject from the Spice Girls, is far away hobnobbing with other deposed dictators on the Côte d'Azur.

The corpse that Papa Doc left to rot outside the airport next to a sign that read 'Welcome to Haiti' has gone. Now the only people in Haiti wearing Ray-Bans are officials of the World Bank. The Macoutes – just like the former KGB men in eastern Europe – are all taxi drivers now and the president is a democratically elected former baker called René Préval.

Yet from the moment you step off the plane into the bedlam of Port-au-Prince airport you know that fear and frustration still hold Haiti in a strangler's grip. The country is still evil and it is still, most definitely, a total slum.

Outside the sweaty arrivals hall, the heat slapped us in the face. Dozens of men scrambled for our bags. A taxi driver bundled us into the back of a Mitsubishi truck. It had no suspension and a shattered front windscreen. By Haitian standards this was pretty good. The drive into town was a descent into hell.

There are no real roads in Port-au-Prince, just humped and potholed tracks under tangled wires of overhead cables littered with car wrecks and sleeping dogs. There are no real houses, just tin shacks with sheets of polythene pulled over them to keep out the rain. Every time the traffic brought us to a stop, children with protruding empty bellies and the rust-tinged hair that signals protein deficiency thrust their hands through the window. Only 700 miles from the cafés of Miami's Ocean Drive we could have been in Bangladesh.

In the 1950s scientists devised a bomb that would kill all the people and leave all the buildings standing. In Port-au-Prince the opposite had happened. The infrastructure had been taken over by rats and weeds but three million people were still living there, crammed into a semi-circle of land between the arid mountains and the stinking Caribbean. Three million people, most of them with nothing to do, yelling at each other in sharp, staccato Creole, honking their horns in endless traffic jams and blasting out Bob Marley on antiquated cassette players.

Those three million people have only 8000 bathrooms, so their shit ran through the town in open sewers. Three million people's rubbish lay in vast, rat-infested mountains that our driver kept swerving to avoid.

If you wound up the car window you expired of heat, if you opened it you choked on the uniquely Haitian smell of charcoal smoke, rotting mangoes, sewage and sweat – a smell that Greene oddly described as 'sweet' and 'flowery' and that was to linger in your mind long after all concrete images had merged into one nightmarish blur.

'Oh God,' said my friend Guy in the back. His Hawaiian shirt, bought the night before in South Beach, was stained with sweat. 'Where have you brought me now?'

Why is Haiti such a mess? It started out so promisingly. Mr Smith, Brown's naive American visitor – a kinder version of *The Quiet American*'s do-gooding Pyle, described it as a 'Black Republic – and a black republic with a history, an art and a literature'.

Under the French colonists, Haiti was the richest country in the world. It provided France with three-quarters of its sugar and its exports financed the building of the town houses of Paris and the châteaux of the Loire.

But then a voodoo priest called Boukman led the workers in rebellion against their masters. It was the only successful slave revolution in history. In 1804 Haiti became the world's first black republic. It was a glorious example of David versus Goliath, but it was one that Goliath never forgot. In the Western imagination Haiti would always be a cauldron of African primitivism, a place where slave masters' children were impaled on spikes by the rebellious masses, a cocktail of savagery and black magic just a few miles from America's shores.

The Haitians had beaten the white man so the white man vowed to repay them by treating them as eternal pariahs.

Saddled from the start with crippling debts to France, Haiti immediately began to flounder. Despite its non-racialist origins, power was soon concentrated among the half-caste mulattos. They became involved in internecine power struggles and neglected their infant country. Between 1843 and 1915 Haiti saw twenty-two revolutions – one for every new head of state, most of whom left office by violent means.

In 1915 the Americans, concerned at the burgeoning presence of German merchants in Port-au-Prince, sent in the marines. Not just any old marines, but ones specially selected from the Deep South, because in the words of one despatch: 'They are supposed to know how to handle coloureds.'

During the Americans' nineteen-year stay more than 40,000 Haitians were killed and thousands of peasants were evicted from their lands to make room for the Haitian American Sugar Company.

Worse was to come after their departure, in the shape of François Duvalier, who was elected president in 1957. Many hoped that this mild-mannered, bespectacled country doctor would steer Haiti on to a more civilized course. Dr Duvalier's mildness was overrated. By 1964, when he pronounced himself President for Life, he had overseen the murders of 60,000 people. By 1971 when he died of old age – an exceptional ending for a Haitian leader – one in six of his countrymen were in exile.

When Greene visited in 1963 he found a country where corpses lined the streets and all schoolchildren were forced to attend the execution of two guerrillas in the cemetery. The secret police, the Tontons Macoutes, regularly murdered grandmothers and children just because their name happened to resemble that of a Duvalier enemy.

Duvalier's actions were so surreal they were often farcical. Schoolchildren were made to recite his version of the 'Lord's Prayer'. 'Oh Doc, who art in the National Palace for life, hallowed be thy name.' One Christmas, he decided to deduct $15 from the salary of every civil servant, but in return he rewarded them with the second volume of his essential works.

No wonder Brown reached the conclusion that 'Life was a comedy, not the tragedy for which I had been prepared.' *The Comedians* is full of moments of high bathos – from Mr Smith pressing handfuls of notes on an unwilling and terrified beggar to Jones leaving the sanctuary of a Dutch ship disguised as a pantomime dame.

The Americans saw those horrors but they did nothing. The good Haitian Dr Magiot told Brown why: 'Papa Doc is a bulwark against Communism. There will be no Cuba and no Bay of Pigs here.'

Duvalier's anti-Castro stance ensured that when he died he was succeeded not by democracy, but by his roly-poly, nineteen-year-old son Jean Claude, who married the avaricious Michèle Bennet. In 1985, with the country on the verge of starvation, Michèle decided to fly to Paris by Concorde where she spent $1.7 million on her Christmas shopping. The result was that no money was left in the national coffers to pay for an oil tanker docked in Port-au-Prince with desperately needed petroleum. As generators spluttered out and tap-taps – the brightly painted buses named for the sound of their engines – ground to a halt, the Haitians began to realize that their leader had literally drained the country dry.

A few months later, with food riots escalating, the couple climbed into their BMW and drove to the airport to board a US cargo plane bound for Paris. Their departure marked the end of the longest period of stability Haiti had ever known. Soon, the country had reverted to its habitual routine of massacres, coups, uprisings and revolts.

'A revolution in Haiti does not have the same meaning as it would have here,' ex-President François Légitime, who was overthrown in 1899, explained to the *London Herald* in 1911. 'It is our only way of changing administrations. Here you have an election: down there they have a revolution.' Greene put it another way: 'If an English election is less complicated than an American, a Haitian is simpler than either. In Haiti, if one put any value on one's skin, one stayed home.'

There were to be six more governments before the people of Haiti voted in their first genuinely public elections for a tiny, bug-eyed, manic depressive priest called Father Jean-Bertrand Aristide.

'Titid' was the first democratically elected president in

Haitian history, yet only eight months later he was boarding a plane for Caracas. He had been overthrown by
General Raoul Cédras, whose military faction embarked on
an orgy of rape and murder. The Americans imposed a trade
embargo that did nothing except leave the peasants close to
starvation. In despair, they began building rafts to take them
to Miami.

By 1994, the people of Florida were fed up with the corpses
of dead children – many dressed in their immigrant Sunday
best – washing up on their beaches and spoiling the back-
grounds to their fashion shoots. They put pressure on their
government to invade and restore Aristide. In the face of an
ultimatum, Cédras backed down. Aristide returned for a final
term and then handed over power to his friend Préval.

Yet now, five years on from 'Liberation' everyone agreed
that Haiti was in the worst state it had ever been. There was
the same poverty, the same deprivation, the same fear. For the
past eighteen months, Préval had been unable to form a
government. The last budget had been two years ago.

A few months before we arrived, Préval's sister had been
shot at three times by motorcycle gunmen. She survived, but
her chauffeur was killed. Four weeks after that, Jean-Yvon
Toussaint, one of Préval's leading opponents, was shot dead
outside his home. Préval said it was the act of a jealous lover,
but the murder had all the marks of a formal execution.

The day we arrived in Port-au-Prince, the Haitian police
executed eleven people in the suburb of Carrefour. The head
of police fled to French Guiana. The teachers shut the schools
so their students could demonstrate on the streets.

The nation simmered in a cauldron of hatred and fear.
Préval's people accused the elite – the former Macoutes and
the handful of billionaire Arab families who saw the country
as their personal fiefdom – of trying to spike the wheels of a

popular revolution. The opposition retorted that Préval and his cronies were every bit as corrupt and incompetent as their Marxist tirades against the 'evil bourgeoisie' suggested.

Whatever the truth, it meant that strolls around downtown Port-au-Prince were frequently enlivened by encounters with large and noisy demonstrations. You could hear the yelling and the machine-guns being fired in the air from several blocks away. At times like these our guide, a forty-year-old Haitian named Milfort Bruno, told us there was only one thing to do: 'Run! Run like hell!'

II

It was an unpromising introduction. Yet only twenty-four hours after arriving in Port-au-Prince I was swearing undying love to the place. Maybe it was the effect of the malaria tablets. It was certainly aided by the local rum.

Mainly, though, I was seduced by our hotel – the Oloffson, a rickety Gothic folly, crowned with fairy-tale turrets and hidden among high palm trees. Covered in dainty filigrees, it looked as if it could have been spun out of candy floss. In the moonlight it stood out white and eerie above the city like Sleeping Beauty's castle.

In *The Comedians*, the Oloffson had a starring role as the Trianon, Brown's empty hotel: 'Fragile and pretty and period by day', but sinister by night, when 'You expected a witch to open the door to you, or a maniac butler, with a bat dangling from the chandelier behind him.'

Everything about the place breathed decadence and lassitude. You entered its grounds through high, iron gates and went past a lazily splashing fountain surrounded by lush vegetation. At the foot of the hotel steps was a stone statue of a grinning man in a top hat smoking a cigar. It was Baron Samedi, the voodoo spirit of the cemeteries.

At reception, a girl was sleeping, her head cradled in her arms. To the left was the mahogany bar whose back wall was the solid rockface of the mountain the hotel was built on. On the wall was a portrait of a black Virgin Mary made entirely out of sequins. The wooden floor creaked, the ceiling fans turned slowly. As we mounted the spiral staircase to our room, a rat ran across our path. All that was missing was Miss Havisham, asleep in an armchair in the corner.

In its brief heyday, when Haiti was as much a part of the jet-setter's itinerary as Monte Carlo, John Gielgud stayed here. Noël Coward sat on the veranda. Mick Jagger wrote 'Emotional Rescue' in his bungalow overlooking the 'blue-tiled bathing pool' – the same pool where the fictional Brown watched two guests making love.

Later, of course, the only body in the pool was the mutilated corpse of the Secretary for Social Welfare, while the only guests were the indomitable Smiths.

Today, the only people staying at the Oloffson were two American aid-workers and their children, while the pool contained nothing worse than a child's plastic boat and a thick layer of slime.

The Oloffson inspired Greene to write an article entitled 'The Mechanics of Running an Empty Hotel' – an article, however, which no one had been able to trace. In the manager's office Greene's reply to one scholar hung framed behind the desk.

Dear Mr Palm,

Thank you for the letter and the photographs and if you are in communication with Mr Moorse [sic] give him my good wishes for the future. I don't think it would be wise to send him a copy of The Comedians. I am afraid I don't remember and have no copy of my essay on the economics of running an empty hotel. As for the interview you must excuse me. I have a tremendous amount of work to do and not many years to do it in.

Yours sincerely,

Graham Greene.

Mr 'Moorse' was 41-year-old Richard Morse, half American and half Haitian. He was tall and stooped, with a matted rasta ponytail and lugubrious face. The questions put to Brown: 'How did a man like you ever come to settle in Port-au-Prince? How did you ever become a hotelier? You don't look like a hotelier', applied equally well to Richard.

His answer was well-rehearsed. After graduating from Princeton, he had first come to Haiti in 1985 to stay with his aunt and research voodoo music. 'Baby Doc was about to flee. I didn't speak a word of Creole and I was beginning to get pretty pissed off,' he said. 'I decided I either found a job or I got out. Then one day I was in the back of a taxi with a voodoo priest who used to give massages to the guests staying at the big hotels. He said: "Do you want to own the Oloffson?" I said: "I'm not sure." He said, more pointedly: "Tell me you want the hotel. Say yes, say yes, say yes." So I said: "OK, I want the hotel." He said: "Good. Give me $20."'

'And did you?'

'Sure I did. And look at me now, for Chrissakes.' He glanced around the room ruefully. 'An American businessman in Haiti. The voodoo must have worked.'

Like Brown, Richard had learned that a Haitian hotel was not a guaranteed money spinner. 'Whenever we have a coup the place fills up with journalists – but I can't enjoy it because I'm too busy worrying that the bastards will come and take the place over.'

For now, Richard's grasp on the Oloffson was shaky. His lease from the Haitian Sam family had run out two years ago. Several bigshots were determined to take the hotel over. To put Richard out of business, they had bribed some local ministry to start on a programme of 'road repairs' outside the hotel, which made it impossible to drive up to the front door.

'To have a drink here, you have to wade through a mud-bath,' Richard said. 'Most people give up and go to the Holiday Inn instead.' The year before, during the annual carnival, his rivals had run the Oloffson float off the road. Nine people were killed and forty-two injured.

Richard smiled wryly at the memory. 'If I have to go, I have to go. The spirits will know when my time is up. I don't want to be like my predecessor, Suzie Seitz. When they finally forced her out, she was so angry she set to work stripping the place. By the time I arrived, she'd taken all the wires out and the floorboards up. I think I'd like to leave with more dignity.'

'What does Suzie do now?'

'She runs the tourist board in town.' He snorted. 'Funnily, they don't send many tourists to the Oloffson. Not that there are any tourists to send.'

III

At least there were no coups this week in Haiti, just the usual tensions stewing in the Caribbean sun. If the truth be told, you could have a good holiday in Haiti. No, really.

'The island to which we were bound was no longer an attraction for tourists,' wrote Greene and, indeed, one of the best things about the place was that all the fat couples from Walsall were getting married and contracting dysentery on the other side of the border in the Dominican Republic.

In Haiti, the beaches – if a little dirty – were deserted. The hilltop suburb of Pétionville had some of the best restaurants in the world and there was never any need to make a reservation. The hustlers that could make life so uncomfortable in Jamaica were non-existent. What was the point of asking for money when nobody had any? McDonald's had no plans to open an outlet in Port-au-Prince, although there had once been a branch of Kentucky Fried Chicken. It had had to close through lack of custom. The Haitians found its food disgusting, a fact which made me love them all the more.

In the grounds of the Oloffson, the sewage stink was masked by exotic flora, and the shrieks of angry demonstrators sounded quite quaint when listened to from behind high walls. Guy decided that the safest place for him was the pool and there he stayed for the first three days, buried in his book and ignoring my every enticement to take a walk into town.

I ended up being shown around by Milfort, who ran a souvenir shop at the end of the Oloffson's drive. Surely, I asked him, things were getting better in Haiti. After all, they could hardly get much worse. He shook his head. 'This is the worst I have ever known my country.'

'But you have democracy now.'

'But at least with the Duvaliers we knew where we were. We knew where the fear was coming from. Now we are still afraid, always, but we are not sure of what.'

We were walking in single file along the Rue Capois, the road that led from the Oloffson to the Champ de Mars – the tatty square that symbolized the town centre.

Walking in Port-au-Prince took considerable skill. First you had to master breathing through your mouth, to keep the smell out. Then you had to learn how to leap over the potholes and open sewers, while avoiding the dozens of women in faded cotton dresses, squatting on thin legs at the side of the road, angular wrists on their knees, guarding a pile of dried beans or wrinkled avocados. 'They will have walked for maybe ten hours to come here,' Milfort said. 'They will maybe make a few *gourdes* – one US dollar – and then they will walk back.'

Milfort was a former worker on a cruise ship. When his wife died, he had had to leave his job to care for his handicapped son. The week before I arrived his brother had been killed in a bus crash on the way back from the Dominican Republic – a twenty-hour round trip he had made every ten days to buy firewood. Every time Milfort talked about him his eyes filled with tears. Milfort could not read or write but he had been to England once, accompanying a Haitian dance troupe.

His eyes shone at the memory of London. 'You have the tap-taps [buses] there on two levels. And you have the men who sit outside the supermarket all day just drinking beer. I ask "How can they do this?" and my friend tells me: "The government pays them to do it." What a wonderful country you live in!'

We passed the National Palace as white as toothpaste with wide green lawns. In the ruin of Port-au-Prince it stood out like a child at an orgy. Yet Papa Doc had tortured his enemies here in an iron maiden, a device shaped like a coffin with an interior spiked with stiletto blades. In another room, the raw flesh of beaten prisoners was rubbed with citrus juice, red pepper and a dilute solution of sulphuric acid.

Today its pure white walls were unblemished, apart from a splash of loopy blue graffiti. '*Jésus, L'Unique Solution*', it read.

Milfort was shocked. 'In Duvalier's day [Haitians never call him Papa Doc] this could never have happened. He would have tortured and killed the man who did it and all his family, too.'

Like most Haitians, Milfort felt no love for Papa Doc, yet he was nostalgic for an era when the Haitian trains – had there been any – would have run on time. I had asked Milfort to show me the Columbus statue where Brown and Martha held their secret trysts. 'It is gone,' he told me. 'When Jean-Claude left, the mob pushed it into the sea.' He sighed. 'Truly, there is no respect any more. In Duvalier's time you could sleep easily in your bed. Now there is no discipline. During carnival I was actually mugged in the street. Sometimes I wish the Macoutes would return and knock some sense into people. I tell you, there is no hope for my country.'

This may have been so, but it was hard to feel that way when you were sitting on the Oloffson terrace, downing rum punches and watching *le tout* Port-au-Prince enjoy the evening cocktail hour. Greene spent his nights in Port-au-Prince gambling and brothel crawling, but today the casino had long closed and the threat of Aids had sent the Dominican prostitutes scampering home across the border.

Now, missionaries curled up on the Oloffson's rattan sofas and sipped lime juice. UN employees drank the local Barbancourt rum and discussed the best place in town to find Landcruiser parts. Towards the end of our stay, a group of moustachioed men with tattooed biceps propped up the bar with bottles of the local Prestige beer. They looked like a bunch of Ozzy Osbourne roadies and this is exactly what they turned out to be. They were in town to work with Richard and his 'Punk-voodoo' band RAM, whose music appears on the soundtrack to the film *Philadelphia*. 'Man, once you've seen Ozzy bite the head off a live bat, this voodoo shit don't scare you none,' one said.

Most evenings, you could expect a guest appearance from

Aubelin Jolicœur – a name that translates as 'little dawn, pretty heart' – but who was better known to readers of *The Comedians* as the gossip columnist, Petit Pierre.

Small, dapper and balding, Jolicœur's uniform was a tropical white suit with a Paisley handkerchief dangling from the breast pocket. A silk foulard was wrapped Noël Coward-style around his neck. One hand carried a silver-topped black cane, the other was usually employed caressing the knee of a female guest.

Jolicœur was seventy-five years old. 'You don't look it,' I said sycophantically. 'Of course! People give me thirty-five, forty,' he cried. I had been thinking more in terms of sixty-five. 'I have the vitality of my forties,' he continued. 'But my disappointment is that I live too long.'

On my second visit to Haiti, it was not so easy to track down Jolicœur. I was given the telephone number for the Park Hotel, a ten-minute walk from the Oloffson but a whole day to reach on the Haitian telephone system. When finally I got through he sounded grumpy and distracted – a million miles from the giggling man 'who swung from wall to wall on ropes of laughter' that I remembered.

He said he would call me the following day, but no call ever came. When I tracked him down that evening, he had reverted to the old Jolicœur. 'Oh dear lady, I am over-whelmed,' he breathed. 'I have done my utmost to call you, but it has been so difficult. I am feeling so very stwessed about this.' Jolicœur spoke perfect English but he could not quite master the r's.

He came to the Oloffson at noon the following day and hauled himself on to a bar stool. He ordered a Coke, kissed my hand distractedly and launched into his memories of Greene.

'We were originally introduced by Mr Truman Capote,' he recalled. 'No kidding. He said: "Monsieur Jolicœur, have

you met the celebrated author of *The Power and the Glory*?"
He was here on assignment for *Paris Match*. Later, he said that
if he had described me as he knew me, I would have looked
like an angel among devils.'

He paused, distracted by a made-for-television movie playing on the silent screen above the bar. An American housewife
was picking her daughter up from school. Suddenly, he turned
back to me. 'You must know my dear, that my country is on
the brink of a *lavalas*. Do you know what a *lavalas* is? It is a
landslide.'

In Greene's day, Jolicœur had been the first Haitian PR
man. A cultured man from the southern town of Jacmel, who
liked to boast that he had fathered seven children by seven
different mothers, he used to greet visiting celebrities at the
airport and then write up their stays in his gossip column in
Le Nouvelliste. 'A travel magazine called me Mr Haiti,' he said
wistfully. 'I made this place a mecca for tourism. I introduced
Mr Greene to Roger Coster, the manager of the Oloffson
hotel. I took him to all the parties, I introduced him to
everyone.'

Of Jolicœur, Greene wrote: 'He was believed to have some
connection to the Tontons. For how otherwise had he escaped
a beating up or worse?'

Jolicœur pre-empted such questions. 'Duvalier used to say:
"If Aubelin Jolicœur is doing it there is nothing to fear."
Because I have nothing to do with politics. I have my own
politics. Some people thought I was a Tonton Macoute but it
was simply that I was myself. I used to be a one-man show.
Aubelin was *sans parallel*. Duvalier would want to show the
country to someone important so he would send for me. But
now they have killed tourism, they have killed my country,
everything is destroyed. *Oh, là là*, it's terrible. I cry in my bed
at night.'

In fact, Jolicœur had been known to earn Brownie points
from the regime by informing on critical foreign journalists.
Under the brutal junta of Henri Namphy, he had been
appointed Secretary of State at the Ministry of Information.
Today, he was paying the price. His gingerbread mansion had
been repossessed by Aristide's men. He no longer even had a
car. He was dependent on the kindness of others, a kindness
that was in increasingly short supply. 'He asked Richard to
give him a room at the Oloffson but he said no,' Milfort told
me. 'In fact, Richard won't even give him credit any more.'

I signed for Jolicœur's Coke and ordered him another one.
He leant forward and touched my knee. 'You know, Graham
Greene never experienced hardships here,' he said. 'It was all
hearsay what he wrote. It was a novel. There were political
assassinations then, but that was all. At least there were no
murders. Today it is worse, worse, worse, ten times worse
than it was under Duvalier. Then at least we had a government.
Today it is anarchy. I want to die.'

'What, right now this minute?' I exclaimed.

He laughed for the first time. 'No! When I am with you I
want to live. You are such a pretty girl. But once there were
so many of you. If I did not mention one of them in my
column, she would cry. But now it is June, high season, and
the hotel is empty. Darling, once I would have loved you.
That doesn't mean that I don't love you now, but it is different.
I made a time that was really fantastic and I shouldn't be seeing
what I am seeing now. It's a shipwreck – *un naufrage.*'

He declined my invitation to lunch. The last I saw of
Jolicœur, he was picking his way across the trenches that
surrounded the Oloffson. His white slacks were splattered in
mud and his silver-topped cane was sinking into the mire.

IV

Jolicœur's time was up. A new Mr Haiti was abroad, a Mr Haiti who might like to buy the Oloffson but would never dream of drinking there, a Mr Haiti who lived high above the grime of Port-au-Prince in the suburb of Pétionville, where people live clean and have too much to eat.

There are video rental shops in Pétionville and Internet cafés. There are boutiques selling the latest designs from Paris. There is a country club where the noticeboard advertises specially imported fillet steaks.

This is the home of the MREs – the Morally Repugnant Elite, a name an exasperated American diplomat gave to the top layer of Arab and mulatto families who have reduced Haiti to its present plight.

Fair-skinned, handsome and utterly vacuous, they sit outside the cafés of Pétionville sipping iced coffees, chattering on their mobiles and complaining about their children's exorbitant school fees. They have been educated in America or at the Sorbonne and their language is French with only enough words of the Creole that is spoken by 95 per cent of the population to get through to the servants.

The wives would like to move from this stinking hell-hole, to America or France, but that – of course – is impossible because how could their husbands then organize the drug trafficking that has made them so rich and their country so poor. Colombian cocaine has been slipping through Port-au-Prince en route to Florida for decades – at an estimated profit to the MREs of $200 to $300 million a year. Aristide did nothing to endear himself to these people when he attempted to stop this trade. In his first year in power 4000 pounds of cocaine were seized by the authorities. In his second year, the amount confiscated was zero. Titid had learned that democracy came with a price tag. Today one fifth of all America's nose candy has passed through Haiti.

'We despise Préval,' said Sami, an Arab businessman, sitting by the pool of El Rancho, the 'luxurious, Americanised hotel', where both Greene and Brown stayed on their first visits to Haiti. Dozens of Toyotas were parked in the drive and screaming children ran barefoot across the Italian marble floors. A sign by the bar read: 'All firearms are expressly forbidden by order of the management'.

'But the only way we will make money is to leave him alone,' Sami continued. 'Otherwise the Americans kick up a stink, there is another trade embargo and my wife drives me crazy because our Swiss bank account is frozen and she can no longer go shopping in Paris.'

Just as in Sierra Leone, the Lebanese have a disproportionate influence on affairs here. They control the Big Star supermarket downtown, the art galleries in Pétionville and the burgeoning crack trade. I had been given Sami's number by a retired Irish missionary who had lived in Haiti for twenty years. 'Ring him by all means, but don't grow to like him,' he told me with a wink.

Sami lived in the mountain village of Kenscoff, behind high walls topped with shards of jagged glass. He has a faux-oak front door, a parlour full of reproduction furniture and a fireplace to make the winter nights more bearable. His servants are known as *restavecs*, meaning 'staying with' – children aged between six and fifteen, whom Sami bought from their peasant families in return for broken promises of an education.

'We hate the cold, but the violence downtown gives us no choice,' he said. 'We have dozens of weapons stockpiled to protect us from the poor. My neighbours used to keep grenades in their basement. When there was a riot they would throw them into the crowds. If they blew a few boys' feet off they were happy. When the Americans came, they searched our houses and confiscated everything. A few hours later we bought another lot.'

After a few days in Port-au-Prince, it was a shock to visit Pétionville, to breathe through your mouth again, to watch people living rather than just surviving. There were astonishing things in Pétionville like rubbish trucks and traffic lights and a one-way system. 'Yeah, well they chose to introduce that on the first day of the new school year, when all the parents were bringing their little babies into town after a six-week break,' said Eleanor Snare. 'The chaos had to be *seen* to be believed.'

Eleanor was Boston born and California bred. She was tall and pale with straw-yellow hair. Her face was stained with nicotine and age spots, with bushy black brows shading pale blue eyes.

Decades of smoking menthol Comme Il Faut cigarettes had left her with an alarming cough and a voice like a cheese-grater. Her favourite expression was 'To make a long story even longer', but she was never dull. At every loud noise, she would jump theatrically. 'I thought it was gunshot,' she would explain.

'Haiti is a strange place,' were her opening words to me. 'The place hits you like a strobe, all the colour and noise and smells. And it's full of strange people. You're never quite sure how they came to be here.'

So what was Eleanor's story? 'Well, I met a nun in California,' she said vaguely. 'She was working here and she persuaded me to visit. So I came and I never left. It's a funny thing. I hate the heat and my French is atrocious. So what kept me here for so long? Well, I suppose it is Haiti. Either you love it or you get out, and despite all the problems I still love it.'

Until recently, Eleanor had been the head of the Haitian–American Institute downtown teaching generations of children English. 'Baby Doc was in my class. The other kids hated him, they called him basket head, but of course I always had to give him top marks.' Over the years she had adopted several Haitian children.

'How many?' I asked eagerly.

'Oh, I can't remember. They're brutes, all of them, brutes. But at least they aren't starving to death any more. Although, having said that, one of them is recovering from typhoid and another was recently in a car accident. He bumped into the back of a Suzuki at some lights. He wasn't hurt but he has to keep a low profile for a while. If he's seen on the streets the driver's family might stone him to death.'

Eleanor and I were standing high above Pétionville, at Boutilliers, a once-popular viewpoint centre for the tourists. Half a dozen souvenir sellers sat forlornly on the rocks. At the sight of us, they leapt to attention, thrusting bad paintings and polished conch shells under our noses. '*Pas aujourd'hui, mon ami,*' said Eleanor kindly in a strong American accent. They did not argue. 'Look,' she said.

Below us Port-au-Prince steamed in the heat, a dense smudge dimly visible through the pollution. There was the port, the stadium, the bulbous yellow spires of the cathedral that looked like a pair of udders turned upside down.

The tin roofs of the *bidonvilles* – which even that connoisseur of misery Mother Teresa had been moved to describe as 'Fifth World' – sparkled in the sunlight like cast-off chocolate wrappers. From here it was clear that Port-au-Prince was not a city surrounded by shanty towns, it was a shanty town that had swallowed a city.

Beyond, were fields of sugar cane and beyond them mountains, brown and sun-scorched and stripped of trees. From an aeroplane it is obvious where Haiti ends and the Dominican Republic begins. The country where the tourists go is green and velvety, the other resembles Greene's '. . . backbone of an ancient beast, excavated from the clay'.

To add to its litany of woes, Haiti has probably the worst ecological record in the world. When Christopher Columbus landed in the 'Pearl of the Antilles', 75 per cent of Haiti was forested. Today, the figure stands at 7 per cent. Almost every tree has been cut down for firewood or arable land, although without trees there can be no topsoil, the essential layer of dirt which nourishes crops.

'The Haitians should see that if they cut down trees the crops won't grow,' said Eleanor. 'But they don't – or if they do, they don't care. There is no sense of community here. The elite drive around in their $15,000 jeeps and it doesn't occur to them that this is obscene, and the poor think only of what they will get for firewood in the market, not how their actions will affect their children's lives.'

She sighed as she looked out across the fetid bay. 'You have to find some beauty here, but I have to say it is getting harder and harder. Once I used to tell my students to stay here and rebuild their country. Now I tell them to get out while they have a chance.'

Eleanor's students were taking her advice. 'If you want to consult a Haitian doctor go to Ghana,' Dr Magiot told Brown and today there were more Haitian doctors in Montreal or Boston than in the whole of Haiti.

Once gone, few Haitians returned. Some, however, had no choice. Take Richard, who I met one morning outside the Holiday Inn on the Champ de Mars. 'Hey lady,' he whispered in my ear. 'Do you want voo-doo? A sunny beach? A boyfriend? A girlfriend? Are you English? Do you know Maggie O'Kane from the London *Guardian*?' More proof of the

Haitian adage that any *blanc* – as all foreigners, even black ones, are called – is either a journalist, a missionary or an employee of the American embassy.

Richard was a skinny young man in a striped T-shirt. He had pencil-point pupils, jerky limbs, the anxious expression of a Haitian and the accent of a taxi driver from the Bronx. 'My fee is negotiable,' he said. 'I haven't eaten in days. I wish there would be another coup. Then I'd be making $150 a day.'

For a dollar Richard told me his story. 'I was born in Port-au-Prince, but my family moved to New York City when I was five years old. I spent all my life there, then five years ago I stole a Ferrari. So they sent me to jail for grand larceny. When my time was up, they said: "We are deporting you on grounds of moral turpitude." Before I knew it, I was back in this shithole.' His eyes swivelled furiously. 'I paid my taxes like a good American citizen and look how they paid me back.'

The Americans love dumping things on Haiti. Murderers from Boston, heroin dealers from Miami, hookers from New Orleans all wander the crowded streets of Port-au-Prince trying to make a living. They are easy to spot, because many of them wear dreadlocks, a style the Haitians, a conservative bunch, find ridiculous.

'There was almost no crime here, until the Americans decided to show us how it was done,' Eleanor said. 'Once if you bumped into a prostitute at night she would say "*Bonsoir chérie*" and try to bum a cigarette. Now she would probably murder you for a few dollars.'

Other things the Americans had recently ditched on Haiti included large quantities of toxic waste and medicines that had passed their sell-by-dates or failed FDA tests. Recently scores of children had been killed by a diarrhoea medicine that had been deemed unsafe for the US market. Little had changed since Dr Magiot told Brown how American mill owners in Haiti: 'Grind grey flour for the people out of imported surplus wheat – it is astonishing how much money can be made out of the poorest of the poor with a little ingenuity.'

There is virtually no indigenous Haitian industry, but there are dozens of American-owned factories in Port-au-Prince, such as the Rawlings baseball plant where hundreds of Haitian women are paid $2.70 a day to produce every ball used in the American league. A spokesman admitted that 'it would cost a fortune' to produce a similar number of baseballs in the US.

If the Americans cannot leave some nasty deposit, they take something else away. Until 1983 the Haitian peasants had a banking system based on the number of pigs they owned. Not only did these pigs determine such matters as a son's education or a daughter's dowry, they also tilled the soil, acted as a household dustbin and, in a matter of time, became the stuff of some celebratory dinner.

But then the Americans heard of an outbreak of African swine fever in Haiti. Worried that this would spread to their own herds, they decided the best course of action was to eradicate every one of their neighbour's pigs. Compensation was pitiful at best, at worst non-existent. The new pigs that they imported did not eat old mango skins and household waste but corn imported from Iowa, which the peasants could not afford. 'I think our pigs eat better than we do,' Milfort said once.

Not only did this act destroy the peasant economy, it also dealt a body blow to the Haitian religion. Pigs are essential to voodoo because Erzulie Dantor, the voodoo equivalent of the Virgin Mary, had called the Haitian peasants to freedom in their dreams by telling them to kill a Creole pig and in its blood write: 'Liberty or Death'.

'Ever since they killed all the pigs, the spirits come to tell me they are angry,' Edgard Jean-Louis, a coffin maker and voodoo priest told me. 'They are angry with the government who took away their food, because that's what they eat. If you are holding a ceremony for them and you don't have a pig, it's as if you didn't hold it.'

Because voodoo, of course, is what makes Haiti tick. It is voodoo that makes Haiti so feared by mightier nations and voodoo that helps the Haitians escape from the horrors of their everyday reality. 'I am not against voodoo,' said Dr Magiot. 'How lonely my people would be with Papa Doc as the only power in the land.'

Outside Haiti, voodoo seems weird and scary but there it fits as neatly into its surroundings as Boots into the British high street. Voodoo is everywhere and no one turns a hair. Middle-class Haitians take the spirits every bit as seriously as a German theology professor worships Jesus Christ. 'Hello,' Eleanor cried, waving regally at a tall man in a Hawaiian shirt, limping across the Oloffson terrace. 'I know he's a *houngan*,' she whispered to me.

'A what?'

'A *houngan*. A voodoo priest.' She exhaled smoke from her Comme Il Faut. 'He's a Macoute as well.'

In the Iron Market, in downtown Port-au-Prince, you can pick up your voodoo paraphernalia along with some dried cuttlefish and a packet of Hyde Park cornflakes. There are little red dollies just waiting to be used as pin cushions, there are Barbie dolls pickled in rum bottles, there are miniature coffins emblazoned with tinfoil skull and crossbones. The whole place is so unutterably bizarre that you keep thinking it must just be a show for gullible tourists until you remember again that there are no tourists, only you.

At the entrance to Frantzy Antoine's voodoo temple – or *hounfor* – in the slum of Bel Air on the northern edge of

Port-au-Prince, we were greeted by a mural of a devil dancing with a pitchfork. Inside, we were in Frantzy's home. There was one room about 30 feet by 10, with tin walls and a dirt floor. The grandmother was crushing herbs with a pestle and mortar. The air was full of smoke from the iron stove. Two children were dancing to the radio and two men sat chatting on a camp bed. That was the extent of Frantzy's furniture.

The only clue that you were in a voodoo temple was the brightly coloured streamers that hung from the ceiling like the aftermath of a children's party and the wooden pole that ran down the middle of the room that acts as an 'aerial to catch the passage of the Gods'.

For the first time, I had persuaded Guy to abandon his sunlounger in favour of an excursion to a genuine slice of hoo-doo. Frantzy beckoned us into a room about the size of a pantry. We were in the sanctuary. It was dark in there and unbelievably hot. 'No electricity,' he smiled. 'There's a power cut as usual.'

He lit a candle, so we could see the altar. It was as cluttered as a tart's dressing table, with necklaces, cups, cakes of soap, creepy plastic dolls, silk scarves, mirrors and gaudy chromo-lithographs of the saints, the sort you would expect to find in a Sicilian grandmother's parlour. There was also a selection of sequinned bottles.

'What's in them?' I asked.

'Moonshine to offer the spirits.'

At the centre of the altar was a shrine to the Virgin Mary. Her statue was surrounded by plastic dollies dressed in red and purple gowns that could have been stolen from a young girl's bedroom in Nebraska. Their synthetic blonde locks were wrapped in satin headscarves. On the wall was a mural of St George spearing the dragon. 'He is my *loa*,' Frantzy explained, wiping the sweat from his brow. 'My spirit.'

Voodoo and Catholicism have a lot in common. Greene, who by now had begun to call himself a Catholic atheist, was amused by this. It is a cliché that 80 per cent of Haiti is Catholic but 100 per cent voodoo; but certainly most people have no problem with worshipping on Sundays in Port-au-Prince's margarine-coloured cathedral and the rest of the week in their local *hounfor*.

Voodoo came to Haiti with the slaves of West Africa. They quickly realized that the best way to continue worshipping the spirits of their ancestors was to hide behind their masters' Christianity. So, Ogoun Feraille, the spirit of war, became St Jacques; Damballah, the serpent, became St Patrick who had rid Ireland of snakes, and Erzulie Dantor, the goddess of impossible perfection, became the Virgin Mary.

The voodoo ceremony described in *The Comedians* was full of Catholic liturgy:

Among the prayers were little oases of familiarity, *Libera nos a malo, Agnus dei*, holy banners swayed past inscribed to the saints, *Panem nostrum quotidianum da nobis hodie* . . . the priest came in swinging a censer, but the censer which he swung in our faces was a trussed cock.

Like Christians and Muslims, voodoo worshippers believe in one God, Bondye, who is conceived – quite reasonably in the light of Haitian experience – as being too remote for everyday transactions. These take place with the *loas*, who represent the various forces of the universe. The aim of a ceremony is to persuade the *loa* to come down from heaven and possess one of the congregation.

The first time I visited Haiti I gave Frantzy some postcards of Princess Diana. On my return, she had pride of place on the altar. Her features had been cut out and pasted to a cloth, a sequinned halo sat over her head and her clothes, depicted in hundreds of blue sequins, were the drapes of the Virgin. 'She is like Erzulie to me,' Frantzy said dreamily. 'She loves any man, whether he is rich or poor.'

The *loas* were like human beings. They felt happy or sad, they looked after the people who paid them attention, but grew angry with others who ignored them.

'I don't serve the spirits because I have no time to do it properly,' Milfort said. 'I am too busy working to feed my family. But it does no harm to respect them. If you don't you may be hit by a car or shot.'

My first voodoo ceremony was a stunning anticlimax. I was hoping for headless roosters, bleeding pigs and satanic orgies. Instead, I got a bit of drumming, a lot of singing, and interminable dancing.

The ceremony was held in the home of Edgard Jean-Louis. We could not use his temple because his sister had gone to Miami and taken the key with her. Edgard was sixty-five, tall, skinny, with the chiselled features of a 1940s film star. He lived a few hundred yards from Frantzy, up a flight of concrete stairs. His garden was a flat roof where a rooster was tethered to a chain, unaware of its destiny. A group of young men chatted and smoked on a sofa made from the ripped-out back seat of a car. From there you walked straight into the dark bare room – with the give-away pole in the middle. A flag depicting a mermaid made out of sequins flashed and glinted like a stained-glass window in the light from the dusty bulb. A pot of basil stood on the sill of the small window to keep the air pure. In the corner was a coffin lined with purple satin and on the floor was a design sketched out in cornmeal, the summons to a spirit.

The congregation consisted of fourteen handmaidens in white dresses and headscarves and six men who played the drums and trumpets. During the ceremony, other men and women wandered in off the street to watch. The tourist contingent consisted of me, Guy, and an Englishwoman called Peggy whom we had met at the Oloffson the night before. Peggy was the kind of woman who would have given Greene's friend Evelyn Waugh nightmares. She wore a cheesecloth skirt, John Lennon glasses and had pioneered underarm hair long before Julia Roberts made it fashionable. She whispered to me that she found Edgard terribly sexy.

Edgard led the ritual chanting to greet first the Catholic saints, then the voodoo *loas*. Then he welcomed one in particular – Ogoun Feraille, the spirit of war. The drummers intensified their rhythm and one of the women leapt forward and fell on the ground as if pushed by an external force.

Clambering back on to her feet, she stumbled around the room. Like Brown's servant Joseph, she was being 'ridden' by the *loa* and she moved: '. . . in a circle, the pupils of the eyes turned up so high that I only saw the whites.'

When she lurched into the onlookers, the other women restrained her. Suddenly she began to dance a jerky version of the Charleston. Then she fell on the ground and flailed like a caught fish. Edgard and one of the women held her down. A moment later, she sat up blinking and bewildered, as if she had been snatched from a deep dream.

Guy was yawning. I was embarrassed in the same way you might feel witnessing a bunch of Christians talking in tongues. Peggy had shut her eyes and had opened her hands palm upwards to the ceiling, as she swayed and muttered.

But something else was happening on the floor. Edgard's eyes were angry and bloodshot and his lips curled back to reveal his teeth. Milfort was impressed. 'He has the spirit,' he said. 'I have never seen that before.' Edgard staggered around the room, grabbed a fat woman who had just arrived and pulled her into the centre. He held both her hands, looked deep into her eyes and spoke to her gravely. She shrugged and turned away. He pulled her back and continued to lecture her. 'He is telling her off because she is not taking her medicine for her bad leg,' Milfort said. 'If she does not take it, she will not get better.'

There was more singing, a conga, and then everybody did the twist. Edgard collapsed on a chair and lit up a big cigar. He dragged on it heavily and then popped it in a drummer's mouth. A woman spun round and round the pole as if trying to send herself into orbit.

When the music stopped, everybody fell to the floor laughing, sweating and calling for water. The woman who had earlier been possessed by the warrior god started checking her make-up in a compact. Others lit up cigarettes and chatted. Guy and I stood like Prince Charles with our hands behind our backs. Peggy ran to Edgard, grasped his hands and launched into a torrent of earnest gush.

'You must come and visit me in England,' she said.

Edgard smiled graciously.

'You can come and stay in my cottage in Suffolk. It's four hundred years old.'

'I don't mind that,' said Edgard.

'That was a short ceremony,' Milfort said as we picked our way home over the rubble. 'In the countryside they often go on for days. People fall asleep for hours. Nobody minds.'

Voodoo has had a bad rap in the West. True, there are occasional animal sacrifices and wild dancing, which before the age of rock 'n' roll must have looked like satanic writhing to foreign visitors.

Today, a ceremony looks only mildly more exotic than an end-of-term disco, while the mindless babbling is no more bizarre and only slightly more boring than your best friend after a couple of lines of coke.

But there is an evil side to voodoo, even if foreigners almost never see it. Most peasants ask the spirits to do good, but some want them to harm their enemies. There are *bokors*, black magicians, who for a price will turn people into werewolves or zombies – slaves with fully functioning bodies but no minds.

In the market, I found a statue. It had a plastic doll's head and a bloated papier mâché body. Its arms were made of fabric and covered with dozens of tiny Mickey Mouse stickers. 'Those are *djabs*,' Milfort told me casually. 'Evil spirits. I wouldn't buy it if I were you.'

There are voodoo secret societies bound by oaths of allegiance to the devil and with a status similar to the Mafia's. 'One night I looked out of my window and I saw a secret society marching by,' Eleanor told me. 'They were all carrying coffins and there was a complete, eerie silence. Sometimes they would click two stones together. I was terrified. If they'd seen me, they'd have eaten me.'

Eleanor was a cynical old bird, so this was scary news. She told me she had been the recipient of voodoo spells for both good and evil. 'I twisted my ankle and my housekeeper cured it with orange peel. But then when they were trying to get rid of me from the Institute, they put voodoo powder on my pillow and it burned my face.

'Most people think I'm an eccentric nut,' she continued. 'But I have seen what I have seen. And the truth about voodoo is that it is like electricity. It's everywhere and its powers can be harnessed for good and evil.'

Papa Doc was quick to exploit the powers of voodoo for his own ends. He recruited *houngans* from all over the country into the Macoutes. His lucky number was 22, so he stuck 22 pins into a doll in the shape of his sworn enemy John F.

Kennedy and rejoiced when he was killed on 22 November. He took pains to dress in the top hat and glasses of the most feared *loa*, Baron Samedi, and to address the nation in the Baron's whiny, nasal voice.

But perhaps the most destructive aspect of voodoo is the fatalism it encourages. Haitian proverbs are full of hopelessness. '*Dèye mòn, gin mòn*', is a favourite. It means: 'Behind the mountain is another mountain.'

'Haitians never think anything is their fault,' said a French aid-worker I met in the southern town of Jacmel. 'If the harvest fails, it wasn't because they didn't work hard enough, it's because the spirits didn't will it. If their daughter has diarrhoea, they don't listen to me when I tell them to boil their water. They'd rather spend the money on a new pair of trousers than on fuel. When she dies, they say she was cursed by a *bokor*. Such stupidity – it can drive you crazy.'

'It's true,' agreed Eleanor, when I put this to her. 'If I was a Haitian I would be so angry at the way my country had suffered. But they just shrug and call it fate.'

Yet occasionally voodoo could empower. It was at a voodoo ceremony in Bois Cayman in 1794 that a priest called Boukman drank a pig's blood and exhorted the people to rise up against the army of Napoleon Bonaparte.

In *The Comedians*, a voodoo ceremony acts as a political baptism of fire which cuts across class barriers and persuades both the intellectual bourgeois Philipot and the servant Joseph to join the rebel army in the hills. When Greene wrote *The Power and the Glory*, he saw religion as something that transcended politics; now it acted more as a kind of cultural glue, galvanizing the people into action.

During the ceremony, Joseph is transformed from a limping servant into Ogoun Feraille. 'Joseph was no longer Joseph . . . he ran without a stumble.'

In the same way, a downtrodden wife can be possessed by Baron Samedi and spend an evening smoking cigars and talking dirty. A beleaguered peasant can spend a night as Erzulie with a painted face and a flirtatious manner. Voodoo helps some of the most wretched people on earth transcend their existence. 'Spirits and demons are only the projection of man's own emotional impulses,' Freud wrote in *Totem and Taboo* and Dr Magiot calls voodoo: 'The right therapy for Haitians.'

V

Certainly, of all the people I had met in my travels, Haitians seemed the least in need of a spell on the shrink's couch. It took me a long time to work out how I could feel so happy waking every morning in the wasteland of Port-au-Prince. Eventually, I realized it was because the Haitians were happy – or at least pretended to be. When I went down to breakfast the girls at reception rolled about with laughter when I attempted to greet them in Creole. On the terrace, two German tourists were asking the tuxedoed maitre d' if they could leave their bags in the room after the noon checkout.

'*Non*,' he said.

'But why not? I do not understand what is the problem?' said Mr German.

'*Non*, I think this is strictly against regulations,' said the maitre d', an irrepressible smirk crossing his face.

'I am not with you? Why I may not do so,' continued the German. He looked around in bafflement as the staff all doubled up with laughter.

'He's joking,' Guy said gently.

'But . . . still I am not understanding. What is the joke, please?'

That is not to say that Haitians are simple souls, who don't want clean bathrooms and Tesco Metros like we do. They are just gloriously bereft of what the French journalist de Tocqueville described as 'That strange melancholy which often haunts the inhabitants of democratic countries.' Haitians had bigger things to worry about than my friends at home in a land of relative peace, parliamentary democracy and Lara Croft, and sometimes that meant they were more fun to be with. The wretchedness of the place never ceased to amaze me, but when I think of Haiti what I remember most is the laughter: at the driver of our beaten-up jalopy wolf whistling at a pretty girl; the man being dragged along the street by a pig on a lead, so fast that his feet could hardly keep contact with the ground.

What entranced was not just the cliché of hope among misery, it was the flamboyance that could not have existed in more sanitized surroundings. From the relative safety of the Dominican Republic, where Greene finished his report for the *Sunday Telegraph*, he concluded that the businessmen at the next table's talk of 'dollars and percentages' were irrelevant to Haiti. 'Haiti produces painters, poets, heroes and in that spiritual region it is natural to find a devil too.' It was obvious why Greene was so attached to the place, for in the medieval squalor of Port-au-Prince it was easy to be shocked, but impossible to be bored. Everything was shot through with an irresistible vitality. 'There might be little food in the land, but there was always colour.'

Every tap-tap was like a miniature Dali, decorated with the cheery scarlets and yellows of a gypsy caravan and topped with jolly slogans: '*Que Dieu te bénisse*', '*Merci Maman*', '*Terry I love you*', which sounded like dedications from callers to a Radio 1 phone-in.

In the countryside, where people lived in mud and palm-leaf

huts, where there were no schools, or electricity, clinics or
running water, every door and window frame was alive in
throbbing pinks and violent blues. Even the graves that surround each settlement are hallucinogenic masterpieces with
the crosses painted lime green and violet.

If Haiti has contributed anything to the world, apart from
killer zombie movies, it is art. The canvases of the great Haitian
painters: Philippe Auguste, Ramphis and Stevenson Magloire
and Andre Pierre hang in penthouses in New York and Milan
and are exhibited in Paris and San Francisco. Greene was an
enthusiastic collector and described their style as: '. . . forms
caught in wooden gestures among bright and heavy colours –
a voodoo ceremony, black clouds over Kenscoff, banana trees
of stormy green, the blue spears of the sugar cane, golden
maize'.

'I remember I sold him a Philippe Auguste for some really
ridiculous amount – like $50,' recalled Issa El-Saieh, sipping
Turkish coffee in his gallery with pine floors and high-
shuttered windows that sat on a vertiginous hill behind the
Oloffson. 'Today it would fetch $10,000 minimum. Not that
I'm in this game for the money, but still . . . I must have been
out of my head.'

Of the many people I grew to love in Haiti, Issa was perhaps
my favourite. Now eighty years old, he had been born in
Haiti into a family of rich Palestinians from Bethlehem. 'I am
descended from the Crusaders on both sides,' he said. 'My
grandfather came here to put the president on his knees. But
don't call me one of the elite. The one thing I have never
been is one of them.'

Issa wore a check shirt and white slacks. He had bright eyes,
a wiry body and sounded like Woody Allen on speed. His
parents did not want him growing up in Port-au-Prince, so at
the age of five they sent him to New York. In America, he

learned to play basketball and became a jazz musician playing
tenor sax and clarinet. He gave me a CD with him on the
cover in a lounge suit holding a clarinet. He had sleek black
hair and a Colgate smile.

'Charlie Parker was nuts, but I loved Ray Charles,' he
recalled. 'He said to me "Do you wanna know what the worst
thing is about being blind? When you masturbate you don't
know if anyone is watching." The happiest days of my life
were when I was playing with those guys in New York.
Or maybe not, maybe the happiest time was when I was
overthrowing presidents. I overthrew quite a few, although I
never succeeded with Duvalier.'

Issa returned to Port-au-Prince to make money. 'Besides,
honey, this is where I was born!' He opened the country's
first department store and in 1957, the year Papa Doc took
power, he decided to open a gallery. Issa and Greene had been
good friends. 'I remember him coming here as if it was
yesterday,' he said. 'He used to sit in here chatting to me, but
he would insult any American who came in. Some of them
were really nice people, but he hated them. He was a maniac,
he just didn't like Americans at all, at all, at all.

'His big thing was the Catholic church. This guy was really
Jesus bitten. He had to put a cross this big on his pillow every
night that he stayed at the Oloffson.'

'Why? Was he frightened of voodoo?'

'I don't know, honey. That was just the way it was.'

Greene had made his usual request to Issa. 'He wants me to
take him to a house of prostitution. I can't say that I have
never been to a place like this. It would look like I wasn't a
man,' he giggled. 'Well, I hear that Georgette has a nice place.
Everybody tells me that to get there you turn right at the Shell
station on the Carrefour road. So we walk in and everyone's
staring at me. The people there all buy their clothes from my

mother. I sit there like I'm used to the place and he looks at the chicks and goes upstairs with one of them. I don't drink but I order a rum and Coke, so it looks like I know what I'm doing.'

On another occasion, Greene announced that he wanted to meet the Papal Nuncio, an extremely dangerous suggestion in the time of Duvalier. 'I arranged it so my car would break down a little bit past Carrefour at three o'clock, just as the Papal Nuncio would happen to be driving by. He would see a broken-down automobile and would offer Graham Greene a lift back into the city and that gave them a chance to talk.'

Issa had a walk-on appearance in *The Comedians* as Hamit, the Syrian above whose shop Brown and Martha used to meet. 'Greene was in Santo Domingo when he found out I had been arrested by Papa Doc,' Issa said. 'So he killed me off. Poor Hamit, found dead in a sewer on the edge of Port-au-Prince. I guess that Greene assumed that no one who was thrown into a Haitian jail would ever come out alive. He probably died thinking I was dead too.'

'Why were you arrested?'

'The CIA intercepted a $20,000 arms shipment and someone decided I must have been the guy who tipped them off.' He rolled his eyes in mock innocence.

'And was prison terrible?'

'I'm a pretty cool guy. I can handle any situation. So prison was the best thing that ever happened to me. I lost thirty-six pounds. Kept it off to this day.'

Issa and I spent many happy hours flirting together. 'Honey, you make my eyes go *big* and *red*!' he would cry when he saw me, before launching into some rambling piece of gossip. 'The only reason Clinton gives a damn about this place is because Hillary has the hots for Préval's wife. She's one of those. Didn't ya know?'

His house was a warren of cavernous rooms with canvases stacked ceiling high. Dozens of hangers-on lounged in the yard and the basement was a maze of studios, where artists painted pictures of green jungle full of zebras. 'I remember that sonofabitch Robert Redford. He comes in here, doesn't say hello, shuffles around. So impolite. Then he says: "How much for this painting?" I say: "Ten." He says: "$10?" and gets out his wallet. I say: "I don't think so, buddy. $10,000."'

Why in this desiccated excuse for a country did art flourish so? 'It all comes down to voodoo,' Issa said immediately. 'The Haitians drove out the colonists so early that the religion had a chance to thrive here like nowhere else. Add a pinch of French to a hundred African tribes and you get a unique mix. Then stir in that Haitian lack of logic, which can be so frustrating to the Western mentality, and what you end up with is an art which is the envy of the world.'

VI

Greene became a champion of Haiti. He wrote letters to *The Times* about it and had questions asked in Parliament about America's coddling of the Duvaliers. He was delighted that his criticisms had needled Papa Doc. 'A pen, as well as a silver bullet, can draw blood,' he boasted in *Ways of Escape*.

Yet Greene's anger, once again, was laced with an irrepressible cynicism. The revolutionary overtones that permeated *The Quiet American* are still there in *The Comedians*, but muffled by a stifling sense of helplessness. The novel celebrates courage, rather than hope. Despite his experiences in Cuba, Greene's support for Communism still owed more to his hatred of Americans than to any belief in a permanent solution.

'Haiti was not an exception in a sane world: it was a small

slice of everyday taken at random,' Brown reflects, a fair summary of the conclusion Greene was arriving at after three decades of investigating hell.

Events have proved him right. Haiti is in a worse mess than it has ever been in before, a mess that has defeated the best efforts of the Communists, the Americans, the missionaries and the *houngans*.

There were no political solutions to the chaos, no escape from its bloody history. In Sierra Leone, people feared for their children's future, struggled for answers and strove to forgive the aggressors. The Haitians rarely talked about their situation and seemed unconcerned that their country was heading towards the abyss.

I was still having a good time, though.

On my last night at the Oloffson, I met a middle-aged Belgian. He was 'in construction' and on intimate terms with every trouble spot in the world.

'Haiti is the worst place I have ever visited,' he said.

To me, it seemed the best. My suitcase upstairs was crammed with exotic souvenirs and my head was pleasantly muddled from a glass of neat Barbancourt five-star. Even Guy had been seduced, to the point where he had decided Haiti was going to be the destination for his hypothetical honeymoon.

'I was in Rwanda just after the genocide,' said the Belgian. 'There were corpses everywhere in the street, but there were also little old ladies with brooms, cleaning up the mess. Here it is every man for himself. When a peasant finds trash in his backyard, he chucks it over the wall so it becomes his neighbour's problem. There is no government, no law and the people have no conscience.'

Jolicœur was playing backgammon in the corner. Richard Morse was checking his e-mails in his office. The lights flickered sensing an impending storm and mosquitoes nipped at my ankles.

'Dinner is served,' said the laughing maitre d'.

We ate lobster and drank champagne. The first thunderbolt of the evening cracked just as a nearby vigilante let out a rat-a-tat-tat of gunfire. I caught Guy's eye. 'Don't worry,' I lied. 'It's just a car backfiring.'

6. Paraguay and Argentina

'Yes, it's very peaceful,' my aunt said.
'Only the occasional gunshot after dark.'

TRAVELS WITH MY AUNT

I

When we entered the Paraguayan tourist office in Asunción on Avenida Presidente Franco a young man jumped up from behind a dusty desk hidden under the stairwell and advanced on us with an extended hand. 'Welcome to Paraguay!' he exclaimed. 'I am so happy to see you. I noticed you walking down the street yesterday and I was so disappointed when you didn't come in.'

His name was José. 'You are the first tourists I have seen since February,' he said to Victoria and me as we leafed through a pile of faded brochures advertising the land of 'Sun and Adventures'. It was the end of April. 'It's because of the crisis. No one wants to come here.'

'Why?' I asked hopefully. 'Is it dangerous?'

Through the grimy window, I could see money changers waving sheaves of guaraní – the local currency and mouthing 'Any US dollars?' – just as they had in Greene's day. An Indian tapped on the glass pointing at a tray around his neck laden with Julio Iglesias cassettes. Across the street, under the colonnades there were stalls offering steak knives, a blood testing kit, contraband Chanel No 5. Strapping blonde women loaded shopping into four-wheel drives. A weary looking Korean guarded a kiosk festooned with copies of *Playboy* from around the world. Almost everyone carried a wooden or plastic gourd from which they sucked systematically through a plastic straw. They were drinking *maté*, the local tea, said to act as a mild narcotic and to be responsible for the state of profound apathy that pervaded everything Paraguayan.

'No it's not dangerous. Not really. But people never come anyway. The latest situation was the last straw. You are the only tourists in Paraguay.'

II

Paraguay is famous for nothing except obscurity. Like Haiti, no one can find it on a map. 'Is Paraguay where Uruguay is?' asked one friend, when I told her of my latest destination. No one has ever knowingly met a Paraguayan. And this, of course, makes the country the perfect hiding place for every sort of fugitive.

To Greene's Aunt Augusta, the elderly heroine of *Travels With My Aunt*, Paraguay is the perfect 'journey's end'. After a lifetime of transgressions, she and her Italian war-criminal lover, Visconti, settle there to spend their twilight years dabbling in a spot of Paraguay's 'national industry': smuggling. Their fellow expatriates are a living Chamber of Horrors. 'Martin Bormann is just across the border in Brazil and the unspeakable Dr Mengele of Auschwitz is said to be with the army near the Bolivian border,' Aunt Augusta says.

To a sleaze collector, Paraguay is like a penny black or an autographed first edition. If anywhere symbolizes Greeneland it is this tiny country locked between its giant neighbours of

Brazil, Bolivia and Argentina. In Paraguay, Greene ended his lifelong quest for depravity. In his fiction, he allowed Aunt Augusta to wallow in the amorality of Asunción, yet his own feelings – expressed in a *Sunday Telegraph* article in 1968 – are of firm disapproval for this 'land of deep tranquillity . . . where wind blown oranges lie ungathered along the country roads'. 'What price', he asks, 'is the lotus-eater prepared to pay for his tranquillity? Here he will pay not in dollars for a luxury suite with double windows against the traffic (there is no traffic), only with the half-closed eye and the prudent pen: to live here one would be charged in the quite small currency of the conscience.'

Greene went to Paraguay in 1968 when it had been ruled for fourteen years by General Alfredo Stroessner, the kind of military dictator who makes Augusto Pinochet look like a softie. In *Travels With My Aunt*, Greene's digs at the General were relatively subtle. Greene saved his real attacks on the regime for *The Honorary Consul*, published in 1973, the story of a bunch of blundering Paraguayan revolutionaries based over the border in Argentina. Their leader, Rivas – a former priest – describes the situation in his homeland: 'People like the General make law and order. Electric shocks on the genitals . . . Keep the poor ill-fed and they do not have the energy to revolt.' Rivas is the son of a rich Asunción lawyer. 'My father paid a lot of money to the Colorado Party so there was no trouble for him when the General came to power,' he says, recalling how his father once sacked a gardener because he had stolen a few pesos from a garden seat.

There were revolutionaries like Rivas – but men like his father were more common. Paraguay ran on expediency and few complained at home or abroad. 'In this blessed land of Paraguay,' says Visconti, 'there is no income tax and no evasions are necessary.' Augusta's nephew Henry Pulling adds:

There had been unpleasant stories in Buenos Aires about [the General's] early rule – enemies tossed out of aeroplanes into the jungle, bodies washed up on the Argentine shore of the two great rivers with their hands and feet bound with wire, but there were cheap cigarettes on the street and cheap whisky in the stores . . . and even the bribes were not unreasonable if one were doing well and could pay regularly . . .

Today, there is still no income tax in Paraguay, whisky costs only $3 a bottle and cigarettes are around 50 cents a pack. The country is a haven for international terrorists, organized criminals, and every imaginable species of common hustler – such as Greene's Czech manufacturer who tries to sell Visconti two million plastic straws on the basis that he could persuade the people to drink *maté* through them.

Paraguay had not always been so venal. In the eighteenth century it was generally regarded as a utopia, thanks to the work of the Jesuit missionaries who organized the Guaraní Indians into craft-based communes 'without a thought of gain or personal advantage', according to Robert Cunninghame Graham, a British historian. 'Food was abundant, poverty was unknown, and its correlative, riches, equally unknown.' Even that old cynic Voltaire was moved to describe their work as a 'triumph of humanity'. But then the Spanish conquistadors grew jealous of the missionaries' power and sacked the monasteries.

From then on it was as if somebody had switched the lights off. Today in the Paraguayan jungle American missionaries hunt for Stone Age tribes and you can still find the descendants of an Aryan colony, set up by Nietzsche's sister, Elisabeth. In the thorny wasteland of the Chaco desert, Moonies worship in heavily guarded farms and school lessons are still taught in German to blonde children in plaid shirts and dungarees, great-grandchildren of pacifist Mennonites who fled their country rather than fight in a war. Post apartheid, hundreds of white South Africans fled here knowing that they would receive a warm welcome.

Asunción is one of the few capitals in the world still to retain a Taiwanese embassy. The right-wing Nicaraguan dictator General Anastasio Somoza escaped here after his deposition, and lived happily for many years in Asunción until he was gunned down in the street one day for failing to keep up his bribe payments to Stroessner.

Travels With My Aunt is the story of hidebound Henry, a retired bank manager from Surrey, who enjoys a dull domesticated life of the sort that made Greene shudder. He meets his flamboyant Aunt Augusta at his mother's funeral. Together they travel the world. Gradually Henry stops worrying about his dahlias and ends up married to the Asunción chief of police's daughter and running his own smuggling business.

Like everywhere in Greeneland, Paraguay runs on unpredictability. Henry begins to appreciate that the best way to enjoy life is to know that at any minute it may be snatched away. 'Tomorrow you may be shot in the street by a policeman because you haven't understood Guaraní . . .' his aunt points out. 'My dear Henry, if you live with us you won't be edging day by day across to any last wall.'

My friend Victoria and I arrived in Paraguay on a connecting flight from Buenos Aires. Like Greene, we stayed at the Gran Hotel del Paraguay, a former 'millionaire's house' to the west of the city with carved pineapples on the gateposts and a garden full of orange trees, just like Aunt Augusta's. On the patio toucans swung from their perches in rusting green metal cages and late at night you could hear the *thwock* of tennis balls, as the children of the Paraguayan elite took lessons from a pro on the floodlit clay courts.

In the wood-panelled lobby, two elderly women dressed all in black spent every evening playing bridge at a round table draped with a flowery cloth. They looked like Joan Crawford and Bette Davis. Victoria and I always greeted them politely but they glared at us in return and their bony hands shot to their powdered jowls as if we might snatch the pearls that nestled there. A man in a checked shirt sat slumped on a sofa watching us suspiciously with his boss eye. A dwarf laden with carrier bags full of whisky edged nervously past us.

No one seemed to like us at the Gran Hotel. The reception-ist was a bulbous-nosed woman with a squint, dressed all in black. Her father, we learned, lived across the road in one of the many sumptuous mansions that flourish in the suburbs of Asunción. He had been a minister in Stroessner's cabinet and he had known Graham Greene.

'We would very much like to meet your father,' I said.

She looked at me as if I had just vomited on the carpet. 'Not possible!' she said and turned her back.

'Why?'

'He is too old.'

'Well then, please will you give him a letter? If he wants to see us after that, it's up to him.'

She stared at me in patent disbelief, and then turned to the boss-eyed man and addressed him in high-speed Spanish, of which I could understand the words 'foreigner', '*Daily Mirror*', 'as if . . .'

'I don't work for the *Daily Mirror*,' I said.

The entire room was looking at me as if I was carrying the Ebola virus.

We did have one friend. 'English!' said the bellboy who escorted us to our room. He was small and skinny, middle aged with floppy black hair, curranty eyes and thin nervous lips. He wrung his hands continuously as he spoke. '*La Principesa Anna* stayed here once you know?'

'Really?' It seemed unlikely.

He told us that dinner was at eight. It was 8.30 already so we went to the dining room. It was deserted. We asked for a menu. The bellboy, who had replaced his grey uniform with a white tuxedo, looked at us strangely. 'I said dinner was at eight.'

'We know. Here we are.'

It was another half hour before he produced menus and another twenty minutes before he took our order. Ten minutes after that, two silver-haired Germans and their guests – two young and noisy local girls in tight leggings – arrived. They returned repeatedly to the buffet to heap their plates with croquette potatoes and clinked wine glasses to cries of 'Salud!'

Cockroaches ran across the tablecloth. We ate river fish and drank Chilean wine. The high walls were decorated with murals of trellises of vines and flowers in pastel blues and greens. The masks of comedy and tragedy floated above the words *In Vino Veritas*. It was the motto of Madame Eliza Lynch, who had once lived here, a woman who, according to her English doctor, 'could drink more champagne than anyone I have ever met without being affected by it'.

Madame Lynch was the Irish-born mistress of Francisco López, one of the least known and most bloodthirsty dictators in history. His qualities, as listed by his biographer, Robert Cunninghame Graham, consisted of 'sadism, an inverted patriotism, a colossal ignorance of the outside world, a megalomania pushed almost to insanity, a total disregard for human life or human dignity [and] an abject cowardice that in any country in the world but Paraguay would have rendered him ridiculous'.

López did everything he could to destroy Paraguay by pushing it into the suicidal War of the Triple Alliance with its neighbours Brazil, Argentina and Uruguay. It lasted from 1865 to 1870 and resulted in the loss of 55,000 square miles and 80 per cent of Paraguay's adult males. Towards the end boys were being sent into battle with painted moustaches. For decades afterwards, polygamy flourished in Paraguay and most important jobs were held by women.

López had had suspected traitors deposited in ant hills to be eaten by ants, or put out in the sun with their eyelids cut off. While his population were eating the bark from trees, he kept a fine cellar of vintage champagnes. He killed two of his brothers, tortured his sixty-year-old mother, and was about to sign her death warrant on the day he was finally captured and killed by enemy forces.

A woman of consummate ambition, his mistress Eliza encouraged him in his quest for power. The dining room we were in had been her ballroom, where she taught Asunción high society the polka and gallop and forced the society ladies, who despised her, to donate their jewellery to the 'war effort'.

Today the preferred way to get around the room seemed to be on hands and knees. As the room filled it became clear that a substantial number of guests at the Gran Hotel were less than one year old and, judging by their squashed expressionless features, native Guaraní Indians. Their parents, however, were usually blonde and their comments about the buffet were made in French or English. 'They have come here to adopt,' said the bellboy. 'It is easy to do in Paraguay. The regulations are not very strict.'

Back in our room we turned on the news. There was a report on car clamping, which had been introduced to Asunción that very week, including vox pops with outraged citizens, horrified at this infringement of liberty. 'That was the nine o'clock news,' said the presenter.

'I thought it was ten o'clock.'

I rang reception. 'Is Paraguay in the same time zone as Argentina?'

'No, *Señora*. We are one hour behind.'

III

But in Paraguay, you sensed that you were not one hour behind Argentina but twenty years. Henry noted when he arrived in the city:

. . . it was a very Victorian town. One soon ceased to notice the cars – they are an anachronism; there were mule carts and sometimes men on horses, there was a little white castellated Baptist church, a college built like a neo-Gothic abbey, and when we reached the residential quarter I saw big stone houses with bosky gardens and pillared porticos above stone steps which reminded me of the oldest part of Southwood, but in Southwood the houses would have been split into flats and the grey stone would have been whitewashed and the roofs would have bristled with television masts. In place of the orange and banana trees, I would have seen neglected rhododendrons and threadbare lawns.

The whole city felt as if it had been doused with air freshener. The breeze brushed softly against your cheeks and 'in spite of the dirt and fumes of old cars the air was sweet with orange blossom'.

Today downtown consists of a few ailing skyscrapers and some shabby squares. There are no clothes shops but dozens of dressmakers; no supermarkets, but a German delicatessen selling bratwurst and Knockwurst, pickled herrings and pumpernickel bread. We passed the Munich bar and its rival – Bavaria. In a café just off Plaza de los Héroes, run by a Korean mother and daughter, we drank tea from chipped flowery porcelain cups while the Beatles played in the background. At the central railway station, a steam engine was sitting on the tracks – the last on the continent still to be in use. The only element of Greene's Asunción that was missing were the trams, which had clattered up and down the city's hills for years after their retirement from Brussels, their walls lined with notices in Flemish and French prohibiting spitting. Now they had been replaced by a fleet of equally ageing buses.

Paraguay's isolation is no accident. The conquistadors ignored Paraguay, because it lacked gold. The few who did settle there often married into the ruling Guaraní families and adapted to their society. 'The upper classes kept up an appearance of wearing European clothes but only when in Asunción,' wrote Cunninghame Graham. 'Upon their own estates they wore linen jackets and trousers, and passed a good deal of their time swinging in hammocks that they kept moving with a naked toe touching the ground . . . all classes and both sexes smoked continually.'

Decrees from the empire arrived late or not at all. Slavery and serfdom flourished in Paraguay decades after they were abolished elsewhere. When the Paraguayans deposed their Spanish governor and declared independence in 1811, the Spanish government declined to contest the action because the colony was so insignificant and economically unimportant. José Gaspar Rodríguez de Francia soon emerged as the strongest member of the revolutionary junta, and in 1814 he declared himself dictator for life.

El Supremo liked to dress all in black, apart from a scarlet cape, and passed a law that everyone in the country should wear a hat so they could doff it when he passed. He recognized that Paraguay was unable to compete economically with her neighbours. The Spanish elite were executed and those who remained were forced by law to intermarry with the Indians. He sealed the borders and proclaimed a state of total self-sufficiency. Newspapers and fiestas were banned and he seized the property of landowners, merchants and the church.

Francia ruled by terror. John Parish Robertson, who claimed to be the first Englishman to visit Paraguay during his dictatorship, described the cells where Francia held his opponents: 'They are small, damp, vaulted dungeons of such contracted dimensions, that to maintain an upright position is impossible in them, except under the centre of the arch. Here it is that, loaded with irons, with a sentinel continually in view, bereft of every comfort, left without means of ablution, and with a positive prohibition to shave, pare their nails, or cut their hair – here, in silence, solitude, and despair, the victims of the Dictator's vengeance . . . pass a life . . . to which death would be preferable.' A contemporary remarked that no one knew that Francia was human until he was dead.

Francia, however, was merely an appetizer to what was to follow. He was succeeded by Carlos Antonio López, a man of prodigious appetite described by an Argentine contemporary as 'a great tidal wave of flesh . . . a veritable mastodon', who constructed the railways and docks and built up the army. He was succeeded by his son, the aforementioned Francisco, who brought the country to its knees in the War of the Triple Alliance. Thirty years afterwards, just as Paraguay was beginning to recover, another stupid war broke out against Bolivia over non-existent oil in the Chaco, an unpopulated desert region. Another 100,000 men were lost. It said much for Asunción that the cathedral was tucked away and insignificant, while one of the most splendid buildings in town was the

Pantheon of the Heroes, modelled on *Les Invalides* in Paris, where General Estigarribia – the man responsible for this last fiasco – lay in sepulchral splendour, guarded by ramrod soldiers in full dress beside the bodies of Francia and López senior and junior.

'These men were megalomaniacs, psychopaths,' said our Argentine friend, Eduardo Seferian, whom we met later on our travels. 'But the Paraguayans still view them as heroes leading their plucky little country into wars that destroyed everything. I suppose one person's bloodthirsty tyrant is another's idol.'

After the Chaco War, a round of dictatorships, coups and civil wars followed, until the country came under the 'rough hand' of Stroessner, who ruled his country for thirty-five years. Stroessner's human rights record was horrific, but, as usual, the Americans tolerated his atrocities in return for a strict anti-Communist line. 'We and the General are like that,' says Tooley, Greene's CIA man raising his thumb and forefinger. In 1989 Stroessner was finally deposed in a coup and Paraguay enjoyed its first democratic elections.

Today Stroessner lives quietly in exile in Brásília, although polls show that the Paraguayans, far from cursing his name, would have no objection if he returned to Asunción to die. They also show that Paraguayans are less enamoured of democracy than other Latin Americans. But why should they be when corruption is still rampant, economic growth has tailed off, and more than a third of the population are living in poverty? There is no tradition of political protest in Paraguay. As Tooley explains: 'Who's going to make a fuss about an odd body or two? The General keeps the peace – that's what the people want after the civil war they had.'

Yet, suddenly it seemed that things might be changing. A month before our visit Paraguay had almost seen a revolution

– the 'situation' José in the tourist office had referred to. It was triggered when the Vice President, Luis María Argaña, was shot dead by gunmen in the pay of the President, Raúl Cubas. Such events were so normal in Paraguay that normally no one blinked an eye – but this murder hit a nerve. Suddenly, the Paraguayans realized they might lose their new democracy. There were riots in the street. Demonstrators demanded Cubas's resignation. The army shot at protestors from city rooftops, killing eight young men and injuring sixty. Finally Cubas fled to Brazil to join his old chum Stroessner in exile and a new coalition government was installed.

We walked down the hill to the port, where Henry Pulling disembarked from the river boat that had carried him from Buenos Aires. A fishing boat was unloading. A few yards away stood López's Gothic presidential palace that had been built by five-year-old boys under the direction of Alonzo Taylor, a British architect. The design was said to have been originally intended for Keble College, Oxford, but came second in the competition. A few policemen in grey raincoats and peaked caps slouched around the entrance.

In the neighbouring square, the Plaza del Independencia, where Henry observed soldiers goose-stepping in front of the cathedral, a small crowd had gathered outside the salmon-pink legislative palace. They were chanting slogans and waving placards in the air: '*Asesino*' '*Corruptos*' '*Traidores*'. Beside them on a plinth that in Henry's day bore 'a very early tank', was an array of fading wreaths to the men who had been killed. Paraguay's tiny middle class – 'well meaning men and women of the left', according to Greene but 'not the stuff of revolutionaries' – was determined no one should forget this moment, the nearest their country had ever come to insurrection. In the colonnades of the Palacio they had mounted an exhibition of photographs: cars burned, mounted policemen squared up to a mob, young men in Che T-shirts charged at riot shields, and men were carried away on their friends' shoulders, their faces streaked in blood.

Yet according to the British ambassador there was still a way to go before revolution. 'Recent events were very much confined to that Plaza,' he said. 'Everywhere else, life went on as usual. Major football matches were played. But at least someone was making a bit of noise.'

It had not been hard to get an appointment with the ambassador. I had rung up and tentatively requested a briefing.

'He's free now,' said his secretary. 'Why don't you come right over?'

The embassy was in a new building in the smart suburbs. When we signed the visitors' book, I noticed that the last entry was six weeks ago.

'It can feel a little isolated here,' the ambassador giggled. 'Princess Anne did visit once though.'

He was a youngish, bland man who seemed fazed at the direction his career had taken him. 'Still, I feel quite hopeful for this country now,' he said. 'When Stroessner went it wasn't the work of the Paraguayan people, it was because a colleague betrayed him. At least this time people did stand up in the face of the police. I think they suddenly realized that they had a democracy and they had better treasure it.'

Stroessner learned he had been ousted one afternoon in 1989 when he was visiting his favourite mistress. His nemesis was his military chief of staff and his son's father-in-law, General Andrés Rodríguez. Everyone expected that one nasty dictator would simply be replaced by another and was surprised when the elections Rodríguez promised actually took place.

The surprises stopped here, though. Stroessner and Rodríguez's Colorado Party won by a landslide just as it had won every puppet election for the past thirty-five years. 'Argaña, who was murdered, always said that the people would vote for Donald Duck if he was the Colorado Party candidate,' the ambassador said.

Yet support was gradually petering out. The ambassador continued: 'Cubas had 54 per cent of the vote, a fact he frequently alludes to, saying "I have the overwhelming majority."' But then Cubas, he went on to explain, was nothing more than a puppet. The real power in Paraguay belonged to his friend, General Lino Oviedo. Oviedo, who was known as the 'Bonsai horseman' because of his diminutive stature, had been jailed for ten years for plotting the assassination of the former President, Juan Wasmosy. After only a year, however, Cubas released him and sent him to live in Argentina. Now Oviedo plotted the overthrow of his enemies from a ranch that belonged to his dear friend President Menem. Increasingly, I had the feeling that we had walked into the pages of a Tintin book.

We went downstairs, to find the first secretary, an ebullient Scotsman who looked about nineteen, in conversation with a silver-haired man with a broad flat face, whom he introduced as Hernando. 'We're just discussing what we could do to honour the Paraguayan navy,' he said. In a landlocked country, this came as surprising news.

Hernando Silvero, OBE, had been working at the British Embassy for nearly forty years and had served as Greene's interpreter during his visit. He ushered us into an office with one eye on his watch. The concept of overtime does not exist in Paraguay and everything stops at four. 'Greene was not a great speaker. He didn't ask too many questions, but it took him only perhaps a minute to encapsulate an observation which might have taken other people many years,' he said, sitting in an armchair and surveying us disapprovingly over the top of his spectacles. 'We visited a couple of places where he wanted to go . . .' He leant his chin on his fingertips and smiled. 'Some first-hand exploring of human nature. But he is dead now so I won't say any more.

'He also attended a rally of the Colorado Party because he wanted to see how much support the government had. Everyone was in red because it was absolutely essential to show your devotion to the Party by wearing a red tie and not only that, it had to be combined with a red handkerchief which you wore in your breast pocket. He noticed that although it was very hot and people were perspiring, no one dared to wipe their brow. You couldn't desecrate the symbol of the Party.' Hapless Henry did not know this and was thrown in jail for blowing his nose on a red handkerchief outside the Colorado Party headquarters on National Day.

Greene always liked to boast that he had upset Stroessner by telling a party of school children about the bogey-man figure of Fidel Castro. Silvero was not sure. 'If anybody of importance came to Paraguay, Stroessner made sure someone took an interest in them but it was never very oppressive. Stroessner was so certain of his destiny and of his position that he never really suspected anyone could subvert it.'

Silvero had been most impressed by Greene's observations of the 'sad Guaraní' songs accompanied by a harp that played constantly on the radio. 'When Greene visited, Paraguay was coming out of a long period of sadness and melancholy and we were not inclined to cheerfulness. We had only just opened up our radios to Argentina and the rhythmical go-go style and still we preferred the sad wailings of the harp. To us being sad and melancholy is a way of enjoying ourselves.' The same, of course, could be said of Greene.

We asked him about Stroessner, whom he had grown close to when he 'advised' him on policy for the Falklands War. 'He was a man who inspired a lot of respect and a lot of loyalty in a way which it would be impossible for the Western mind to understand. He was not rude. He was not someone who imposed his presence. People just had a natural respect and a natural fear of him. He was like a medieval king. If he touched somebody he transferred his power to them and if people were close to Stroessner, they had a lot of power. I refused to laugh at his jokes and he liked me for that. I remember going to a wedding once and people queued to touch my hands just because I was in favour.'

In the tradition of all great Paraguayan dictators, Stroessner had encouraged an insular mentality in his landlocked nation. 'He was always telling us how efficient and good we were, and that was what we wanted to hear. The Paraguayan people are very *machista*. They like to think that they don't need the rest of the world. The Americans keep trying to pressure us to take the opinions of the world into account. But the ruling party couldn't care less what anybody thinks.'

Today, Paraguay still makes no attempt to woo the outside world. The country does not maintain a single tourist office abroad. To be fair, its attractions are limited. Even the diligent Lonely Planet struggles to find reasons for visiting the country. It comes up with the 'hydroelectric projects at Yacyreta and several national parks, although access is difficult to most of them'.

'There's birdwatching,' said the ambassador, after a long pause. 'And the Iguazú Falls, but they're not even in Paraguay.'

Victoria and I had already visited the sandstone ruins of Trinidad, once the most important Jesuit mission on the continent. They were situated down a dirt road marked only by a sign that read 'Paraguayans owe . . . to the tourism industry'. The missing words had been ripped out. There were no postcards of the site, no bar, just a ticket seller who looked amazed, but not particularly pleased, to see us. We had the place to ourselves all day. Across the border in Argentina, we learned, similar sites were filled with coach parties.

There was, however, one major tourist attraction in Para-guay – Ciudad del Este, formerly Puerto Stroessner, that the President had named a free port, thus anointing it as the headquarters of the country's celebrated smuggling industry. Ciudad sits in the eastern corner of the country tucked neatly between the borders of Argentina and Brazil making it an ideal base for contrabandists. 'What have they got to smuggle?' Henry asks. 'Scotch whisky and American cigarettes,' explains Tooley, the CIA agent. 'You get yourself an agent in Panama who buys wholesale and he flies the stuff down to Asunción. They are marked "goods in transit", see. You pay only a small duty at the international airport and you transfer the crates to a private plane . . . Then your pilot takes off to Argentina just across the river . . . You unload into trucks and there you are. You've got your distributors waiting with their tongues hanging out. The government makes them thirsty with duties of one hundred and twenty per cent . . . [but] All the goods that come in from Panama don't go on in the Dakota. What do the police care if some of the crates stay behind?'

Most of the stuff that stays behind ends up in Ciudad, which pulls in $14 billion a year as opposed to Paraguay's official GDP of $9 billion. There are 15,000 shops crammed into Ciudad's twenty blocks, as well as hundreds of stalls selling merchandise of extremely dubious quality. You can buy or sell anything there so long as it is not made in Paraguay. It sounded like my idea of paradise.

We travelled to Ciudad on a wheezing bus with worn red leather seats that took us through the sprawling outskirts of Asunción, past Korean video stores, flower stalls, breeze-block shacks and liquor shops. The countryside was a tangle of shiny banana leaves with sleek brown and white cows grazing in lush pastures. The Swiss influence was at work here in A-frame timber houses and restaurants named Tyrol. By the roadside were fruitsellers – hard-faced Indian women in blue and green robes – and boys who waved baskets of empanadas and fried chicken at us.

The bus stopped everywhere to drop off old men with darned cardigans and to let on travelling booksellers who would dump their box by the driver and then walk up and down the aisle muttering as if to themselves about their new romances and tracts on digestive health. No one appeared to pay the slightest attention to these spiels, yet at the end half a dozen hands would wave their guaranís in the air demanding service. At one point we passed through a tiny town with an enormous stadium on its outskirts. This, the driver explained, was Colonia Iguazú, a colony set up by the Japanese government for expatriate cotton growers. A little later, we saw a sign pointing to Nueva Australia.

Our first impression of Ciudad was a two-lane, smog-choked bridge that acts as the frontier between Paraguay and Brazil. It was jammed with lorries, vans and private cars – Brazilians crossing the border to pick up goods at tax-free prices which no one seriously expects them to declare. The thin pavement that ran alongside was just as busy with Brazilians bent double under overloaded satchels full of the fruits of a spending spree. Small boys pushed towering hand-carts laden with fridges, videos and stereos. We arrived at the Brazilian frontier. A policeman was sucking on his *maté* gourd in the shade. 'Will you stamp our passports?' I asked. He laughed at me. No one wants evidence of their trips in and out of Ciudad.

Now we were in Foz do Iguazú from where we wanted to visit the Falls – despite Tooley's judgement that they were

'Just a lot of water.' As soon as you crossed the border, you realized what a time warp Paraguay was languishing in. Less than a mile from Ciudad men wandered the street bare chested and in skimpy shorts. Women swayed past in hot pants and skimpy vests. There were hoardings everywhere for Coca-Cola and Toshiba. I remembered the women in stuffy Asunción wilting in their pantyhose and knee-length skirts, the men in their tidy suits, how in the absence of neon we had fumbled our way along the night-time city streets. When we checked our watches we were unsurprised to learn that Brazil was one hour ahead.

We returned to Ciudad the following day. Everyone warned us to be careful there. After all, three tonnes of cocaine moves through the city every month, not to mention vast quantities of Paraguayan-grown marijuana. Body parts are for sale, as well as false identity papers for the country of your choice. Murder costs $1,000 for a non-white victim, a Caucasian only slightly more. Ciudad is a home-from-home for Colombian drug cartels, Chinese Triads, Japanese Yakuza, Italian Mafiosi, Russian gangsters and Nigerian bandits. Ciudad is where Hezbollah based itself while planning the 1992 bombing of the Israeli embassy in Argentina that killed twenty-nine people. The Egyptian El Said Hassan Ali Muhammed Mukhlis, a suspect for the tourist killings in Luxor, as well as bombings of the US embassies in Kenya and Tanzania, lived there for five years. In 1998, he was arrested by Uruguayan police as he left Ciudad to plant a bomb in Britain. But all we found were showcases full of Kevin perfume, muffin makers, paddling pools, ice-cream scoops in the shape of pigs that oinked when you squeezed the handle and trays of fake Gucci watches. I couldn't even track down a pair of fake Levi's.

Hard times had fallen on Ciudad. Three months before we

arrived the Brazilian *real* crashed, losing a third of its strength against the dollar. Now Ciudad no longer represented such a bargain. 'It's been a disaster,' said Khalil, another of those Lebanese businessmen who populated Greeneland, to whom I got chatting in his electrical goods store. 'Last year there were so many people in here you couldn't have put a piece of dental floss between them. Now no one. We need our Brazilians. The whole of Paraguay is feeling it.'

Yet despite the economic situation, the world capital of organized crime had the atmosphere of a country village. At night, Victoria and I walked the city streets without even attracting a catcall. Taxi drivers unfailingly switched on their meters and asked us if the radio was too loud. There were no beggars on the street. At three, everyone in town took a siesta. It made sense. Why pickpocket a tourist when you have a major credit card fraud ring to organize? Ciudad del Este had the safest feel of anywhere in Greeneland.

IV

From Ciudad we crossed back over the border into Argentina and took a smart air-conditioned bus to Corrientes, four hours away and the setting for *The Honorary Consul*. Corrientes is a small colonial city on the banks of the wide Paraná river surrounded by grasslands and cattle ranches. 'My friends in Buenos Aires couldn't understand . . . [why I wanted to go there],' Greene wrote in *Ways of Escape*. 'They said . . . the city had no interest at all.'

Greene's passion for Corrientes was puzzling. He had discovered the city by chance when his riverboat stopped there for half an hour on the way to Asunción. 'When I wanted to write a novel about a man accidentally kidnapped by guerrillas

I calculated that the Tupamaros or the Montaneros [Argentinian terrorist groups] were much too calculating to make such a mistake,' he told an interviewer in 1979. 'If the novel was to be plausible, they had to be Paraguayans, sufficiently cowed by Stroessner's dictatorship to be still inexperienced. Then I remembered Corrientes on the Paraguay/Argentine frontier.' In 1970 he returned there for a fortnight's stay.

Corrientes had penetrated my imagination like the first injection of a drug . . . a few lights along the quay, a solitary sentinel outside a warehouse, a small public garden with something resembling a classical temple, and the slow tide of the great river – those were all on which I based my expectations.

Arriving in Corrientes, I felt inclined to agree with Greene's friends in Buenos Aires. It was lunchtime when our bus arrived there – the riverboat no longer existed, and the only sound was that of barking dogs. The roads were empty apart from a pick-up truck with some shabby Indians in the back. The driver mouthed an obscenity at me. I knew that most of the soldiers who fought in the cold Falklands were from this tropical town and it made me a little nervous. The streets were lined with low modern houses, it was raining heavily and the shops whose 'overlapping signs and slogans stuck out over the sidewalk' giving the place a 'Chinese look' were all closed. Backwater was too vivid a word to describe this town that was 'founded long before Buenos Aires by the *conquistadores* coming from the north'.

We were staying at the Gran Hotel del Turismo, a building designed in the style of a country house with low dark beams and shiny wooden floors. Greene had stayed here too but called it the 'Nacional'; he used its terrace that overlooks a broad curve in the Río Paraná as the setting for the dinner when Dr Plarr, one of the protagonists of *The Honorary Consul*, tries and fails to convince his friends to form an Anglo–Argentinian Society that will write to *The Times* about the kidnapping of the town's honorary consul.

Of all his novels, *The Honorary Consul* was Greene's personal favourite. It is the story of the eponymous Charley Fortnum, a lonely, ageing Anglo-Argentine with a penchant for the bottle who runs a farm outside Corrientes. He falls in love with and marries Clara, a girl from the local brothel, who is grateful for his kindness and his money. Later, Fortnum is kidnapped by Paraguayan revolutionaries who mistake him for the American ambassador and, even when their error is revealed, refuse to release him. They believe that the British government will put pressure on General Stroessner to free some political prisoners in return for their captive's safe release. They are wrong.

Dr Plarr, who happens to be Clara's lover, is summoned by the kidnappers to tend to Charley. He fails to convince the guerrillas of the honorary consul's unimportance. He argues with their leader, his old schoolfriend and a former priest, Rivas, about whether a man of God can justify such bloodshed. Eventually, the police attempt a rescue mission. Plarr and Rivas are killed. Charley survives, having just learned that Clara is carrying Plarr's child.

The warnings to Greene that nothing ever happened in Corrientes proved completely unfounded. On his first day, the local paper reported the kidnapping of a Paraguayan consul from a nearby town after he was mistaken for the Paraguayan ambassador. In *Ways of Escape*, Greene describes his consternation at the news: 'How could I plan a novel so clearly anticipated by reality?' Yet a few days later, Stroessner told the kidnappers to do what they wanted with their captive, since he was on a fishing holiday and did not want to be disturbed. The consul was released and forgotten and Greene felt able to continue with his story.

Perhaps, however, he had been influenced by a different incident. Andrew Graham-Yooll, the Anglo-Argentine editor of the English language newspaper the *Buenos Aires Herald*, whom we met later, was convinced that Greene's story had another source. In 1971 Stanley Sylvester, the British honorary consul and manager of the Swift Meat Packing Company in Rosario, was abducted by a Marxist revolutionary group as he left his home to buy a loaf of bread for breakfast. His captors said that he was an agent of the 'Yankee Monopoly' and as such 'an enemy of the people'. Swift was asked to donate $50,000 in food and blankets to Rosario's slum dwellers. They did and Sylvester was freed one week later.

Graham-Yooll wrote to Greene asking him if he was aware of the incident. 'I received a frosty letter in reply, saying he had never heard of Sylvester and was disturbed by the similarities to the case,' he recalled. 'When I later interviewed him on a visit to BA, he again claimed no knowledge of it, but I fail to see how this could be possible.'

Whatever the truth of the matter, the kidnapping was far from the only excitement during Greene's brief stay in Corrientes. On the second day, a liberation-theology priest who worked in the *barrio*, or slums, was ejected from his church by the archbishop, sparking protests from the congregation. The archbishop was then put under house arrest by the governor.

Another day, a small bomb was found in the cathedral and on the last day a family were drowned when the suicidal father drove them off the jetty into the deepest point in the river.

We had one contact in Corrientes, a Mr Eduardo Seferian, about whom I knew little except that he spoke good English and was very knowledgeable about Greene's stay in the city.

The night before we left Paraguay, we faxed Eduardo explaining the purpose of our journey and asking if we could meet. A few hours later, the telephone shattered my deep sleep. ''Ullo, is that Jew-lee-ya?' said a broad Manchester accent. 'It's Seferian 'ere. I 'ave received your fax and would be delighted to meet you. 'Ow about dinner? I'll pick yew up at the hotel.'

Victoria and I spent a lot of time discussing what kind of man Seferian would be. 'Stooped, elderly, spends a lot of time in the library,' I said. 'Whatever we do we must make sure that we pay for dinner,' said Victoria. 'Why does he have such a strong Manchester accent?' I wondered.

At 7.30, we were waiting in the lobby of the Gran Hotel. A small balding man with a beaky nose and smiling eyes offered me a smooth hand. 'Miss Smith,' he said. 'I am Eduardo Seferian. I think we'll have dinner at my house tonight. There are simply no decent restaurants in Corrientes.'

He ushered us outside to a white Mercedes. 'Allow me,' he said, opening the door. Clearly we were not expected to offer to pay our share of the petrol.

It was night, the rain had stopped and I understood the charm of Corrientes. Nothing had changed since Dr Plarr surveyed the city from the terrace of the Nacional: 'The city was beginning to wake up for the evening hours after the long siesta of the afternoon. A chain of cars drove by along the riverside. The white naked statue in the belvedere shone under the lamplight.'

The narrow streets were full of yellowing autumn leaves. In Eduardo's car we glided past the 'block of yellow flats', one of the city's 'eyesores' where Plarr lived. Its façade was covered in streaks of black mould. In the 1970s the only link between Corrientes and its rival town Rosario on the north shore of the wide river, the colour of 'coffee with too much milk', was by ferry. Now a long bridge joined the two towns. As its foot was the 'white Gothic prison', like a 'sugar decoration for a wedding cake', today an army barracks.

Eduardo was in his fifties, the son of an Armenian father and an English mother. He was born in Manchester, where his father owned a cotton mill. 'But then the slump came and we had to get out so we moved to Romania,' he said, turning right into a tree-lined side street. 'From Romania we ended up here in Corrientes.' And what did he do? 'I own some cotton mills.'

We parked outside a two-storey, modern house behind a high metal gate. We were greeted by barking dogs and a maid in a black and white uniform, like something out of a French farce. Standing in the hall was an older version of Sharon Stone, tall, slim with short blonde hair, high cheekbones and a wide, expensive smile. She wore pinstripe trousers, a blue T-shirt and discreetly expensive silver earrings. 'Hi,' she said extending a manicured hand. 'Nice to meet ya. I'm Muffy.'

We never discovered where the name Muffy came from, but then so many of her details were indefinable. She had the neutral glamour of the jetset, who buy their jackets in the Rome branch of Valentino and their trousers at Dior in Dubai, luxury boutiques so generic they deprived her of any definable background or nationality. Her English was perfect but tinged with a Spanish accent. She was in her fifties although grooming made her appear much younger. In Corrientes she was an even more incongruous figure than Eduardo. 'Where are you from?' Victoria asked her.

'Born in Kansas, but never been back,' she said. 'I live in BA now, except when I'm here with my Edward.'

Eduardo's house was the kind in which James Bond might have entertained Pussy Galore. It had tiled floors covered in thick Persian rugs. A chandelier hung from the ceiling. There was a portrait of the Queen in one corner and a bar whose glass-plated surface protected dozens of photos of Eduardo on the golf course. He opened a bottle of pink champagne. There were nibbles on a tray divided into twelve subcompartments: bite-sized chunks of ham and cheese on cocktail sticks, black and green olives, pistachios and peanuts.

'I can tell yew all about Graham Greene's stay in Corrientes,' Eduardo said excitedly. 'I know exactly who he based his honorary consul on, the one played by Michael Caine in the film. Well, actually, he was based on two people. The first was Michael Roderick Bittlestone. Bittlestone's father was a general in the Indian army. I'm sorry – in the British army in India, because if you said the Indian army, he corrected you immediately. He was born in Baluchistan and he came here to manage a farm. When the war broke out, he volunteered and went back to England. He joined the navy but only twenty-four hours out of Southampton, he was torpedoed. He was saved in a lifeboat, then after two years in the forces, they kicked him out because he was epileptic. He came back here and became destitute. To survive, he taught English. He used to say he had taught the language to half of Corrientes. "Learning English gives you a start in life," he said. He was doing quite well, but he let himself go a little bit.'

'He got into the Indians didn't he?' Muffy asked.

Eduardo took no notice of this. 'Michael decided he wanted to get his British passport back but they said to him "You are Pakistani". He said: "I'm no more Pakistani than the man on the moon." He had to make very strong representations at the embassy and finally he got his passport back. Then I wrote to the British Legion and a gentleman called Mr Walker who was their top man in BA. Luckily, he had been in the same boat as Bittlestone after the torpedo and he remembered him, although Bittlestone hadn't the faintest idea who he was. So he got a pension from the British Legion, which was lucky because he got ill and couldn't get out of bed. He had terrible bedsores. I used to go and see him.'

'You took care of him,' said Muffy.

'I beg your pardon?'

'You TOOK CARE of him.' I began to realize that Eduardo was not wilfully ignoring Muffy, he was simply deaf.

'Well, I did as much as I could.'

'You did everything for him. Physically, mentally and morally.'

We were sitting down now and eating large rumpsteaks accompanied by bowls of french fries. 'We broke our diets for you,' Muffy said.

Eduardo continued: 'Bittlestone felt lonely so he put an ad in the paper saying that he wanted female company but he couldn't afford much. An Indian woman volunteered. But she was a bit of a frivolous person and she put the horns on him as they say, with a man who worked in the coastguard here. After a bit she announced she was expecting a baby. Bittlestone told me that there was a 50 per cent chance he was the father. I said: "Don't be silly." He said: "All right then, 30 per cent." Graham Greene was in town when all of this was happening and he became good friends with Bittlestone. But when he visited the home, he immediately sensed that the wife was playing around and all of that went into the book.

'In the end the mother ran off with this fellow, so Bittlestone ended up bringing the daughter up on her own. He died last year. She must be in her twenties now and she looks Indian, I must say.'

'Why didn't you tell me about the little girl?' Muffy demanded.

'I didn't think you'd be interested.'

'Oh Edward. Don't be stupid.'

'But there was another model for Fortnum too?' I asked. Jock, the terrier, had his nose halfway up my skirt.

'Yes, there was John Cook, the farmer. He was Scottish and his wife was English. They were very nice people, but he liked his drink and he also ran around. He liked to go to the house of ill-repute. He had a farm called *Las Tres Marias* and he was a very shrewd businessman, a solid hard worker, but by ten in the morning he was drunk on a bottle of gin. He went to these parties and pinched the ladies' backsides and things like that. He was always very congested in the face from the drink. He only died last year, and his family all live in BA now, but they have taken terrible exception to the book. They say: "I wouldn't read it for anything in the world. That Graham Greene is a Communist."'

Eduardo had never actually met Greene, having been in Buenos Aires when he was in town. 'But then you're lucky to find me here now,' he brightened. 'Half the time I'm in BA, half the time I'm at my house in Punta del Este. Muffy has a house in Punta too, don't you?'

'Yes, sweetie. That's where we met. I used to jog along the beach and pass Edward every morning. Finally, I stopped and said hello.'

Muffy and Eduardo had been going out for nineteen years, but had never married. When Eduardo told her that two foreign women were coming to dinner, she had taken a taxi to the airport and caught the first plane up to Corrientes.

Like Greene's friends in the capital, Muffy couldn't comprehend her lover's attachment to Corrientes. 'Edward loves it here and his business partner is happy to let him do all the work – he says it's far too rough for him. I make the most of it when I come here. For Christmas, I got Edward to install two bathrooms in this house. Most women would have wanted a diamond ring, but I wanted porcelain. In the mornings, I jog along the riverbank and watch the smugglers unloading their contraband. All my best thoughts come to me when I'm jogging. That was when I realized that I must divorce my husband. Then I do an aerobics class with the women from the town. One said to me, this morning: "Do you know how my husband and I decide who will get out of bed first in the morning? I lift my husband's *pollo*. If it drops to the left side I go, and if it drops to the right, he goes." They make me laugh.'

After Muffy's escape from Kansas, she had been brought up in England and educated at a posh girls' boarding school in Gloucestershire. At nineteen she married a Uruguayan prince. 'We were married for twenty years and had three children before I realized what a mistake I made. I think he still wants me back.'

Eduardo meanwhile had never been married. 'He's a busy man,' his girlfriend told us proudly. 'He owns the local football team, Mandiyu. Who used to train them sweetie? To TRAIN THEM!'

'Eh? Oh. Maradona.'

When Eduardo dropped us back at the hotel, the doorman's eyes grew wide. 'Was that Señor Seferian?' he asked.

'Do you know him?'

'Everyone knows him. He is the man who saved Mandiyu. You just had dinner with him? *Es un ídolo.*'

V

In the morning, the sun was shining and the charms of Corrientes were complete. This was a city of frangipani and avocado trees, small parks, modest statues and 'old colonial houses'. Yet, in reality, the town was a compound of dozens of disparate, foreign elements – proof of the words of Borges, Argentina's most famous writer: 'Our entire country is imported. Everyone here is really from somewhere else.'

Greene's 'bust of an admiral with a homely Irish name' which stood in a small square by the waterfront was a homage to Admiral Dr William Brown, a native of County Mayo and the founder of the Argentine Navy. Eduardo told us that in one engagement during the Independence Campaigns of 1810–25, he ran out of shot for his cannon and resorted to hard cheese to rout the enemy. Eduardo also showed us the Italian Club, where Greene's Englishman Dr Humphries ate goulash prepared by a Hungarian chef, a splendid colonial building painted beige with table football, a bar, and an all-weather soccer pitch at the back. The night before I had been looking for Eduardo in the telephone book. I found him listed after Schweitzer, Schuster and Schoerer. 'Most of us here are half Spanish and half Indian,' Eduardo had said. 'We do nothing but breed cattle and drink *maté* all day. Across the river in Rosario they're all Yugoslavs and Italians and they work hard. We are rivals in everything – football, basketball. We even challenged them to a golf tournament once, although in those days we had no course, just a letterhead. Popescu's father said: "We shall never beat the buggers." I said: "Don't worry, golf is a game for good-for-nothings" and we have been thrashing them ever since.'

Dr Bogdan Popescu was the man we were going to see that morning. His name marked him clearly as another immigrant. He was a clinician who had been born in Romania but had lived in Corrientes nearly all his life. We visited him in his office at the local hospital. He was in his fifties, with a bald head and blue-rimmed glasses perched on the end of a beaky nose. His left eye drooped like a wilted flower. Under his white coat, he wore a suit with a red bow tie. He was very kind and very serious. Greene had met him when he was a young man of twenty-six and used him as his model for Eduardo Plarr.

'In my youth I was admiring of Graham Greene,' Dr Popescu recalled. '*The Power and the Glory* impressed me a lot because it showed the difficulties in your religious beliefs. My English teacher, Michael Bittlestone, told me he was staying in town and that he had taken him to a brothel. Then one evening I was dining with my wife on the terrace of the Hotel del Turismo and he was there. I was very shy in that part of my life but I dared to go and see him. He was very gentle and he invited me to stay at his table. For me it was very emotional.

'We talked about his book and he told me he was here because he wanted Corrientes to be the scenario of one of his novels. He enjoyed very much staying here. Then we talked about his religious beliefs. He was in a shirt, without a tie and very sober. I remember him perfectly. It was a very nice encounter. I understood him and he understood me.'

The result of Greene's stay had deeply impressed the young doctor. 'He described so well our reality. I remember the paragraph about how the doctor had never seen anyone reading in the city. Well, here people didn't read too much. Now we have a university and it's changed, but in that time he was very unusual.'

Dr Popescu was nothing like the dashing Dr Plarr of my imagination, but this last remark made me see the connection between the real man and the fictional character. Like so many Argentinians, both men 'would always be a stranger and would never properly be assimilated'. Popescu's parents had fled the Romanian Communists. Plarr is the son of a Paraguayan mother and English father. His foreign blood makes him the typical Greene protagonist, isolated on the margins of his society.

'I speak Spanish fluently and my wife is from Corrientes, but I wouldn't say I am from Corrientes,' Popescu said. 'I feel very comfortable here, but sometimes I am not well adapted. At times, I feel like a stranger, not because the people here are not very kind but because the Latin American concept of life is not like Europe. I can't speak for all Europeans, but my parents lived for work, for self-realization. Here, they live for fun, for the *joie de vivre*. They are more natural people and they have more fun, but they lack rigour. They have no desire to educate themselves or to live responsibly.

'That is why there is such a big contrast between poverty and riches here. This is one of the poorest provinces. One in ten people are illiterate here, other people can read and write but they don't know how to interpret what they are reading and writing. Equipment and drugs are inadequate. I don't think you can be happy if the people around you don't have their minimal needs, but the Corrientinos are happy because they sing songs and go to carnival.'

Like Plarr, Popescu had devoted himself to helping the poor of the *barrios*. This was exceptionally brave behaviour in the early 1970s when anyone showing compassion for the disadvantaged was likely to be labelled a subversive, and risked becoming a target of the military government's men in sunglasses who drove Ford Falcons and helped undesirables 'disappear'. I could see shades of Greene's revolutionary priest, Rivas, in Popescu too, especially as he recalled what had been gnawing at his soul that evening at the Hotel Turismo. 'I was very idealistic and I was also very concerned with ideas of religion,' he said. 'I found the Catholic religion had aspects that were very severe and were not realistic about what really happens in the world. There was no tolerance in that time and Greene saw that that was what I was thinking.'

'Did you recognize yourself in the novel?'

'Some friends of mine said I was the doctor,' Popescu said with shy pride. 'I don't know. I would be so pleased to be that person.'

I asked him if I could take his photograph. 'No, thank you. I would rather not,' he said as he shook our hands. 'I am so different now from how I was then. I would rather be remembered as the young man.' Later, Eduardo told us he was suffering from myasthenia gravis, an autoimmune disorder that had also afflicted Aristotle Onassis and given him the same droopy eyelid.

The following morning, Eduardo drove us to 'Señora San-chez's' brothel, where Fortnum met Clara. The Corrientinos knew it as *El Tiburón* – the shark. We found it in the suburbs, a low white building with 'no exterior signs to differentiate her establishment from the other houses in the respectable street'. It had a red tin roof with fleur-de-lis running along its rim. At the front a low white wall was crowned with green metal railings. 'They were to stop people bringing their horses in,' he giggled. 'You could get straight off yer horse and into bed.'

Eduardo stopped a passer-by and asked him what went on there. 'Once it was a – you know,' he smirked. 'Today, it is a student hostel.'

Eduardo drove us to the airport past the *barrios*, an untidy collection of tin-roofed shacks on the marshes on the edge of town. 'The people there have no bathrooms, but they all have televisions,' said Eduardo as we purred past in the Mercedes. 'Mind you, I'd do the same. You can only have a bath once a day, but you can watch television the whole time if you feel like it.'

He had done everything he could to secure us a passage on a boat down the River Paraná. 'But there are no boats these days,' he said wistfully. 'It's such a shame. I remember making

that journey myself in the 60s. There was a swimming pool
on board and you dressed for dinner. But the best thing was
the jungle that lined the river. You could hear the mun-kays
'owlin'.'

VI

Buenos Aires was in gridlock. The students were on strike and
were blocking the roads. Outside Aeroparque airport six lanes
of traffic honked, fumed and tried to find a way out of the
morass. Volkswagens bumped over the central reservation.
Taxis bowled along the pavement. A green Fiat and a black
and yellow taxi sat in a stubborn head-to-head like two stags
with their horns locked. Businessmen dismounted from the
airport bus and ran frantically through the traffic towards their
flights. Other passengers trudged along the verge like pilgrims,
wheeling their suitcases behind them. A television cameraman
arrived and ran from car to car collecting outrage.

We had already been late leaving Corrientes because lightning had hit some vital piece of airport equipment. Now we
had been sitting in the traffic for one hour and had perhaps
moved a hundred yards. Our taxi driver had slicked-back grey
hair and heavy-lidded eyes. '*No puede ser,*' he chanted dolefully.
'I don't believe it.' He swapped indignation with the other
drivers. He called his wife on his cellphone. 'She's not here,'
squawked a female voice over the hands-free monitor, 'she's
gone to the hairdresser's.'

Ahead of us to the west, the sun was setting over the
apartment blocks. Behind us on the bank of River Plate were
the mock Tudor towers of the Buenos Aires fishing club.
Victoria buried herself in the guidebook.

'According to this, Argentina is the most underpopulated

place on the planet,' she said with a wry look out of the window.

VII

Of all Graham Greene's travels, those to Argentina seemed to have attracted the least attention. Yet he visited there several times in the late 60s and early 70s, and both *Travels With My Aunt* and *The Honorary Consul* contain episodes set in Buenos Aires.

Perhaps Buenos Aires has never been considered part of Greeneland because Greene so clearly disliked 'the skyscrapers, the traffic blocks, the sirens of police-cars and ambulances, the heroic statues of liberators on horseback'. He was uncomfortable among the anomalies of the 'great sprawling muddled capital with its *fantastica arquitectura* of skyscrapers in mean streets, rising haphazardly and covered for twenty floors by Pepsi-Cola advertisements'. Most of all, however, he disliked Argentinians. At the time of his visit the military dictator General Videla was ridding society of all subversives. Yet the bourgeoisie epitomized by Plarr's mother, with her passion for sticky cakes, seemed unmoved by the kidnapping, torture and murders. 'She read no newspaper and never listened to the radio, and Harrods and her favourite tea shop remained open throughout all the troubles.' Harrods, of course, was the best shop in town – the only branch outside London, established in 1913 with all the bricks, ironwork, woodwork, cement, windows and installations sent from England. At the moment, however, it was closed for renovation.

This was a country that made its fortune exporting beef to Europe during the two world wars and that harboured Nazis and Jews in equal measure. Its military leaders had killed far more people than Pinochet, yet nobody even remembered their names – let alone attempted to bring them to justice. Once Greene might have felt a frisson at being surrounded by such evils, now in old age his sympathies lay staunchly with the kidnappers in Corrientes.

'Greene had an aversion to Buenos Aires,' said Andrew Graham-Yooll. 'He knew that there was an elite living off vast tracts of land and cattle, and he also knew that there was a guerrilla movement springing up. He liked to shock a society which saw reds under every bed by telling people how much he admired Castro. I remember accompanying him to the cattle show of the *Sociedad Rural Palermo*. He turned to me and said, "Isn't this a bore? Is there anywhere we can go and get a drink?" After that, someone came up to me and said: "I don't know what that man's doing here. He's a Communist."'

As usual, Greene disliked discomfort and the establishment in equal measure. When he visited he usually stayed with his literary agent Victoria Ocampo, a scion of one of Argentina's most prominent anti-Perónist families, in her palatial house in the smart riverside suburb of San Isidro.

'Ocampo was in an unhappy marriage from the word go, so she went into the big-name friendships with the most extraordinary people like Greene and Borges,' Graham-Yooll said. 'He must have enjoyed staying there, he would have had a great view from his bedroom of the river and when he came into town for cocktail parties and press conferences, he would have had a chauffeur-driven limousine. Yet, I still can't imagine that he was anything but hostile to the place.'

'Why?' I asked. We were sitting in the scruffy offices of the *Buenos Aires Herald* near the wide Río de la Plata. Outside the traffic screeched past; inside there was the loud creaking of a printer disgorging the copy of the following morning's edition.

Graham-Yooll looked surprised that I even had to ask. He himself had been sent into exile during the military junta and had only recently returned to his native land.

'Well,' he said. 'This is a very easy city to hate. It's my city and I live right in the middle of the smoke and the noise, just three blocks from Harrods and when I step out it's an awful place. There's the level of pollution, the level of noise, the broken streets, the poor service in many situations.

'And then there's the isolation. When Greene was here, Argentina could quite easily have been an island. We didn't care about the rest of the world. We ate steaks, we played football, we had the tango and we distrusted all foreigners. We thought they were all spies.

'Even the telephones didn't work in those days. You had to get down on your hands and knees and beg the operator to let you call your mum across town. In Chile, you could pick up a handset and be connected to anywhere in the world. I don't know if Greene had to use the phone terribly much, but he wouldn't have liked it if he did. Oh, we're terribly isolated. Just think about it. This is the last place the plane gets to before it turns back again.'

I found it hard to grasp the point of Buenos Aires. It was too far away from anywhere and when you finally arrived all you found were McDonald's and Wendy's and Burger Kings. The shops sold 'really English' tweed jackets and Barbour waxing kits. The cafés had pretensions to be French and the trendiest restaurants were all Italian. In the nineteenth century, Buenos Aires had been an immigrant's dream, a bigger and richer version of Europe with statues, cobblestones and whole buildings shipped in. The Colón opera house is billed as 'Just as magnificent as La Scala.' In the harsh surroundings of Latin America Buenos Aires represented unimaginable sophistication. People called it the 'Paris of the Americas', but if you knew the genuine article you could only be disappointed.

As a South American country it failed too: there was none of the romance you felt in its Latin neighbours. There was no Indian culture to give the place perspective and depth, because the early settlers had slaughtered all the natives. Instead of the undulating beat of salsa, the city moves to the anguished rhythm of the tango whose dancers entwine and separate with eyes averted, in a physical enactment of the joyless lust of the bordellos where the dance's roots lie. The corrugated-iron houses of the La Boca quarter, painted all the colours of a tube of Smarties, may have launched a thousand tourist brochures, but when we visited there we found that the gaudy façades consisted of a single street and concealed dilapidated slum dwellings.

Only the diet seemed authentically Argentinian. The room-service menu in our hotel read: 'Loin steak, full-breaded beefsteak, Neapolitan breaded beefsteak, beefsteak with french fries or salad, loin beefsteak with some salad, omelette'. A stuffed cow in the window of the restaurant next door lured in the punters.

We had lunch at the Café Richmond, in Calle Florida, once the Argentine version of Bond Street or Fifth Avenue, with shops selling furs, perfumes and European antiques. Now it was lined with tatty record shops and fast-food outlets. Plarr's mother had loved nothing better than to sit here 'in unrelieved black before a plate of sweet cakes'. For all I could see, she was sitting here still on a red leather chair, surrounded by elderly women in pearls. The walls were panelled with mahogany, brass chandeliers hung from the ceiling. A sad rubber plant sat in the corner. Waiters in green waistcoats and red bow ties hovered around a misted-up cake counter.

The best table, in the window, had been taken by three old

ladies, with pussy bows around their necks and Home Coun-
ties accents. 'Of course, all along she had been having an affair
with her publisher,' cried one, forking her rum baba and
gulping her glass of red wine.

They were Anglo-Argentines, products of what at the time
of the First World War was the biggest British community
outside the Empire. They had been born in BA and educated
there at St Hilda's School for girls, speaking English better
than Spanish and keeping their heads down during the Falklands War. When they visited Britain they splurged in M&S.
When they returned to BA for the long summer, they spent
every Sunday at the Hurlingham Club on the outskirts of the
city, preparing sandwiches for the post-cricket teas. Only
with their children's generation had they begun to witness
'inter-marriages'. The Swedish, the Germans and the Yugoslavs maintained equally rigid communities. 'In America, they
would have become American the minute they stepped off
the boat,' Eduardo had said of them. 'Here they hang on to
their identity for generations.'

Victoria and I should have blended with these sober people,
carrying furled umbrellas, but if anything we were more of a
novelty in BA than we were in Paraguay. People nudged us
as we passed and asked us for the time, to determine our
accents. They seemed desperate for our approval, but expected
us to hate them.

One afternoon, Victoria dropped her purse in a café. When
she returned an hour later, it had gone. It was Victoria's own
fault and it could have happened anywhere. But the manager
was mortified. The woman sitting at our table put her head in
her hands with embarrassment.

'Things like this happen in the Argentine,' she said in
night-school English.

She was wearing a fur jacket and her face bore the stamp of

some skilful surgery. In the café's gilt-framed mirrors, I could see a hundred people just like her, in soft leather jackets and designer jeans. They talked on their mobiles and flicked through copies of *Elle*. It was impossible to imagine a crowd more svelte.

Yet according to the newspapers, Argentina was a mess. 'What has become of us?' wailed the headlines. Unemployment stood at 14 per cent. Prices were far higher than in Europe or America. Shortly after we left an aeroplane crashed on to the same road where we had sat with our angry taxi driver, killing sixty-seven people. 'It's a wonder it didn't happen earlier,' said the leader writers.

The Argentinians did not accept their lot. Every day there were fervent demonstrations against corruption in the law courts, or at the government's treatment of the elderly. The student marches made us late for our 'girl's night' at Clemmie's, a friend of a friend, and someone, we were told, typical of the Argentine upper classes. Clemmie was twenty-five, blonde and pretty and worked in an art gallery. She was getting married in November, but for now she lived with her parents next door to the Alvear Palace, the city's smartest hotel, in an apartment filled with oil paintings and bronzes of horses. Clemmie's mother was Argentinian. She had softly spun candy floss hair and smelt of Joy perfume. Her father was British. 'S'pose I'd better kiss you, everybody bloody does here,' he grumbled.

Clemmie's friends wore pearl earstuds and velvet Alice bands. They sat in a circle around a glass coffee table, gossiping and helping themselves from two-litre bottles of Coke and Diet Coke. 'What would you like to drink?' Clemmie asked us.

Victoria and I looked at each other. 'Wine,' we said.

This caused a bit of a stir. Clemmie was gone for a long

time. She came back with two glasses filled with ice cubes. 'We didn't have any wine in the fridge,' she apologized.

To the girls, Victoria and I were as bizarre and far more fascinating than two Guaraní Indians. 'Are you married?' they asked us, timidly. They were all engaged and every Saturday that winter was booked up with someone or other's reception at the Hurlingham. 'Not married? A boyfriend?'

'Yes, but I'm not planning to get married,' I said.

'No,' said Victoria. They gazed at her in wonder. 'But you are in your thirties,' said one.

Another girl sidled up to me on the sofa. 'Tell me, in England do girls usually drink wine in the evenings?' she said in tones that implied 'Do English people often shoot up in public?'

Clemmie announced that we should order empanadas. 'How many would you like?' she asked, the phone tucked under her chin. 'Two?'

'Three,' I said.

Everyone else ate just one. I remembered that Argentina has the highest incidence of anorexia in the world.

Most of the girls were going to honeymoon in Miami, where Argentinians are known as the *Demidos* – gimme two – because goods are so cheap there that they always buy in bulk. 'Don't go shopping in Argentina,' they implored us. 'It's far too expensive.' They lived at home because they could not afford to move out.

These tales of hardship confused me. Who lived in the cypress-shaded streets? What about the shopping malls I saw everywhere, with their ice-rink floors and opulent boutiques? They were busy twelve hours a day. Who was spending money there?

Clemmie laughed. 'No one actually goes there to buy anything,' she said. 'We just go there to meet our friends and be seen.' A phrase swam into my head and wouldn't leave: fur coat and no knickers.

VIII

Muffy, on the other hand, probably wore a fur coat *and* fur knickers. She had returned from Corrientes to her apartment in BA. When we rang her, she told us somewhat reluctantly that Eduardo had insisted she took us to lunch at the Hotel Lancaster, where Greene's Henry Pulling had stayed en route to Asunción. On occasion, Greene had stayed there, too, claiming it was the only place in town with good linen sheets. It was an undistinguished Georgian building, slotted into the towering *belle époque* buildings of the Avenida Cordoba, just a few blocks from Harrods. The dining room was a light, bright room with low chandeliers and rococo chairs. Grey-suited businessmen talked in low voices and forks tinkled against china. Muffy, looking gorgeous in a grey suit, regaled us with scurrilous stories about Prince Andrew and Fergie – a regular sighting on the BA circuit since her mother ran off with an Argentinian polo player. She broke off to study the menu.

'Jeez! Willya look at these prices?'

She clearly wasn't sure if she liked us or not. I looked for the cheapest thing on the menu. 'I'll have a salad.'

'I'll have the pasta,' said Victoria. She was speaking with difficulty, having been bullied that morning by the bored employee of a beauty salon into having her non-existent moustache waxed.

'Will you? Well, we'll have mineral water with gas. The bubbles fill your stomach so you eat less. I'll have the salad to start and then I think the *setas*. Oysters. Delicious!' A thought

occurred to her. 'Are they in season?' she asked the waiter.
He wore elbow-length white gloves.

'Yes, *señora.*'

'Then where do they come from?'

'The woods near Buenos Aires. Picked this morning,
señora.'

'The woods? But they're seafood aren't they.'

'No, señora. *Setas* are mushrooms.'

'I never did get the hang of this Spanish,' she said happily.

We got quite drunk and everybody relaxed. 'Do you know
how to eat pasta?' Muffy asked Victoria. 'You twist it around
your fork like so.' A moment later, she leant across the table
and flicked Victoria's hair. 'You know, you should dye this.
The grey is showing through.'

I was beginning to understand that Muffy didn't hate us,
she felt threatened by our freedom to travel the world and the
bond we shared with Eduardo over Graham Greene. 'So why
aren't you and Eduardo married, Muffy?' Victoria retorted.

'I don't know. He is my darling, but he just won't do it.
Once I got so fed up with him not asking, I left him. I took a
cruise round Europe for a year to get him out of my system
but it just didn't work. I think the real problem is his sister.
He's devoted to her and she hates me. I never have said a
word against her, but still she makes him afraid to marry me,'
she said. She glanced around the room conspiratorially. 'I
think she's a *witch.*'

'Maybe she thinks you're after his money?' I said.

'I hardly think so, darling. After all, I'm a *Rockefeller.*'

After that, I didn't feel guilty about ordering pudding and
coffee. The bill for three was $220.

After lunch, it was back to Muffy's apartment hidden behind
glass and metal doors on Avenida 9 Julio, the widest street in
the world. A maid waved at us from the kitchen as Muffy

whisked us through light and airy rooms, stopping at the grand piano covered in photos of beautiful women and handsome men. 'That's my son's wedding – he's living in Miami now. That's my daughter's – she was a naughty girl, got pregnant at sixteen and insisted on keeping the baby. That's my brother with my sister-in-law. She murdered him, but I still adore her.'

She showed us a copy of *Gente!*, a publication so excessive it made *Hello!* look like the *Church Quarterly Bulletin*. On the cover was a picture of a slightly startled Muffy cheek to cheek with a shorter, swarthy man. 'Muffy Rockefeller dances the tango with President Menem,' read the caption.

Even by the standards of this continent, the President was a flamboyant man. When his wife annoyed him he had an army officer forcibly remove her from the presidential palace. When he was accused of marital infidelity, he retorted: 'I am not a philanderer, I am a seducer.' His latest girlfriend, a 41-year-old psychologist, was credited with finally succeeding in persuading him to kick his coke habit. 'He's a villain,' Muffy declared. 'You know he had a face-lift recently. He went on television with his face covered in bruises. When they asked what it was, he said it was a wasp sting! Hah!'

At the wheel of her BMW, a present from Eduardo, Muffy gave us a tour of her Buenos Aires. 'There's the Alvear Palace Hotel. Whoops!' She waved at an angry fellow motorist. 'When I was nineteen and I wanted to marry my Uruguayan Prince my father sent me to stay there. He said: "See if after a week you still like Argentina." I didn't, but I was so in love I married him anyway. Mistake! You know, I never would have believed it but I wonder if women really need to get married. I think I'm turning into a feminist.'

We drove on through the chic suburbs of Palermo. Paraguayan maids dragged at the hands of grumpy schoolgirls in tartan skirts and blue blazers. Women in dark glasses walked dachshunds whose bellies scraped along the ground. 'See the mansion to the left? My best friend lives there. She used to be the mistress of Jimmy Goldsmith. Hey! You're from London, you must have known him!'

We slowed down to accommodate the daily quota of demonstrators chanting, waving flags and banging cheerfully on our bonnet. As the engine ran, Muffy entertained us with her conspiracy theories. Menem's son was a drug runner, his daughter ran a brothel, a politician who murdered a journalist and then committed suicide in shame was, in fact, alive and well and living in Brazil.

Such rumours were as much a part of the Argentine diet as *Alfajores*, the cloying biscuits of condensed milk, so adored by Plarr's mother. Why did these crazy stories thrive in Buenos Aires? I asked Muffy.

She thought for a moment. 'You know,' she said, 'the Argentinians are very self-critical. They know their country is in a mess. Look at them – always marching and protesting. Yet ultimately they also know they can do so little about it. There's a feeling here that nobody cares what happens to ordinary people. They've voted for this government and they've paid for it – yet no one expects to be served by it. Some of the time, they're angry but most of the time they're just cynical. We joke about it. We tell each other these stories to try and outdo each other. When it becomes amusing, it no longer seems real.'

Yet you could distance yourself too much from reality. The following afternoon, we were in a taxi inching through traffic around the Plaza de Mayo, past the Casa Rosada, the presidential palace, whose original colour came from whitewash mixed with pigs' blood. A crowd had gathered on the square. 'It's *las madres*,' said the driver.

The mothers of the Plaza de Mayo march through the square every Thursday afternoon at three. They have been doing so for twenty-four years, since Videla started his 'dirty war' against their children. On the ground, among the pigeon shit, were the white-painted outlines of bodies. They looked as if they had been vaporized by a neutron bomb. Each bears a name and a date of their disappearance. Many are much later than the re-introduction of civilian rule in 1983: Sergio Duran 6/8/92, Susana Escobar 24/2/91, Agustín Ramirez 5/6/88.

The mothers wore linked arms as they walked round and round two-by-two. Elderly and dumpy, with handbags crooked into their elbows and support-stockings wrinkling around their knees, they looked like members of the Women's Institute on a day trip to the seaside. Only the hopeless message of their white headscarves – 'Let the disappeared reappear alive' – revealed who they were.

There are 2000 'Mothers' in Argentina, maybe a hundred were present that day. As many as 20,000 people are thought to have disappeared. Elvera had come all the way from Tucumán in the north east to march. 'I do it once every six months,' she said.

Her daughter, Estela, had been a student at the University of Tucumán. In 1979, she was twenty-one. One afternoon, she kissed her mother goodbye and went to a café to meet some friends. She never returned.

'Maybe she was tortured, I hope they killed her straight away,' Elvera said emotionlessly. 'I wonder sometimes – was her body dropped into the river from an aeroplane? Is she in an unmarked grave? I would dearly like to visit it.'

The horror ran deeper than this, though. Many of the women who were murdered had been pregnant at the time of their disappearance. Most gave birth to their babies in detention centres, before being tortured or killed. Some of the children were dumped in orphanages, but others had been adopted by the families of the men responsible for the killings.

Many of the grandmothers had spent the past two decades trying to trace these children. Most had been unsuccessful, others found the children unwilling to learn about their horrific origins and furious at being asked to denounce the only parents they had ever known.

It was Argentina that hardened Greene's beliefs and was to ensure that in the last decades of his life he was to become more and more entwined with the left-wing revolutionaries of this huge, cruel continent. Videla's deeds have gone unreported or been forgotten. In 1985, he had been tried and jailed for life, but shortly afterwards Menem had pardoned him.

'We still walk the streets next to these killers,' said Elvera. 'None of them were punished for what they did. There is no memorial to our children. People say it is hard to live with memories, but it is harder to live without them.' I remembered Andrew Graham-Yooll telling me that most Argentinians regarded the mothers as an anachronistic embarrassment. They wished they would go away.

Surrounded by vendors selling hot peanuts and mini-Argentinian flags, the women had become a tourist attraction. There was even a *Madres* café now, selling T-shirts and coffee mugs. The only people who watched them march were Dutch women wearing Hard Rock Café sweatshirts and clutching bags from Kelly's gaucho souvenir shop. They signed petitions and took photographs as the mothers continued their endless, circular march. Traffic howled round the Plaza and the words of Greene's revolutionaries in the *barrio* floated into my head. 'They have forgotten us.'

EPILOGUE: Berkhamsted

In a bizarre profession anything which belongs to an everyday routine gains great value – perhaps that was one reason why . . . he chose to return to his birthplace

THE HUMAN FACTOR

There are so many souvenirs. The red voodoo doll with stuffing like pubic hair oozing from the seams. A pair of black feather-trimmed high-heeled mules from the mall in Buenos Aires. A brown silk handbag patterned with gold flowers haggled for in the backstreets of Hanoi. Another doll – this time a Zapatista, a black ski mask over its face and clutching a toothpick machine-gun.

Occasionally, there is news. An aerogramme from Sierra Leone: 'Madam Smith, although we met only once in the camp with the British High Commissioner I believe this relationship will enable us to be good friends. For now things are not really good with me. I appeal to you to assist me with whatever you can assist me. Will you please tell me in your reply what kind of business you would like to do with me: diamond, gold or any other?' From Cienfuegos, Cuba, a letter. 'It is your friend Sara. How are you? I am very, very and very happy because soon I think Eric comes to visit me soon.' From San Cristóbal, daily e-mails from human rights organizations: 'Yesterday the president of the San Cristóbal diocese was detained and beaten by caciques from Tzetelton in the

Chamula diocese. He was investigating the imprisonment of three people in that community who do not participate in the caciques' form of Catholicism and who are therefore denied access to drinking water and whose children are not allowed to enrol in school.'

Nothing has changed in Greeneland, yet so much has happened. As I write, in Mexico, Don Samuel Ruiz, protector of the Indians, resigned on his seventy-fifth birthday. The Vatican was reluctant to appoint his 'co-bishop' Don Raúl Vera to succeed him but finally bowed to international pressure. Sierra Leone is in uproar. The expedient peace accord that gave power to Foday Sankoh is in tatters; the rebels are on the rampage; Ecomog has been replaced by ineffective UN forces, Britain has sent in the Paras and Peter Penfold has been recalled. The rhetoric of *doi moi* in Vietnam turned out to be just rhetoric. Foreign investors are continuing to flee. The Q Bar has closed down. The Party has cut the working week by eight hours to forty, despite the fact that everyone wanted to work and complained about not having the money to spend on a day off.

Fidel is stronger than ever thanks to Elian Gonzalez, a young Cuban boy whose mother was drowned on the way to Miami. Cuban exiles in Miami demanded he stay with elderly relatives there rather than returning to his father in Cuba, a stance that even by American standards appeared unreasonable. On the eve of its second round of democratic elections Haiti is sinking even further into its mire. Paraguay's coalition government has broken up because the Colorado Party refused to countenance economic reforms or give any power to its rivals. Only in Argentina, where a new president, Fernando De La Rúa ousted Menem at the elections with the promise of bringing his country's former military leaders to justice, is there any spark of hope.

There was one more place I wanted to visit in Greeneland, a place that held no interest for me at the beginning of my travels, but which now, after everything I had seen, appealed. It was Berkhamsted, a quiet town in the heart of the English commuter belt – and to many the epitome of dullness. But it was also Greene's birthplace and the setting for his last great novel *The Human Factor*.

When Greene returned to Berkhamsted at the age of thirty-three, before setting off to Mexico to research *The Lawless Roads*, he was filled with revulsion. 'You couldn't live in a place like this – it was somewhere to which you returned for sleep and rissoles by the 6.50 or the 7.25.' To him, the town symbolized passivity and moral decline.

Yet towards the end of his life Berkhamsted began to mean something quite different. Since *Brighton Rock*, Greene had been drawn outside modern society, to seek what lay behind the trappings of technology and civilization. Now, at seventy-three, he realized that the best way of escape might lie in returning to one's roots. In *A Sort of Life*, his first volume of autobiography, published in 1971, Greene wrote of his home town: 'Everything one was to become must have been there . . . I feel it would be strange if . . . I were not brought back to die here in the place where everything began.' None of the bile of *The Lawless Roads* poisons his new vision. Instead, Greene's hero, Maurice Castle, finds a refuge here from his work in London as a double agent and the machinations of the superpowers. Home has come to mean peace.

Berkhamsted is only forty minutes from Euston. I went there on the morning train, travelling against the tide that Castle joined every day. 'He knew nearly all the commuters by sight – he was even on nodding terms with some of them.' At Berkhamsted, I followed Castle's route home, 'the longer way . . . across the canal bridge, past the Tudor school, into

the High Street, past the grey flint parish church . . . then up
the slopes of the Chilterns towards his small semi-detached
house in King's Road'. I knew enough about Greene by now
to know that all these landmarks would still be standing. Only
details – filtered through the prism of boyhood memories –
would have changed. The canal was still shaded by weeping
willows, although the 'strange brutal canal workers with blackened faces like miners', who shouted insults at Greene and his
nanny had long gone. Now their barges housed artists and
jewellery makers. New desirable homes had been built at the
water's edge, a cul-de-sac behind them bore the name
'Greenes Court'.

Berkhamsted School, the minor public school, where
Greene, the headmaster's son, passed ten wretched years from
seven to seventeen, still dominated Castle Street, 'part rosy
Tudor, part hideous modern brick the colour of doll's-house
plaster hams'. Today, its female head has renamed it Berkhamsted Collegiate School, College Campus; the sixth form
is co-educational, caters mainly to day pupils and boasts a
school house called Greenes.

Round the corner, at the top of the High Street, stood the
Norman parish church, where Castle stops to pray for his
stepson, Sam. Further down the 'broad dignity' of the High
Street had been abused after the First World War by the
erection of the new cinema with its 'green Moorish dome'.
Greene's unworldly father allowed his boys to watch the
first Tarzan movie there in the mistaken belief it was an
'educational film of anthropological interest'. Then the building was considered the height of 'dubious taste', today it had
been replaced by its contemporary equivalent, a Tesco's store.
The half-timbered building across the street, once WH Smith,
where Greene shoplifted a copy of *The Railway Museum* and
The Abbess of Vlay, now housed a hairdresser's. I looked in

vain for Greene's 'curious individual Berkhamsted faces' with 'pointed faces like knaves on playing cards, with a slyness about the eyes, an unsuccessful cunning' but all I saw were blank-eyed pensioners and tired women pushing prams. Everyone else was at work in London.

Back on the High Street, I stopped at the King's Arms where Daintry – MI5's lonely security man – telephoned his report on Castle. 'Please note we observe a smart casual dress code – no jeans' read a sign on the door. I sat in an armchair by the vast unlit fireplace and ate a plate of sandwiches from a low round table and eavesdropped on the couple entertaining her ancient mother, on day release from her old-people's home. 'We have aerobics on Thursdays,' she was telling them. 'It's really rather fun.'

A little further down the High Street I turned left up a 'steep villaed hill' that was King's Road, where Castle lived in a small, semi-detached house with a 'gaudy' stained glass of *The Laughing Cavalier* over the porch. Greene based his description of the house on his Aunt Mary's, now demolished, and invented a number for it – 129. Cars sped past me; in the commuter belt no one walked. The red-brick houses sat silently behind privet hedges, burglar alarms set to deter further investigations. The police station that offered Castle false security still stood on the corner.

After lunch, I retraced my route, back down King's Road, but then continued past the station, under the railway bridge and on past the 'ruins of a once-famous castle, which had withstood a siege by Prince John of France', the 'new houses' which had been there a quarter of a century and up the long muddy road that led to the wide expanses of Berkhamsted Common. Here, surrounded by the 'smooth olive skin of beech trees and last year's quagmire of leaves', Greene, aged twenty and suffering from unrequited love, played Russian roulette with a revolver found in his brother's cupboard. It was one of the first salvoes in his 'war against boredom', a war that would take him 'on an absurd and reckless trek through Liberia . . . to Tabasco during the religious persecution . . . to the French War in Vietnam'.

In his childish imagination, Greene romanticized the Common as a haunt of spies, in adulthood he was able to make it the place where Castle drops his report for his Communist paymasters. Yet in *The Human Factor*, the Common is also the scene of a domestic idyll. Castle, his wife, Sarah, stepson Sam and colleague Davis have an autumn picnic there and afterwards play hide and seek. In sadder times, Castle remembers this scene. For by now Greene no longer perceived the family as some kind of a hideous trap. All that matters to Castle is his own little unit. 'We have our own country,' Sarah tells her husband. 'You, me and Sam.' Towards the end of his days Greene was realizing that all that really mattered was the abiding power of love.

Castle was not allowed to end his days in Berkhamsted and nor was Greene. He died of intestinal cancer in Switzerland in 1991 and is buried near Vevey. Towards the end of his life, the travelling tailed off, but he never stopped picking at the scab of the human condition. His travels had shown him that the Communists who employ Castle are as disdainful of human relationships as their capitalist enemies. The Church's answers had proven inadequate. 'Perhaps I was born to be a half believer,' Castle tells his wife. Greene had reached the same conclusion.

Yet in Greene's final philosophy, this was no bad thing. 'I think, the only message that I would wish to convey is fallibility,' he told Karel Kyncl in *Index on Censorship* in 1984. 'It is difficult for an imaginative man to be cruel without feeling shame at cruelty.' The greatest gift, Greene had concluded, was doubt. I sat on Berkhamsted Common and thought of Greene being received into the Catholic church. The baptismal name he chose for himself was Thomas – the doubter. Then I thought of Castle fending off sleep until he hears his beloved wife breathing peacefully beside him: 'Then he allowed himself to strike like his childhood hero Allan Quatermain, off on that long slow underground stream which bore him on toward the interior of the dark continent where he hoped that he might find a permanent home, in a city where he could be accepted as a citizen, a citizen without any pledge of faith, not in the city of God or Marx but the city called Peace of Mind.'